Devotions

Eileen H. Wilmoth, senior editor

J pray that
you may have
your roots and
foundations
in love

(Ephesians 3:17 *Today's
English Version*).

January

*Photo by Paul Ling is of Andrew and
Laura Wood while serving as missionaries in Ukraine*

January 1

His Power, His Purposes

Turn from your wickedness and pray to the Lord (Acts 8:22, *New Living Translation*).

Scripture: **Acts 8:14-24**
Song: **"More Love, More Power"**

Few people understand the truism of the statement, "Absolute power corrupts absolutely." Most people have not experienced absolute power. We live a life that is measured by limitations. Wouldn't it be great if only we could do whatever we chose, whenever we wanted?

Sometimes we look at those whose power seems complete, and we envy them. When the commander orders, the troops obey. When the boss speaks, his subordinates do his wishes. With just a signature, a monarch binds a new law on everyone in the land. By a rhythmic move of his hand, the conductor controls a whole symphony.

We who subconsciously long for more power should not be too hard on the converted sorcerer Simon. He, like many today, had made his living by doing what those around him couldn't. God forgave his immature wish to use God's power for his own selfish purposes. God will forgive us if we make the same mistake today.

O Father, we praise Your name and we are grateful that You have all power. Help us to live by Your commands. In Jesus' name, amen.

January 1-5. **Mark A. Taylor** is vice president of church resources at Standard Publishing, where he has served for more than 25 years.

Your word is a lamp to my feet and a light for my path

(Psalm 119:105, *New International Version*).

Our door is open, and the light is on. Please join us as members of God's great family, and we'll begin our day with a song, a Scripture, a meditation, and a prayer.

This devotional book is designed to lead us to concentrate on a special verse from God's Word each day. These devotions are linked to the topics based on the Home Daily Bible Readings in the International Sunday School Lessons. In each devotion, we will find anecdotes, illustrations, and stories that will make us laugh, cry, and long to draw closer to one another and to God.

Find a home in your neighborhood and take time today to meditate and pray for the family who lives in this home. May we open our homes to those in need and in so doing, allow the love of Christ to be seen in us. May we be an open door to happiness and peace in our families, our communities, and the world.

Pray for the Christian family members whose photos are on the monthly pages of this book. Notice that some use this daily devotional as part of their Bible reading and devotional time each day.

Some of our immediate and extended family members, both here in the office and around the world, have written our daily devotions for us. Christians around the world—ministers, homemakers, college professors, lawyers, businessmen and women, college students, college presidents, and teachers—both young and old have joined us as they lead us in our daily meditations and prayers.

Let's spend time in prayer and ask God to bless us all to His glory. When we see a church building, a stained glass window, or a cross, let's pray for the church family.

The beauty of God's world is all around, and it can help direct us to His love in Christ Jesus, our Lord and Savior. When we see a bird, a flower, a tree, a mountain, or a snowfall, let's glorify God. We are His children, so let's feel His beauty penetrate our hearts and souls

As the editor of this book, I pray that we will all let it direct our thoughts and prayers to God. I pray that together as the family of God, we will "share the light of the world" with those around us. May we all do God's work here on earth.

"To him be glory in the church and in Christ Jesus throughout all generations, for ever and ever!" (Ephesians 3: 21, *New International Version*).

Eileen H. Wilmoth, senior editor
Devotions™ and *365 Devotions*™ and *Devotional Companion*™

Pursuing the Passion

"Anyone who puts a hand to the plow and then looks back is not fit for the Kingdom of God" (Luke 9:62, *New Living Translation*).

Scripture: **Luke 9:57-62**
Song: **"I Would Be True"**

Our garage offers testimony to my son's fleeting boyhood interests. In one corner is a set of beginner's golf clubs, flanked by a rejected hockey stick, a basketball, a hardball bat, and a long-forgotten tennis racket.

Each item served him well as he discovered his skills and interests. But he soon focused on the things that he has continued to pursue into adulthood.

Some people live without ever settling on a passion. They never stick with anything long enough to become excellent at it or to derive real satisfaction from it.

Some people pick up and put away gods like my son moved from sport to sport. They become attracted to Christ, but later His demands seem hard and His promises too distant. Just as the people Christ met in His time on earth, some people today are too preoccupied with living to stay focused on the Lord of life. The challenge to them, and to us, is to keep looking forward to the prize that awaits the faithful (see Philippians 3:14).

Dear Father, when we are discouraged, comfort us with Your presence and energize us with Your purpose. When we are tempted to turn away, remind us of the prize You have promised to the faithful. In the name of Christ, we pray. Amen.

The Best Banquet

"Look! Here I stand at the door and knock. If you hear me calling and open the door, I will come in, and we will share a meal as friends" (Revelation 3:20, *New Living Translation*).

Scripture: **Revelation 3:14-20**
Song: **"Turn Your Eyes upon Jesus"**

The party is shaking the whole frat house. The pounding bass of the stereo shakes the walls and reverberates into the neighborhood. Pressed together in a sweaty mass, the college students are possessed by the noise and preoccupied with each other.

They don't hear the gentle rap, tap, tap at the door. They don't see the quiet messenger gripping an envelope and peering through the front window. They won't receive what he is bringing. Is it a gift? A check? An invitation? A scholarship announcement?

They will not know because they can't hear and they won't see. They are having fun. But they may miss the promise of a better life than they ever thought possible.

Like the church described in today's passage, they think they have it all, but what they have will soon fade and crumble. They—and we—must consider the offer of the One at the door. At His mansion, around His throne, is a never ending celebration that satisfies like no other.

Forgive us, dear Father, when we believe that our accomplishments, our possessions, and our abilities are enough. Help us to see our poverty, to acknowledge our utter dependence on You, and to ready ourselves for the banquet feast in Heaven at Your feet. Amen.

Surprised by Yesterday

How do you know what will happen tomorrow? For your life is like the morning fog–it's here a little while, then it's gone (James 4:14, *New Living Translation*).

Scripture: **James 4:13-17**
Song: **"Be Thou My Vision"**

For some people, marking the New Year is an exciting time. They make plans. They commit to resolutions. They envision the future.

For some, just the opposite is true. The coming of a New Year means they're a little older. They have a little less time to realize their dreams. Their health isn't what it used to be. A New Year brings new worries, new responsibilities, and new problems. For these people, the New Year is depressing.

For me, it's somewhere in between. When I look back at the twelve months just past, I'm always surprised. It's not that I've made no progress nor reached any goals. It's just that each year I'm struck by so much that has happened that I never would have anticipated. A death. An illness. An engagement. A birth. A resignation.

I shake my head and ponder again the truth of today's Scripture. All of my yesterdays prove that I can't predict my tomorrows. All I can do is to trust them to God.

Help me, Lord of life, *to remember the futility of boasting in my plans. Teach me to trust in You. Give me strength as I seek to glorify You. Give me grace to cope with the unexpected. In the name of Christ, I pray. Amen.*

Deny My Self?

If you try to keep your life for yourself, you will lose it. But if you give up your life for me, you will find true life (Matthew 16:25, *New Living Translation*).

Scripture: **Matthew 16:24-28**
Song: **"All to Jesus I Surrender"**

After Jesus explained to the disciples that He would die, He told them that they, too, must die. And we can assume that they did not understand how they were to take up their own cross.

We can be patient with them, for we ourselves have trouble with this idea. "If any man will come after me," Jesus said, "let him deny himself" (see verse 24).

"Deny my self? But self is at the center of every decision I make! I choose my job because I like the work or because I need to survive. I choose my spouse because I seem special when I'm with this person! I choose my apartment because it's almost as nice as the house I wish I could afford. I choose my friends because they make me feel needed and worthwhile. When have I ever made a decision with a purely unselfish motive?"

Yet Jesus calmly listens to this blustering and reminds us that the essence of life will never be found in any of that. He alone is the source of meaning. Only by living for Him will we discover how really to live.

Dear Father, *help me, as I look at the example of Christ, to learn how to live. Help me to unlock the meaning of life by surrendering my life to His control. In His holy name, I pray. Amen.*

At the Feet of Jesus

Therefore do not worry about tomorrow, for tomorrow will worry about itself. Each day has enough trouble of its own (Matthew 6:34, *New International Version*).

Scripture: **Luke 10:38-42**
Song: **"Does Jesus Care?"**

We live in a busy society. There are lots of things to do, people to see, places to go. Our "to do" lists, written down or in our brains, are miles long. We hear people say that there aren't enough hours in the day. To combat the problem, we add more to the list.

Does Jesus care that we have so much to do and so little time to do it? Yes, He does care. That's why He would rather have us sit at His feet and pay attention to important matters. Jesus prepares us to face the day by giving us what we need first—His teaching.

"But Martha was distracted." Set the table. Fix the food. Are there enough chairs around the table? Why isn't Mary helping? It sounds a little like us at times. We're busy doing everything except listening and studying at Jesus' feet: too busy to read the Bible and too busy to pray. Some are too busy doing the Lord's work to stop and pray about the Lord's work.

Dear heavenly Father, *help us to slow down from our "busy-ness" so that we can hear Your words. In Jesus' name, we pray. Amen.*

January 6-12. **Don Stowell** and his wife, Sharlene, minister to a church in Cincinnati, Ohio. They have three teenage daughters.

The Lord Has a Plan for Your Life

That everyone who believes in him may have eternal life (John 3:15, *New International Version*).

Scripture: **John 11:1-6**
Song: **"He Lives"**

We understand the urgency of the news. A relative calls and says that a loved one is sick and in the hospital. Our hearts race, our blood pressures go up. We get to the hospital as soon as we can. After all, to us, it's an emergency. For us, it's important that we be there.

Jesus had been to the home of Lazarus and his sisters, Mary and Martha. They were close friends with Jesus.

Now we hear that Lazarus is sick, and Jesus is in a different city. The urgency of the message seemed to indicate a very serious illness. It wasn't just a cold. But Jesus "stayed where He was two more days." Why didn't He sense their urgent need for Him to come right away?

The answer comes from Jesus, and we need to pay close attention to it: "This sickness will not end in death . . . it is for God's glory so that God's Son may be glorified through it." First, there is the promise. Then there is the reason. You can't ask for more, even in times of great anxiety. The Lord has a plan. We aren't always sure of the plan, but we must allow Him to use us for His glory.

Thank You, God, *that You love us enough to prepare us for eternal life. In all of our worry, anxiety, and questions, You continue to lay out Your plan for us. In Jesus' name, we pray. Amen.*

Trust Walk

"I am the light of the world. Whoever follows me will never walk in darkness, but will have the light of life" (John 8:12, *New International Version*).

Scripture: **John 11:7-16**
Song: **"He is Able to Deliver Thee"**

When I was in a youth group many years ago, the "Trust Walk" was popular. It required the youth to be paired off, one of whom would be blindfolded. The sighted person would lead his or her partner on the walk while avoiding obstacles along the way. The blindfolded youth had to trust the partner not to lead him in the wrong way.

That's what the disciples had to do. They had to trust Jesus, who planned to go back to Judea where the Jews had tried to stone Him. But He was on a mission. Lazarus had died, and Jesus had to go to reveal the glory of the Lord, even if it meant facing opposition.

The work of God is at hand. To decide not to do it is to walk in darkness where there is the possibility of stumbling. When we walk by ourselves—that is, without the Lord—we risk avoiding His light. However, when we walk with the Lord, even if we don't understand things, He will lead us through. And we can trust Him.

When Jesus says, "Let us go," then let us go.

O Lord, today I will begin listening to You more closely. It is Your light that helps me see. It is Your voice that leads me in Your understanding. In Jesus' name, I pray. Amen.

Knowing the Power of God

"Lord, . . . if only you had been here, my brother would not have died" (John 11:21, *New International Version*).

Scripture: **John 11:17-27**
Song: **"I Sing the Mighty Power of God"**

When we are facing tragedy, it is our nature to find someone or something to hold on to that will give us hope. We believe that this emotional attachment is the answer (or will lead us to an answer) to our afflictions. In this passage of Scripture, Martha is the first to speak to Jesus. From the earlier instruction at her home, she has learned about their extraordinary Friend. She knows the Lord and what He can do. Mary stayed home, probably to mourn the loss of her brother.

But Jesus knew that the death that many were aware of was only for a short time. His power would soon be seen. "I am the resurrection and the life. He who believes in me will live, even though he dies"(see verse 25). Those words fulfill His promise that "this sickness will not end in death" (see verse 4).

Martha not only held on to the words He spoke, she held on to Jesus. He would not be the Christ, the Son of God, if He did not have the power to give life. So she ran and got her sister Mary and told her that Jesus had come. Now they had hope in the mighty power of the Lord!

Dear God, in our weakest moments, You are our strength. Your power will lift us up and show us the best of life. May we hold on to You. In Jesus' name, we pray. Amen.

He Mourns With Us

When He saw the crowds, He had compassion on them (Matthew 9:36, *New International Version*).

Scripture: **John 11:28-37**
Song: **"God Will Make a Way"**

I have preached the sermon at many funerals and memorial services. In almost every service there were tears of sadness. Some were mixed with tears of joy. We understand sadness, and we who are in the Lord understand tears of joy. The tears of joy tell of the assurance for the one who has died in the Lord.

Jesus put Himself in our place. His good friend Lazarus had died a physical death, and he had been in the grave four days already. When Jesus came to the tomb, He was overcome with human grief, and He wept. Those around Him saw His great compassion and love for His friend.

There were others in the crowd that day who wept with Jesus. They had been witnesses to the power He possessed. They knew that He had healed the blind and the lame. They knew that He could have healed Lazarus "if only He had been there."

Today, Jesus shows His compassion; He was deeply moved by the sadness of the people. Today He shows that He understands our sorrows. And today He shows that there is great power over death and the grave.

Thank You, Father, for sending Your Son to mourn with us. You know what we need. May we have the compassion that You have for Your children. In Jesus' name, we pray. Amen.

January 11

Prayer Comes Before Resurrection

"Father, into your hands I commit my spirit" (Luke 23:46, *New International Version*).

Scripture: **John 11:38-44**
Song: **"It Is Finished!"**

Two things impress me about the Scripture text. The first is the trust and devotion of the Son to the Father. It is in the prayer of Jesus that He shows His understanding of the power to raise one from death to life. Jesus wants us to trust God enough to pray to Him and to acknowledge that He sent Jesus into the world.

The second impression is that the Word spoken by Jesus is powerful. When the Word is spoken, it is done. The winds and the waves obeyed Him at His command. The demons came out of the possessed man. The fig tree withered. Now it was time to show that obedience is expected from the grave. Jesus commanded: "Lazarus, come out!" To the amazement of the crowd, Lazarus came out. Death had been swallowed up in victorious life.

Prayer trusts that the living God will show His power. His power is shown in raising Lazarus to life. This means that anytime, anywhere, when it seems best to God, He will demonstrate His power in some magnificent way. Jesus said, "Did I not tell you that if you believed, you would see the glory of God?" (see verse 40). We have!

Your Word continues to amaze us, Father. You have revealed to us the assurance for life. We thank You and praise You! Help us remember that prayer changes things. In Jesus' name, we pray. Amen.

Preparing for Death

From that time on Jesus began to explain to his disciples that he must . . . be killed and on the third day be raised to life (Matthew 16:21, *New International Version*).

Scripture: **John 12:1-8**
Song: **"My Tribute"**

A relatively short time had passed since Lazarus was raised from the dead. Jesus was back in Bethany at Lazarus' home where he and his sisters, Mary and Martha, hosted a dinner in Jesus' honor. This was, perhaps, a moment of irony: Jesus raised Lazarus from the dead, and now Jesus is preparing for His own death.

Martha was doing what she did best—making dinner and serving her guests. Mary paid attention to the spiritual things. She took the purest of perfume and anointed Jesus with it. To her, it was a sacrificial gift. Since it was costly perfume, it was like giving all she had as a gift. When Mary wiped Jesus' feet with her hair, she showed ultimate devotion for her Lord.

Jesus gave His all as a sacrificial gift. His ultimate devotion was death on the cross to remove our sins. In the presence of His disciples, Jesus accepted the gift of anointing "for the day of my burial." Is that all? No, because the Man who would go to the cross and die for us would show us life again. He is our Savior today!

Father, thank You for life in Your Son Jesus. Show us how to honor Him with our lives. As with the perfume Mary used, may we smell the sweet fragrance of Your presence. In Jesus' name, we pray. Amen.

January 13

U-Turns Allowed

I have prayed for you, Simon, that your faith may not fail. And when you have turned back, strengthen your brothers (Luke 22:32, *New International Version*).

Scripture: **Luke 22:24-34**
Song: **"I Have Decided"**

Been there. Done that. How quickly we use that modern cliche when someone tells us of an experience they've had. Perhaps the incident was an embarrassing action. Most of us relate to daily happenings in the lives of each other. We laugh together at our human foibles or offer a sympathetic smile and nod.

Are we as quick and positive in our response when a brother or sister has stumbled in their Christian walk? Certainly we are not to smile at wrongdoing and sin, but a negative attitude toward a person is not right either. How should we respond?

Jesus gave us an example when He warned Peter of his upcoming denial. "When you have come through a time of testing, turn to your companions and give them a fresh start" (see Luke 22:32).

Recall your times of stumbling and reach out. Make a call or visit. Write a note. Remember God allows u-turns.

***Dear God**, how easy it is to see the failures of others. Remind us of Your forgiveness. Show us the way to reach those who need to turn back to You. In the name of our wonderful Redeemer, we pray. Amen.*

January 13-19. **Joyce Anne Munn** is a retired elementary teacher. She continues to teach creative writing and serves on the national board of Christian Educators.

What's Your Response?

Give an answer to everyone who asks you to give the reason for the hope that you have. But do this with gentleness and respect (1 Peter 3:15, *New International Version*).

Scripture: **Luke 22:54-62**
Song: **"I Have Decided to Follow Jesus"**

A drama team at church recently gave a thought-provoking skit. An unusual technique showed the actors' thoughts on a screen above their heads. Two men were having a conversation. One of them was shown to be thinking of asking the other about his faith. He soon did just that, and the Christian seemed stunned and muttered an answer. His thoughts were about not knowing what to say and wondering how to get away. The seeking man persisted, but the Christian made an excuse to leave. As he started to walk away, however, his thoughts changed, and he decided to talk to his friend. During the rest of the skit the men were in conversation about Jesus.

We don't blatantly deny Christ. But do we quickly exit the room when the discussion turns to religious matters? Such reactions probably come more from fear about how to respond than from being ashamed of our faith. Nevertheless, the result could be the same: someone who needs to hear about Jesus doesn't because of us. Don't deny your Savior by not being prepared to talk about Him. Ask God for courage to be a faithful witness.

O Lord, give us the courage to speak for You. Thank You for the ones who shared You with us. In the name of Jesus, we pray. Amen.

Let's Go Fishing

Therefore go and make disciples of all nations, baptizing them in the name of the Father and of the Son and of the Holy Spirit, and teaching them to obey everything I have commanded you . . . I am with you always, to the very end of the age (Matthew 28:19, 20, *New International Version*).

Scripture: **John 21:1-6**
Song: **"Fishers of Men"**

When I was young, my dad started taking an afternoon a week off from work during the summer months. During our special time we went fishing in the stream behind our house. My job was to dig the worms and get the poles, bucket, and tackle box ready. Soon we'd head for our favorite spot. We rarely caught anything—maybe a bluegill or two. Now I realize Daddy's purpose for those jaunts wasn't to catch fish. Instead, it was to spend time with me, building special memories in my heart.

Aren't we much the same in our Christian life? We love spending time with our heavenly Father, worshipping in a beautiful sanctuary. We treasure those times and special memories. Jesus spent time alone with the disciples, but then He challenged and commanded them to "go fishing" for souls. That challenge extends to us today. Let's obey Jesus' command to be fishers of men and head for the stream where fish are biting.

Precious Father, *thank You for the time to worship and adore You. Father, help us to realize You want others to share this same blessing. Give us a desire to "go fishing." In the name of Jesus, we pray. Amen.*

Dinner's Ready

Then the angel said to me, "Write: 'Blessed are those who are invited to the wedding supper of the Lamb!'" And he added, "These are the true words of God" (Revelation 19:9, *New International Version*).

Scripture: **John 21:7-14**
Song: **"Come and Dine"**

Most people enjoy eating. Christians are no different. Take a look at restaurant parking lots after worship services on Sundays. Most patrons heading in the doors appear to be wearing their church clothes. Check the church calendar for special events that include food. There's nothing wrong with eating, although some of us have likely overindulged a few times. If a survey were to be done, though, most people would probably respond that their reason for enjoying these times is the fellowship. We linger after the food is gone, perhaps talking about families or some new church program.

Peter and John were excited to see Jesus again and spend time with Him. He had even prepared a meal for them and the five others who had been out fishing.

We, too, can look forward to such a time with Jesus in Heaven. We're invited to the wedding feast and then will continue forever in fellowship with Him and all the saints. Praise God!

Dear Father, thank you for inviting us to Your heavenly feast. We look forward to spending eternity with You and all those who have accepted Your invitation. In the name of Jesus, we pray. Amen.

God Sees Clearly

The Lord does not look at the things man looks at. Man looks at the outward appearance, but the Lord looks at the heart (1 Samuel 16:7, *New International Version*).

Scripture: **John 21:15-19**
Song: **"To the Work"**

Things aren't always as they appear. I once saw a drawing of a shadow, which showed a bowlegged cowboy ready to reach for his guns. Another picture showed what was actually casting the shadow. An artist had done an amazing job of arranging animals to create this illusion. A gorilla was being held up with two animals with long tails. Their ears formed the guns, their bodies the legs, and their tails were the boots. The gorilla's arms, head, and body formed the same for the cowboy. A buzzard's body and the long tails of two other birds created the hat shadow. Appearances can be deceiving!

Are things in your spiritual life as they appear? Do people see you as a faithful Christian? What does God see? He looks on the heart. Jesus asked Peter about his love and said, "Feed my sheep." What is He calling us to do for Him today? Do we love Him? Are we feeding His sheep and taking care of His lambs, as He desires?

All-seeing God, forgive us when we do not reflect You. Make us aware of any deceitfulness in our actions. Increase our desire to faithfully feed Your sheep. In the name of the Chief Shepherd, Jesus Christ, we pray. Amen.

Lost!

In the same way, I tell you, there is rejoicing in the presence of the angels of God over one sinner who repents (Luke 15:10, *New International Version*).

Scripture: **Acts 2:37-42**
Song: **"Seeking the Lost"**

While shopping at Wal-Mart, I heard the speaker blare: "Code Adam." That means a child is lost. Employees appeared from everywhere, walking up and down the aisles. Within minutes, the child was found. Smiles were visible on faces throughout the store. Surprisingly, in about ten minutes, the same thing happened again. Employees again walked the aisles. They were concerned for a lost child. As before, the youngster was located. Days earlier, a young girl was lost in the woods not far from our town. When she was found safe, those searching for her had smiles of joy and tears of relief

God has a plan for rescuing the lost also. We're His agents to go into the world to find them. The message we are to call out is clear: "Repent and obey Him." Are you responding readily to seek for the lost? Do you pray for those who don't have a Savior? Let's take part in God's rescue plan. We'll see many smiles, and even the angels will rejoice when a lost one is found.

Wonderful Redeemer, *create in us a desire to seek for those who do not know You. Teach us to be aware of those wandering lost and alone. Forgive us when our own busyness keeps us from Your eternal rescue operation. In Your Son's loving name, we pray. Amen.*

Follow Your Heart

Can you fathom the mysteries of God? Can you probe the limits of the Almighty? (Job 11:7, *New International Version*).

Scripture: **Acts 3:1-10**
Song: **"I'll Go Where You Want Me to Go"**

A mother and her children were involved in an accident. She and her daughters were not seriously hurt, but as she reached her son, she realized his injuries were critical. She fell to her knees and began praying. About the same time, a paramedic was driving down a nearby road. For some inexplicable reason, he says, he turned his car around and headed to the other highway. He quickly encountered the accident and stopped to help. A nurse came upon the scene at the same time. They administered first aid until the ambulance arrived. Coincidence? Not likely. Such events have been called "God-incidences."

Peter and John were in the right place at the right time. The man at the Beautiful Gate who was healed by them surely didn't consider their being at that location when he was a coincidence. He immediately praised God for healing him. Have you felt a strong urge to change your plans or perhaps to call or write a friend? Listen to your heart. God still works in mysterious ways.

Dear Father, help us to be aware of Your presence in everything we do. Help us today to be Your servants that help the world to know You. We want to serve You. In the name of Jesus, we pray. Amen.

Jesus Is on Trial

Cast all your anxiety on him because he cares for you (1 Peter 5:7, *New International Version*).

Scripture: **John 18:28-32**
Song: **"God Will Take Care of You"**

People were in the process of falsely accusing Jesus, but God was watching over His Son.

A friend told me about the time that he observed a lifeguard on a beach. A lot of people were enjoying the ocean, some riding the waves, and others falling down as the waves hit them. But the lifeguard continued to look over the scene from his elevated position. He was alert to any situation that might require his immediate help. A short distance away, there was a man sitting on a beach. He was also intently looking at the ocean. His eyes, however, were intent on a little boy paddling in the waves near the shore. Paying no attention to the roar of the ocean and the laughter of the crowd, the man concentrated on the safety of one little boy—his son!

As my friend spoke to me, I realized that both these men portray God in His relationship to us. Not only does He watch the entire world to see all of His children, but He also concentrates His attention on each of us.

Dear Father, help us to know Your presence in us when we face difficult times. We pray in the name of Jesus, our Lord. Amen.

January 20-26. **Kenneth Meade**, now retired, ministered to the Church of Christ at Manor Woods in Rockville, Maryland, for more than 45 years.

Jesus Is Asked if He Is a King

He hath on his vesture and on his thigh a name written, KING OF KINGS AND LORD OF LORDS (Revelation 19:16).

Scripture: **John 18:33-37**
Song: **"Come, Thou Almighty King"**

Who is Jesus to you? It's important that we remember what He did for us and that our lives are a witness to who He is. God needs people who will stand up for His Son and let the world know who Jesus really is.

I was getting my hair cut the other day when my barber asked a strange question. We have been friends for years, and he knows I am a Christian. We talk often about the Bible and the church. I keep praying that he will open his heart to the Word of God.

This day, he surprised me by asking, "Who is Jesus— really?" I could tell by his voice that he was honestly searching but that he really didn't understand that Jesus is the Son of God who became the Savior of the world. I was able to share my faith in Jesus with him. My friend has been to church a couple of times since, and I'm hoping that he'll some day give His life to Jesus and let Christ become his King of kings and Lord of lords.

When Jesus is King of our lives, we make every effort to do those things that are pleasing to Him.

God, we thank You for sending Your Son to earth. We are grateful that He died for us. We have hope for the future because He is alive. We want to live with You forever. In Jesus' name, we pray. Amen.

Pilate Forces the Crowd to Choose

For me and my house, we will serve the LORD (Joshua 24:15).

Scripture: **Matthew 27:15-19**
Song: **"I Choose Jesus"**

It isn't always easy to make the right choice. Sometimes we don't know the true value of our choice.

At the Press Exhibition in Cologne, Germany, there is a display that shows the relationship between the printing trade and the postal services. The decoration represents a huge eagle, and the effect is very striking to the eye. But as one looks more carefully, one discovers that it consists of hundreds of thousands of postage stamps issued during an inflationary period in the nation's economy. Viewed from a distance, they produce a grand image. The closer a person comes to them, however, the more he notices that they are all of inflated amounts. They bear large numbers but have little worth. This mighty facade, though appearing costly, has no real value.

Think before you make a decision. Never choose anything that would not honor Christ. The most important thing is not to have riches and fame but to know that you have Jesus in your heart. Remember that all decisions have lasting consequences. When you always think about what God wants you to do, He will guide you to make good choices.

Almighty God, *we honor You. Give us the courage always to stand for You when we are tempted to be influenced to do wrong. In Jesus' name, we pray. Amen.*

Jesus Is Brought Before the People

Simon Peter answered, "You are the Christ, the Son of the living God" (Matthew 16:16, *New International Version*).

Scripture: **John 18:38—19:5**
Song: **"He Is Lord"**

Can you picture Jesus wearing a crown of thorns and a purple robe as Pilate stood Him before the people? He hadn't done anything wrong, and yet He was beaten and mistreated. Pilate's startling words to the crowd were, "Here is the man!" Even though Pilate wouldn't take a stand for Jesus, there seemed to be something about Jesus that Pilate had difficulty understanding.

Wherever we go in life and no matter what we do, people watch us and wonder who we are. They draw conclusions by what we say and do. What kind of an impression do you want people to have about you? When we think about the answer to that question, it may well determine how we live. If we want people to know that we are Christians, then we must live our lives in such a way that they will see the evidence. Are we kind? Do we protect their reputations even when they aren't present? Are we willing to make an effort to help them in any way we can?

It must have been difficult for Jesus to stand before the people being falsely accused, but He remained faithful.

O Father, thank You for Jesus who did not quit when His life became difficult. We want to be like Him. In His name, we pray. Amen.

The Crowd Cried, "Crucify Him"

Whoever acknowledges me before men, I will also acknowledge him before my Father in heaven (Matthew 10:32, *New International Version*).

Scripture: **John 19:6-12**
Song: **"All Hail the Power of Jesus' Name"**

It's hard to believe that Pilate did not keep the crowd from crucifying Jesus. It's even more difficult to believe that the people called out for Jesus to be crucified.

Have you ever flown in an airplane? In talking with a pilot friend of mine, I said: "I imagine you feel a tremendous responsibility when you're sitting at the controls, thinking about all the passengers who have entrusted their lives into your hands." "No, sir," he replied. "I never think of the passengers when I am flying the plane; I think only about myself!" "What do you mean?" I asked. The pilot replied, "I know that if I remain alert and keep this large aircraft under control, it will arrive safely at its destination, and so will I, and also all the passengers."

God's children are also in a responsible position. What we do affects those around us. When we obey Christ, we honor Him. People around us will see how wonderful He is because they see Him in us.

O God, we want our lives to be effective in helping others know about Jesus and how wonderful He is. Use us to Your honor and glory and give us the strength to stay true to You whether others do or not. In the name of Jesus our Savior, we pray. Amen.

Pilate Releases Jesus

So then, each of us will give an account of himself to God (Romans 14:12, *New International Version*).

Scripture: **Matthew 27:21-26**
Song: **"Higher Ground"**

It seems amazing that people could have been filled with so much hate that they wanted to crucify Jesus. When you read Matthew 27:25, did you notice that they were so determined for Jesus to be crucified that they didn't even care how this would affect their children? We see hate all around us. The world needs more love and respect. Let us make every effort to bring out the best in the people around us.

Poet Shel Silverstein wrote a heart-touching verse entitled, "The Little Boy and the Old Man." In it he portrays a young boy talking to an elderly gentleman. Silverstein has the boy saying, "Sometimes I drop my spoon." "I do that too," replies the old man. "I often cry," continues the boy. The old man nods, "So do I." "But worst of all," says the boy, "it seems that grownups don't pay any attention to me." Just then the boy feels "the warmth of a wrinkled old hand." "I know what you mean," says the little old man.

It is nice when someone understands what we're going through. Let's all try to be there for those in need.

Thank You, God, *for giving us family and friends. May we support and encourage them. Fill our hearts with Your love and let that love flow through us to them. In the name of Jesus, we pray. Amen.*

Jesus Is Crucified

But God demonstrates his own love for us in this: While we were still sinners, Christ died for us (Romans 5:8, *New International Version*).

Scripture: **John 19:13-22**
Song: **"Were You There?"**

It's hard to imagine someone loving us so much that they would be willing to die for us. But that is what Jesus did. He never sinned, and yet He died for our sins.

A minister announced that he would be preaching next Sunday evening on "The Love of God." As the people gathered, they saw a very large painting depicting Jesus being crucified. The minister turned off all the lights. Then he lit a candle and carried it to the painting. First of all, he held it high to illumine the crown of thorns. Next, the light revealed the two wounded hands and then the marks of the spear wound in His side. In the silence, he blew out the candle and left the sanctuary. There was nothing else to say.

What people do shows how much they love. It seemed that Jesus was all alone when He was arrested, tried, and crucified. He knew He was doing the will of His Father. Are we willing to give up our desires to do things that are helpful to others? When we really love someone, we are willing to make a sacrifice for them.

Father, it's difficult for us to understand how much You love us. Help us to be generous as we reach out to help others. Help us to follow the example that Jesus gave to us. In His name, we pray. Amen.

Encouraging Ourselves

Barnabas (which means Son of Encouragement), sold a field he owned and brought the money and put it at the apostles' feet (Acts 4: 36,37 *New International Version*).

Scripture: **Acts 4:32-37**
Song: **"Our God is an Awesome God"**

Our adult daughter, Terri, called and left a message for us. When she did not receive a return call, Terri was concerned. Terri returned home to discover that she had left the message on her own home phone.

Sometimes we need to send ourselves a message. This is often true when it relates to encouragement. The early church had a tremendous impact in the future of Barnabas and his life of encouragement to others. When Barnabas saw the believers selling their property and bringing the money to the apostles, "the Encourager" was stimulated to express generosity. Others at first encouraged him who became "the Encourager."

Scripture encourages us, and we realize that God gives not what we deserve but what we so desperately need.

We are reminded in Scripture of the hope we have in Christ. Therefore, be encouraged with these words.

Thank You, Father, *for the blessings of encouragement. When we are encouraged, let us also learn to encourage others. In the name of Christ, our Savior, we pray. Amen.*

January 27-31. **E. Ray Jones** is a retired minister who now leads church seminars. He and his wife, Betsy, reside in Clearwater, Florida. They have three grown children.

Support Is Encouraging

But Barnabas took him and brought him to the apostles. He told them how Saul on his journey had seen the Lord and that the Lord had spoken to him, and how in Damascus he had preached fearlessly in the name of Jesus (Acts 9:27, *New International Version*).

Scripture: **Acts 9:23-30**
Song: **"How Firm a Foundation"**

Real friends encourage one another. Sometimes we are called to stand up for each other against the world.

Paul would have had a much more difficult time being accepted by the church in Jerusalem had Barnabas not been willing to trust Paul when he said that he had been converted. When someone that others trust expresses trust in us, we see the tremendous impact that trust has on the larger fellowship of Christians.

Barnabas expressed trust in others because he believed in the power of the gospel. When we believe that the power of the gospel can transform lives, we will be more willing to support the new Christian who has been transformed and turned from the sins of the world. This trust is crucial to the new Christian.

When we believe the best about people, we encourage them to be their best. This helps us all to be firm in faith.

O Father, help us to encourage one another. May we live our faith in such a way that those around us will know that You can change the human heart. In the name of Jesus, our Savior, we pray. Amen.

To Encourage, Be There!

When he arrived and saw the evidence of the grace of God, he was glad and encouraged them all to remain true to the Lord with all their hearts (Acts 11:23, *New International Version*).

Scripture: **Acts 11:19-24**
Song: **"Just a Closer Walk with Thee"**

In a high school laboratory experiment, students were told they would be given shocks of various intensities while their blood pressure was monitored. The students were warned that the shocks would be painful but have no permanent damage. Then the experimenter gave the student a choice—wait alone or wait with a fellow subject. Most chose to wait with another student.

The point of the experiment was to show that when we're facing pain, stress, or anxiety, we want another human being around.

Paul had a similar experience. He came from Rome after years in prison, uncertain of his future. When the brothers in Rome heard that he was coming they traveled forty miles to meet him. "At the sight of these men Paul thanked God and was encouraged."

We encourage each other by what we do or just by our presence when we simply show up. Knowing that we are available to our brother, whatever his need, is a source of encouragement.

Almighty Father, *we thank You for Your power. Most of all we thank You for Your presence. Just knowing You care for us puts strength in our bones. In the name of Jesus, we pray. Amen.*

Practical Help Is Encouraging

The disciples, each according to his ability, decided to provide help for the brothers living in Judea (Acts 11:29, *New International Version*).

Scripture: **Acts 11:25-30**
Song: **"Reach Out and Touch"**

It was predicted that a famine would spread over the entire Roman world. The response of the disciples in Jerusalem was to give according to their ability to provide help for the brothers living in Judea. They then sent their gift to the elders by Barnabas and Saul.

This is an example of how a caring church prayed for the needs of others. The church in Antioch not only prayed, they also provided food and clothing.

The need for prayer is great, but so is the need for practical help. Prayer is powerful, but it's unfortunate that sometimes prayer is used as an excuse for not practicing sacrificial service. Scripture reminds us that it does no good to pray that people will be filled when we do nothing ourselves to help see that their needs are met. Our brothers need prayer, but they also may need bread.

The gifts that the elders sent with Barnabas and Saul were a great source of encouragement. By this the Christians in Jerusalem knew their brethren cared and were sacrificing to see that that specific problem was resolved.

Dear Father, *help us not to forget that fellow believers can supply physical as well as spiritual needs. Teach us to walk in You. In the name of Jesus Christ, we pray. Amen.*

Remember Your Commission

After they had fasted and prayed, they placed their hands on them and sent them off (Acts 13:3, *New International Version*).

Scripture: **Acts 13:1-5**
Song: **"Send the Light"**

My ordination service was a most memorable moment in my life. After many years, the memory is still vivid. I remember both the speaker and the elders who participated. Occasionally in the early years of my training, I became discouraged. When this happened I thought of the confidence the church leaders had in me. In latter years when I was tempted to forsake the faith, I remembered their commission to fulfill my calling. In those moments when I was tempted to walk away, I heard their admonition to "stand firm in the faith."

A significant statement that has stayed with me is this, "If you are faithful in preaching Christ, God will go with you and provide you with power for possible results." I've never forgotten these words. And God has never failed to do what He promised.

No matter what task God assigns, He will, through His Holy Spirit, supply the power for victory. His promise will be a continual source of encouragement while we're carrying out our commission.

Almighty Father, thank You for Your commission to us to go into the world and preach the message of salvation. Thank You for providing for us the power of the Holy Spirit that we might fulfill Your will for us. In the name of Jesus, we pray. Amen.

Devotions™

I pray that
Christ will
make his home
in your hearts
through faith . . .
you may have
your roots . . .
in love

(Ephesians 3:17, *Today's
English Version*).

February

*Photo by Chuck Perry is of Aisha and
Kerry Washington at their wedding in
Lexinton, Kentucky*

Victories Encourage Us

They gathered the church together and reported all that God had done through them and how he had opened the door of faith to the Gentiles (Acts 14:27 *New International Version*).

Scripture: **Acts 14:21-28**
Song: **"Victory in Jesus"**

Ray BonDurant went ashore at Normandy with General Omar Bradley. Said Ray, "The general was visibly upset with the loss of so many of his men." What bothered him most was the possibility that all of those deaths might be in vain if they could not successfully break through the German defenses. Ray said, "I shall never forget the look on his face when the report came that the allies had broken through. The battle would still be long and bloody, but the victory was in sight."

We experience victory in the Christian life. One church has a praise report in their Bible class where members can share answered prayer and victories they've experienced in their Christian walk.

When we experience defeat, let us never forget that in the defeat we suffer we will be victorious in Christ. There is laid up in Heaven a crown which the Lord will give, and not only to us but also to all who love His appearing.

Lord, *remind us that in Christ we are already victorious. We have conquered sin and death. Through Christ, our Lord, we pray. Amen.*

February 1- 2. **E. Ray Jones** is a retired minister who is now active in leading church seminars. He and his wife, Betsy, reside in Clearwater, Florida.

Encouragement through Conflict

They had such a sharp disagreement that they parted company. Barnabas took Mark and sailed for Cyprus (Acts 15:39, *New International Version*).

Scripture: **Acts 15:36-41**
Song: **"Let There Be Peace on Earth"**

It was said of Napoleon Bonaparte that war for him was a natural condition. It was only in times of conflict that he really came alive.

Some Christians are addicted to conflict. They don't feel they're being faithful to the Lord unless they're fighting someone over something. In too many situations, the clashes are over petty differences.

When faced with conflict, others are addicted to flight. If they have differences with others they flee. Some change ministries every few years. Others change church membership. Still others just drop out and disappear from church life altogether.

Paul and Barnabas had a conflict that was so intense that they could no longer work together. But they were still together in the faith. Therefore, they could work for the kingdom. Conflict did not separate them from Christ.

We can not have differences so deep that we sever ourselves from Christ or his kingdom.

Dear heavenly Father, *keep us from allowing our egos to separate us from our brothers in Christ. Help us to understand we can have differences, but differences ought not to separate us. In the name of Christ, our Savior, we pray. Amen.*

Choosing to Do Right

For the Lord is righteous, he loves justice; upright men will see his face (Psalm 11:7, *New International Version*).

Scripture: **Acts 25:1-12**
Song: **"Yield Not to Temptation"**

The apostle Paul stood before Festus to defend his faith and his compliance with the laws of Caesar. His enemies had brought serious charges against him, but he remained calm and confident. He knew in his heart he had lived honorably, and he was willing to let his integrity speak for him.

Making godly choices in our lives puts our trust in God to the test. What if our decision to follow our conscience causes us to lose friends? Our job? Our privacy? The earthly consequences of living for God can be costly.

Yet the rewards of a righteous lifestyle far outweigh the risks. The psalmist said, "upright men will see his face" (Psalm 11: 7). In other words, when our hearts are right with God, we can come into His presence without fear. He comforts us and gives us the strength to remain faithful. He forgives us when we fall. He gives us peace in the face of adversity. Like the apostle Paul, we can challenge our fears and do what is right.

Dear God, *we struggle with temptation. Give us the courage to stand firm in the face of conflict. Teach us the satisfaction that comes when we honor You with your choices. In the name of Jesus, we pray. Amen.*

February 3-9. **Larry Ray Jones** is the senior minister of the Northside Church of Christ in Newport News, Virginia. He and his wife, Jane, have two children.

One Way or Another

Now I want you to know, brothers, that what has happened to me has really served to advance the gospel (Philippians 1:12, *New International Version*).

Scripture: **Acts 25:13-22**
Song: **"God Will Make a Way"**

A young mother and father lost their son in a tragic skating accident. Heartbroken, they prayed for God to use the experience to touch the hearts of their unsaved family members. The church friends showered the couple with love. They brought food, offered prayers, gave monetary gifts, and provided encouragement. The couple, though deeply hurt, displayed unimaginable faith. In the weeks that followed, family members began to attend worship with them. God answered the couple's prayer and comforted them with immediate results.

The apostle Paul was facing a most serious trial, but God was using it to proclaim His Son's glory. Because Paul was willing to be God's servant, his circumstances created an open door for the gospel.

When you face a trial that changes the course of your life, you may wonder how God might be using the situation for a higher purpose. Sometimes we cannot understand God's plan, but if we remain faithful, He will show us the way. He gives strength to persevere.

Dear God, *we are confident You will turn every situation into an opportunity. Give us spiritual strength to persevere and the wisdom to discern Your leading. We pray in the name of Jesus. Amen.*

Justice Prevails

Submit yourselves for the Lord's sake to every authority instituted among men: whether to the king, as the supreme authority, or to governors, who are sent by him to punish those who do wrong and to commend those who do right (1 Peter 2:13-14, *New International Version*).

Scripture: **Acts 25:23-27**
Song: **" 'Tis So Sweet to Trust in Jesus"**

A church in the process of relocating found land in a prime location. A contract was prepared and dates were set to close on the property. In the meantime, the local county government banned the use of the site by a church. Church members had promised God they would accept the outcome without complaint. The day after the public meeting another piece of land was discovered. It was even better suited for the church's use, and a contract was signed. The congregation rejoiced and thanked God for leading them in the right direction.

Sometimes governments disappoint us. When this happens, it is our nature to criticize those in authority.

Perhaps Festus treated Paul fairly because he found him to be a man who respected public officials. As a result God was able use Festus to protect His servant.

Government officials face struggles on a daily basis. Reach out to those who have authority over you and demonstrate a servant's heart and a cooperative spirit.

Dear Father, *teach us to love those who have authority over us. Make us an example of Your love. In the name of Jesus, we pray. Amen.*

That's Incredible!

Then Jesus told him, "Because you have seen me, you have believed; blessed are those who have not seen and yet have believed" (John 20:29, *New International Version*).

Scripture: **Acts 26:1-8**
Song: **"Christ Arose"**

In 2001, Harold Stilson at age 101, became the oldest person in history to shoot a hole-in-one. His feat occurred on a par-3, 108-yard hole at the Deerfield Country Club in Deerfield Beach, Florida. It was his sixth ace in eighty years of play. Unbelievable!

Of all the incredible events recorded in the Bible, the resurrection of Jesus is the most pivotal. It confirmed Jesus' authority as Savior and Lord, and proclaimed victory over spiritual and physical death. Earlier He had said, "I am the resurrection and the life. He who believes in me will live, even though he dies; and whoever lives and believes in me will never die" (John 11:25, 26, *New International Version*).

When the apostle Paul had an opportunity to share his faith with Agrippa, the resurrection of Jesus was the central theme of his testimony.

The resurrection is our central theme as well. Paul says we have been "raised with Christ" (Colossians 3:1). The Holy Spirit inhabits us and gives us spiritual power to live a Christian life. Sound incredible? Remember that nothing is impossible with God!

Dear God, *thank You for new life in Jesus. May we be a testimony to the power of His resurrection. In His holy name, we pray. Amen.*

The Power of a Testimony

Here is a trustworthy saying that deserves full acceptance: Christ Jesus came into the world to save sinners—of whom I am the worst (1 Timothy 1:15, *New International Version*).

Scripture: **Acts 26:9-18**
Song: **"Amazing Grace"**

President George W. Bush's past personal struggles with alcohol are well known. His family and friends attribute his victory over drinking to his faith in Jesus. We see his victory in a changed life.

Nothing speaks as loudly as a testimony. Truth can be debated, and statistics can be skewed, but a changed life is difficult to refute. Jesus once angered the Pharisees by healing a man who was born blind. After numerous attempts to discredit Christ, the healed man remarked, "Whether he is a sinner or not, I don't know. One thing I do know. I was blind but now I see!" (John 9:25, *New International Version*).

Paul defended his ministry to Agrippa by recounting his conversion. His personal story was stronger than any sermon he could have preached.

Are we living testimonies of God's grace? Can others see the transforming power of Jesus at work in us? If so, God can use us to open the hearts of those who desperately need Him.

Dear Father, *teach us to be messengers of Your love to the world. Help us to know that the strongest proof is our personal witness of Your power. Help us to reflect Your Son Jesus in our daily lives. In the name of Your son, Jesus, we pray. Amen.*

Consumed by the Mission

But Peter and John replied, "Judge for yourselves whether it is right in God's sight to obey you rather than God. For we cannot help speaking about what we have seen and heard" (Acts 4:19-20, *New International Version*).

Scripture: **Acts 26:19-23**
Song: **"I Love to Tell the Story"**

A few years ago a church in St. Mary's, Georgia, inherited sixty million dollars. After prayerful deliberation, the church decided to put 2.8 million dollars in a foundation that would provide one hundred thousand dollars a year for local ministries. The remaining millions were placed in a benevolent fund for distribution to other churches in need. The members believed God had made them stewards of an opportunity to lift up the ministry of others.

We can look to the life of the apostle Paul and see his example of witnessing for Jesus. Paul had experienced the saving grace of Christ; throughout his ministry he faced opposition and hardship, but his love for Christ and compassion for the lost pushed him onward.

Let us rekindle our compassion for others and open our eyes to the spiritual needs of others. May we walk through the doors of opportunity and share His grace.

Dear Lord, thank You for calling us to share Your grace with others. Sometimes we miss an opportunity because we are afraid of saying the wrong thing. Give us the confidence and the wisdom to speak for You. In the name of our Savior and Lord, we pray. Amen.

February 9

The People God Loves

But the Lord stood at my side and gave me strength, so that through me the message might be fully proclaimed and all the Gentiles might hear it. And I was delivered from the lion's mouth (2 Timothy 4:17, *New International Version*).

Scripture: **Acts 26:24-32**
Song: **"I Am Praying for You"**

An insurance company employed a duck to advertise its product, resulting in a dramatic increase in sales. In commercial spots, the duck tried desperately to tell people about an insurance solution, but no one seemed to hear. The director of communications for the company had one explanation for the success of the campaign. "He's got the right answer, but nobody is listening."

This sometimes describes the frustration we feel when we encounter resistance as we share the message of Jesus. We often ask, "Why won't people listen?"

King Agrippa was impressed with Paul as a person. Paul had effectively demonstrated his devotion to Christ and his concern for Agrippa. The king was moved but regretted that he could not set the apostle free.

Let us speak the truth in love. People see Jesus through us. He is the answer.

Dear God, help us to remember that we live in a disillusioned world. Help us to be living examples of Your love and grace, so that others will not doubt our commitment and sincerity to You. Cleanse our hearts of impure motives and help us to be able to touch the hearts of others with Your salvation. In the name of Jesus, we pray. Amen.

Unlikely People Chosen

Him would Paul have to go forth with him (Acts 16:3).

Scripture: **Acts 16:1-5**
Song: **"Jesus Calls us O'er the Tumult"**

I remember those days in junior high when we had to pick our team members for a game. Since I was not athletically inclined, I was always chosen last, and no one really wanted me to be on their team. It was obvious that I would let them down.

I wonder why Jesus chose Judas on His team. Jesus knew that Judas would betray Him. Yet Jesus had a purpose in the divine scheme of things.

In our lesson today, we see Paul picking Timothy for the ministry. He was the most unlikely candidate for the task. He was young and inexperienced. He came from an obscure family. He was the "son of a certain woman" and his father was a non-Jew, a Greek. And yet, Paul found him suitable.

God can use us, no matter what our background, if we will give ourselves to Him. We will be surprised at how God can use you and me when we surrender.

Dear Father, our God and Creator, we stand before You. We give ourselves fully to You. Help us this day to be used in any way You find fit. Give us the courage to honor Your decision to use us. In the name of Jesus, our Savior, we pray. Amen.

February 10-16. **A. Koshy Muthalaly, Ph.D.** is an ordained minister on the faculty of Southern Nazarene University, Bethany, Oklahoma.

You Are Special

For I have no man likeminded, who will naturally care for your state (Philippians 2:20).

Scripture: **Philippians 2:19-24**
Song: **"Of All the Spirit's Gifts to Me"**

James and John are twins. When they were growing up, they had fun playing tricks on their teachers because the teachers could not tell the twins apart. But when they came home, there was no fooling their mother. She knew exactly how to tell them apart. It wasn't easy to fool her.

Isn't it wonderful that God has made each of us so uniquely designed not only in our physical characteristics but in the way we are emotionally put together?

In the Scripture reading today, Paul writes to the hurting Philippian Christians and says that he will send young Timothy to them. He will comfort them.

Timothy was a pastor at heart. It came naturally to him. When people are hurting, we can be the one who shows love and care. Timothy was that person for the Philippian Christians. Today we can be the special people for someone who is hurting.

We are special in the eyes of God. Each of us has been given gifts that are unique to us. Today we can thank God for making us so special.

Lord Jesus, thank You for making us special, so different, but yet so alike. Thank You for the special gifts You have given each of us. Use us today to bless others. In the name of Jesus, we pray. Amen.

True to the Faith

To Timothy, my true son in the faith (1 Timothy 1:2, *New International Version*).

Scripture: **1 Timothy 1:1-5**
Song: **"I Know Whom I Have Believed"**

Mr. McCartney had worked for his company for the last thirty-three years. Rain or shine, he was there at seven in the morning, and he stayed till his work was done. Lacking formal education, he was not able to climb up the professional ladder. But there was something that everyone knew about Mr. McCartney. If he were given a task, he would finish it faithfully and on time. He was loyal to the company that employed him when he desperately needed a job.

Paul writing about Timothy refers to him fondly as "my own son in the faith." Having watched Timothy grow in his relationship with Christ, Paul knew that Timothy would stand firm in his faith. Young as he was, Timothy was a firm believer. Just as Mr. McCartney in his job, Timothy was a man who could be counted upon to be there and be loyal when it came to matters of faith. He found the ability to stay true to his commitment. He had found Jesus, and he was willing to show others his love and compassion.

We can ask ourselves today whether we can be firm in our faith when we are tested in times of trouble.

Lord, we know that our faith will be tested. Keep us firm when faith is likely to be shattered. Help us to stay true to the faith. We ask for help to stand firm. In the name of Jesus, we pray. Amen.

Is Your Faith Truly Sincere?

When I call to remembrance the unfeigned faith that is in thee (2 Timothy 1:5).

Scripture: **2 Timothy 1:1-7**
Song: **"I Want Jesus to Walk with Me"**

Have you ever listened to a minister and felt that he was a phony? Did it seem that he didn't speak from his heart–that he was not authentic and genuine?

Today we pray for men who are genuine and trustworthy to fill the pulpits of all churches around the world Sunday after Sunday. We long for truthfulness, sincerity, and a lasting faith in God to be seen in the religious leaders of our day.

The true character of a person is especially seen during times of testing. Genuineness comes straight from the heart. There is nothing phony about it. People who know us will be able to see our trustworthiness and genuine feeling for truth.

Paul writing to Timothy says that he was a man of "unfeigned faith," which he learned to cultivate from his mother Eunice and his grandmother Lois. There was nothing phony about his faith and practice. He was true and genuine to the core. When we are genuine, people will want to follow our example and turn to Jesus.

Dear God and Lord of all, help us today to be true to You. Teach us to obey Your words. Help us to live in such a way that the world will know You by our actions. May our faith be an example of love. In the name of Jesus, our Lord and Savior, we pray. Amen.

The Need to Nurture

But Silas and Timothy abode there still (Acts 17:14).

Scripture: **Acts 17:10-15**
Song: **"He Leadeth Me! O Blessed Thought!"**

Some of us love action. We want to always be in the forefront. Ministries that keep us in the limelight are appealing. We sometimes define the limelight ministries as the most important ones. However, it is not always the glamorous ministries that count for eternity. It is often those things behind the scenes that are important.

Remember the time Philip was holding a great revival meeting when God called him into the desert to meet with one man? The man was reading the book of Isaiah as he rode along in his chariot. For Philip it may not have seemed sensible to leave a successful ministry to meet with one man in the middle of nowhere. But it was through that isolated meeting that the gospel was introduced to the continent of Africa!

The Scripture text for today tells us that Silas and Timothy stayed behind to nurture the believers in Berea while Paul went on to a public ministry in Athens. The ministry of discipleship was of great significance for the believers in Berea who were determined to find scriptural answers for their needs.

God may call us to work behind the scenes for a higher purpose.

Lord, *we are ready to go out or to stay behind so that Your work will be accomplished. In the name of Jesus, we pray. Amen.*

The Need for Encouragement

And sent Timothy, our brother, . . . to comfort you concerning your faith (1 Thessalonians 3:2).

Scripture: **1 Thessalonians 3:1-6**
Song: **"We Shall Overcome"**

Discouragement is easy to come by in the work of the ministry. Pastor Joe was faithful in the church. He had given his best years to the congregation, and now the church had voted him out of his position in the church. He was very discouraged and felt let down by his church. But his faith in God was strong as he wrestled with his faith during that tough period of his ministry.

It was just then that he came across an old friend from seminary. What perfect timing! He had a listening ear, and Joe felt better. You see, his friend had the gift of encouragement in the faith. It was not so much what his friend said, but the way it was said. It was the timing of the whole thing. It was God speaking through his friend to meet a specific need. Joe needed that word of encouragement, and it lifted his drooping spirit.

Paul was writing to the Thessalonian Christians in a time of their affliction. He sent young Timothy to encourage them in their faith. Timothy had the gift of encouragement. Will you encourage a fellow believer today? We need each other.

Heavenly Father, help us to have the spirit of discernment to know when to offer a word of encouragement. Give us the heart to love and uplift another because of You. In the name of Jesus, we pray. Amen.

Awaiting the Return

Do thy diligence to come shortly unto me (2 Timothy 4:9).

Scripture: **2 Timothy 4:9-15**
Song: **"Come, Ye Thankful People, Come"**

Jason and his co-worker Keith worked well together. The business prospered because of the harmony between them. They knew how to complement each other's work to make the business succeed. But when Keith had to be called away to take care of his ailing mother for an extended period of time, Jason had to carry on the task of running the business on his own. He had to do Keith's part as well for a time. He then realized how valuable his friend was in the running of his business.

Paul's relationship with Timothy was like that in the work of the ministry. While in a prison at Rome he longed for young Timothy to come and see him in person and to give him a full first-hand report on the work of the ministry. He missed his partner in the work of the Lord.

Today, let us acknowledge the people around us, and let us tell our valuable fellow workers how much we appreciate them. Often we do not realize how important they are to us until life situations change and we long to see and to work with them again. As believers, after our work here on earth we will all see each other in Heaven.

Heavenly Father, we thank You for the good people we work with every day. We are grateful for the way others help us. Teach us to love one another and to express Your wonderful love for all mankind. In the name of Jesus, we pray. Amen.

A Bridge for the Gospel

". . . I am clear of my responsibility. From now on I will go to the Gentiles" (Acts 18:6, *New International Version*).

Scripture: **Acts 18:1-10**
Song: **"We've a Story to Tell to the Nations"**

When I travel from Athens to Corinth, I look forward to crossing the bridge that spans the Corinthian Canal. One can marvel at the straight, deep cut the French dug to connect the Saronic Gulf of the Aegean Sea and the Gulf of Corinth of the Adriatic Sea more than a hundred years ago. Looking down toward the water 170 feet below, one may see a boat going through the canal.

The thought of a canal goes back as far as Alexander the Great and Julius Caesar. In 66 A.D., Nero undertook the building of a canal across this isthmus.

A bridge is an appropriate symbol for ancient Corinth, a city strategically located for the proclamation of the gospel. Trade going between central Greece on the north and the Peloponnesus on the south passed by Corinth, as did trade going east and west across the isthmus. In Paul's day, a five-mile-long causeway was used to haul boats on rollers from one sea to the other.

Corinth was a bridge for the gospel. What would you identify as bridges for the gospel today?

O God, give us boldness to speak the truth. Help us, by Your Spirit, to bridge the chasms that divide. In the name of Jesus. Amen.

February 17-23. **Ward Patterson, Ph.D** is a Christian writer living in Cincinnati, Ohio.

Are You Teachable?

He began to speak boldly in the synagogue. When Priscilla and Aquila heard him, they invited him to their home and explained to him the way of God more adequately (Acts 18:26, *New International Version*).

Scripture: **Acts 18:24-28**
Song: **"Teach Me Thy Way, O Lord"**

In today's Scripture we learn about Apollos. He was a Jew and a native of Alexandria, Egypt. He was learned, especially in the Scriptures, and a gifted communicator. He was courageous and capable of debating with others. But even more commendable, he was teachable.

What a wonderful thing it is to find a person who is both capable and teachable. Over the years, as I have been involved in teaching, the many teachable students have encouraged me. Perhaps they see the relevance of the material they are being asked to master to their lives. Or they simply want to know more about what is being discussed. Or they have honed their attention span in order to master complicated material. They have disciplined themselves to buckle down when learning becomes difficult. They want the truth.

When the teacher finds someone who has the discipline and intellect to accomplish much, but who is also humble enough to be receptive to the knowledge of others, he can feel that his teaching is worthwhile. Priscilla and Aquilla found such a person in Apollos.

Father, help us to be willing to teach and willing to learn. Amen.

February 19

The Network of the Faithful

I ask you to receive her in the Lord in a way worthy of the saints and to give her any help she may need from you (Romans 16:2, *New International Version*).

Scripture: **Romans 16:1-5**
Song: **"Come, All Christians, Be Committed"**

When I was a college student, I was a part of a choir that toured about during the breaks in the academic year. I really enjoyed the opportunity to visit a variety of churches and to stay in the homes of their members. I was struck then, and have been struck many times since, by the network of people that comprise the church.

Paul closes his monumental writing to the Roman church with personal greetings to individuals, churches, and households. He mentions at least 26 people by name. Many of them are unknown to us except for these notations by Paul. But listen to the things Paul tells us about them. Some risked their lives for Paul, some opened their homes for church meetings, some worked tirelessly for the church, some went to prison with Paul, and some endured the testing of their faith.

As Christians, we are a part of a network that stretches around the world. May we be a blessing to one another.

Gracious heavenly Father, we thank You for the community of faith. You have put around us so many people who have encouraged our walk with You. They have loved us and provided for our needs. Help us to be like them, wise about what is good and innocent about what is evil. In the name of Jesus, we pray. Amen.

Listen and Win

Be on your guard; stand firm in the faith; be men of courage; be strong. Do everything in love (1 Corinthians 16:13, 14, *New International Version*).

Scripture: **1 Corinthians 16:13-24**
Song: **"Lord, Thy Church on Earth is Seeking"**

One of the skills a good coach develops is the "pep talk." It is the final words of encouragement he or she gives to the team just before the game begins. It is spoken with great confidence. It reminds the team of all the hard work that has gone into preparing for this game.

First Corinthians 16:13, 14 sounds almost like Paul's pep talk to the church in Corinth. In powerful imperatives, he urges watchfulness, steadfastness, courage, strength, and love.

The story is told that in 1924, when Notre Dame was to play Princeton, Coach Knute Rockne had such a sore throat that he could hardly speak, let alone give his usual rousing pep talk. Instead of hearing their own coach, the Irish players heard the Princeton coach in the next room exhorting his team. "There's the best pep talker in the world," Rockne said. "Listen to him and win with his fight talk." Notre Dame won the game.

Listen to Paul . . . and win!

Almighty God, help us to be prepared for whatever comes our way. Help us to be firm in the face of opposition and strong in the face of ridicule. Help us to hold the truth in love. And help us to be devoted to the service of the saints. In the name of Jesus, we pray. Amen.

Take Your Burden to the Lord

The Lord will rescue me from every evil attack and will bring me safely to his heavenly kingdom (2 Timothy 4:18, *New International Version*).

Scripture: **2 Timothy 4:16-22**
Song: **"Be Still, My Soul"**

I was once lost in the high Himalayas of Nepal, separated from my porter, off my maps. It was a terrifying experience. My porter carried my sleeping bag and warm clothing in a conical basket on his back. In the evening, as we walked along a high ridge, we got separated. The sun began to set, and snow began to fall.

Fortunately, some Sherpa men came along the trail. When night fell, they built a fire and loaned me a blanket.

Alone again the next day, I finally found my way into a small village. That night, in a Himalayan house, I bedded down under a rug in front of a blazing fire.

I could not sleep. I worried about my porter and how I was going to find my way on the next day; I tossed and turned. Finally, the words of a hymn came to my mind: "Take your burden to the Lord and leave it there. If you trust and never doubt, He will surely lead you out."

The next day I found my way to a town where my porter was organizing a search party for me.

Paul knew what it was like to have the Lord carry his burdens. We can too.

Loving God, thank You for standing by us. Teach us to always rely on You. In the name of Jesus our Savior, we pray. Amen.

Be Humble, Gentle, and Patient

Be completely humble and gentle; be patient, bearing with one another in love (Ephesians 4:2, *New International Version*).

Scripture: **Ephesians 4:1-8**
Song: **"They'll Know We Are Christians by Our Love"**

It was a proud day when I received my doctorate. The dissertation had been written and defended. The forms had been submitted and approved. I stood among thousands of graduates awaiting the moment when Dr. J. J. Auer would slip the coveted hood over my head and congratulate me for my worthy accomplishment.

Dr. Auer, with great gravity and reverence, hooded me, and I was now resplendent with the plumage of academia and the ultimate symbols of my degree.

Then, after the ceremonies, I joined thousands of other graduates as they entered a large gymnasium to return their coveted attire to the university. I dumped my symbols of glory onto the five-foot high piles of academic regalia that were rising on the floor. What a few hours before we had treated as symbols of priceless honor, we now treated like refuse at a dump.

Such, alas, is the fate of so many of those things in which we take pride. They shine for a moment, and then their glory is gone.

***God and Father of all**, we pray for the unity of Your church. When disagreements and conflicts come, help us to bear with one another in patience, forgiveness, and love. We pray in the name of Jesus. Amen.*

Each Part Doing Its Work

From him the whole body, joined and held together by every supporting ligament, grows and builds itself up in love, as each part does its work (Ephesians 4:16, *New International Version*).

Scripture: **Ephesians 4:9-16**
Song: **"Our God Has Made Us One"**

Competition often shows the best and worst in people.

An article in *Newsweek* a couple of years ago was entitled, "Attack of the Battle Bots." It told of a new sport where "gearheads" spent as much as $50,000 to create remote-controlled robots to joust one another to the death. Five hundred contestants were expected for an upcoming tournament in California, and coverage of such tournaments was becoming the newest hit on cable TV.

As impressive as such robots are, no one has ever come up with one as flexible, adaptable, and unified as the human body. We are fearfully and wonderfully made, as the psalmist put it (Psalm 139:14). Paul saw the body as a fitting metaphor for the unity and diversity of the church (Romans 12:4-8; 1 Corinthians 12:12-31).

The parts of the church body may be different, but all make their special contribution to what the church body is capable of doing. The purpose of each part of the church body is to prepare God's people for service and bring about unity in the faith and knowledge of Christ.

Dear God, *help us to be involved for good. May we attain the full measure of the fullness of Christ. In His name we pray. Amen.*

Jesus Travels Our Roads

At that time Jesus came from Nazareth in Galilee and was baptized by John in the Jordan (Mark 1:9, *New International Version*).

Scripture: **Mark 1:1-13**
Song: **"One Day"**

In 1873 a missionary from Belgium went to the Hawaiian Island of Molokai to work with the patients in the leper colony there. After working closely with the people for several years, he himself contracted the disease and eventually died of it. Today he is affectionately remembered in Hawaii as Father Damien. His statue stands in the state capitol building, and a high school is named for him.

Jesus so identified with us when He was here on the earth in the flesh that He went through the experiences of temptation. He set the righteous example for us. In His temptation He experienced what we all go through, only He did it without failing.

We read in Hebrews that we have a high priest who has been tempted. It is comforting to know that whatever we may be going through, Jesus understands.

Dear heavenly Father, *thank You for sending Your Son to save us. Thank You that He was willing to feel our pain. In the name of Jesus, we pray. Amen.*

February 24-March 2. **Donnie Mings** and his wife, Charlotte, have been ministering in Hauula, Hawaii, for more than 23 years. They have two children and five grandchildren.

Change of Occupation

At once they left their nets and followed him (Mark 1:18, *New International Version*).

Scripture: **Mark 1:14-20**
Song: **"Jesus Calls Us"**

There was once a farm boy who spent time outdoors, taking care of his dad's livestock. He learned a lot about taking care of the animals, and he even from time to time risked his life to protect them from predators. One day while he was out in the fields, his dad sent someone to call him to the house. He wondered why he was needed, but when he went in, there was a man who amazingly proclaimed that the boy would be the next ruler of the land. What a change the young man, David, experienced.

The fishermen, Peter, Andrew, James, and John were hard-working, just trying to earn a living. They were simple men, without any particular social standing or religious training. They were on the job, by the lake, working on their fishing nets. When Jesus called them, they left what they were doing and followed Him. They obediently became the pillars of the church.

Today Jesus calls to each of us, no matter what our station in life. He pleads with us to follow him. Are we willing to obey the call to follow Him?

Dear heavenly Father, *thank You for the example of the four fishermen who left all to follow Jesus. Please give us the strength to be willing to walk away from whatever hinders our following You. In the name of Jesus our Savior, we pray. Amen.*

Come And See

"Nazareth! Can anything good come from there?" Nathanael asked. "Come and see," said Philip (John 1:46, *New International Version*).

Scripture: **John 1:43-51**
Song: **"He Leadeth Me"**

Bumper stickers on the backs of cars tell us something about the people who own the cars. Perhaps you've seen the one that says, "Don't follow me, I'm lost." Probably that car should not be followed. But we all do some following in life. We have people that we admire, people who have done things we would like to do, people who have gone places we would like to go. We tend to follow such people in some way, doing things the way they do them, copying their lifestyles and heeding their advice. Most people are like sheep needing a shepherd.

There is Someone whom we can follow with complete trust. His name is Jesus. Philip and Nathanael first recognized who Jesus was. They accepted His position as Messiah and His authority to call them to follow Him. Then they went with Him, forsaking whatever they were doing in life, in order to learn from Him and do what He wanted them to do. Jesus is just as capable and trustworthy to lead us today as then.

Dear heavenly Father, *thank You that Jesus is a shepherd we can follow without having to worry. He never gets lost. Thank You that He is patient with us and that He knows our needs. Help us to follow Him faithfully. In His name, we pray. Amen.*

Fishers of Men

Then Jesus said to Simon, "Don't be afraid; from now on you will catch men" (Luke 5:10, *New International Version*).

Scripture: **Luke 5:1-11**
Song: **"Rescue the Perishing"**

What can you take with you when you go to Heaven? Can you take your money? Your car or your house? We invest a lot of time and money in things like music systems, pictures, art, jewelry, and other treasures that are useful during our time here on the earth. These things have to be left behind. But something of great value can be taken with us. We can take people with us: our families, friends, and others that our lives touch. We just have to make sure that they and we are on the right road, trusting in Jesus Christ as the way to Heaven.

The four fishermen Jesus called were used to catching fish. They took fish out of one environment (water) into another environment (air). That meant certain death to the fish. They went from life to death. Now those same four would be working with people instead of fish, and they would be taking them in the other direction, from death to life. You and I can share in that work today. We can help bring people into a saved relationship with that same Jesus, the way to eternal life in Heaven.

Dear heavenly Father, thank You that people are precious to You. Thank You that we can take our loved ones with us as we journey to be with You. Help us to witness to all that we know today. In Jesus' name, we pray. Amen.

A Slave Set Free

So if the Son sets you free, you will be free indeed (John 8:36, *New International Version*).

Scripture: **Mark 1:21-28**
Song: **"Jesus, I Come"**

There are people today who are under some kind of bondage. We see it in the ways in which they live their lives. It may be a chemical abuse, gambling, financial bondage, or a wrong relationship. There are also those who are under a demonic possession that destroys both the body and soul.

Jesus came to "set the captives free." He came to deliver us from the evil one. He came to give spiritual deliverance and freedom from the one who can destroy the soul.

It was the Sabbath day, and Jesus went to the synagogue in Capernaum, along the shores of the Sea of Galilee, and began to teach. The people who were in the synagogue were astonished at what Jesus was saying. There was a man in the synagogue that day that was walking around freely, unfettered in the eyes of society. But he was a total slave, controlled by a demon. Jesus had compassion on him and set him free.

Jesus wants to set us free today as well, whatever our bondage might be. We can come to Him and be free.

Dear heavenly Father, *thank You for freedom in Christ Jesus. Help us to live as a people set free from all bondage. Help us to lead others to You. In the name of Jesus our Savior, we pray. Amen.*

In You, O Father, I put my trust. I bring my prayers and petitions before You that Your name may be glorified!

_____

_____

_____

_____

_____

_____

_____

_____

_____

_____

_____

_____

_____

_____

_____

_____

_____

_____

Devotions

I fall on my knees before the Father, from whom every family in heaven and on earth receives its true name

(Ephesians 3:14, *Today's English Version*).

March

Photo of Paul and Lucille Perry at the celebration of 50 years of ministry is by their son Chuck Perry

Our Greatest Need

That evening after sunset the people brought to Jesus all the sick and demon-possessed (Mark 1:32, *New International Version*).

Scripture: **Mark 1:29-38**
Song: **"I Need Jesus"**

I have a friend who started coming to church because something tragic had happened to one of his children. Many people who know about the Lord put off coming to Him and serving Him until something bad happens or they have some kind of crisis in their lives. Why is that? Perhaps it's because they do not see their need for the Lord until they get into trouble. Jesus calls us to Himself at all times. Not just in a crisis.

In Capernaum, which is on the shores of the Sea of Galilee, people came to the Lord. They came because they saw that Jesus could heal their sickness and deliver them from demonic oppression.

When Jesus healed Peter's mother-in-law, the result was that the whole town came to Him. Jesus was able to heal the sick and then use their need to bring many of them to believe in Him and accept Him as Lord.

Dear Lord, *help us not to wait until we have a problem before we come to You. Help us to talk to You all the time about situations we face in life. Thank You for reminding us that You are our greatest need. In Jesus' name, we pray. Amen.*

March 1-2. **Donnie Mings** and his wife, Charlotte, have been ministering in Hauula, Hawaii, for more than 23 years. They have children and grandchildren.

Galilean Ministry

So he traveled throughout Galilee, preaching in their synagogues and driving out demons (Mark 1:39, *New International Version*).

Scripture: **Mark 1:39-45**
Song: **"Sunlight"**

In recent years archaeologists have unearthed a magnificent Greco-Roman city just four miles from Nazareth, where Jesus grew up. We know it as Sepphoris. From the ongoing excavations we are getting a picture of a place in Galilee that is not mentioned in the Bible. It appears that there was a considerable non-Jewish influence in "Galilee of the Gentiles," as it is called in the Scriptures. We now understand how there could have been a herd of pigs just east of the lake.

Jesus' ministry was active in the Galilee area. It is here that much of His healing ministry took place. We read that He preached in the synagogues throughout all Galilee, and He also cast out devils. Everywhere He went He brought a spoken message of healing for the spirit and soul of man.

There was a greater need to teach the people the things of God because the Gentile presence in the area also meant that there was more pagan influence. Wherever the Lord God is unknown, the need is the greatest, and Jesus spent much time ministering in that environment.

Dear heavenly Father, *thank You for the light of Jesus Christ and His gospel. Help us to follow You. In thy Son's name, we pray. Amen.*

The Aroma of a Forgiven Man

By this shall all men know that ye are my disciples, if ye have love one to another (John 13:35).

Scripture: **Mark 2:1-12**
Song: **"What a Friend We Have in Jesus"**

In Kenya, Africa, there was a funeral for a gentleman who had given fifty years of his life to God to win the Maasai people for the Lord. A Maasai warrior said the following about this man:

"I met this man when I was eight years old. His expression of love was fantastic. He would enter our class singing, 'What a Friend We Have in Jesus.' I can hear him . . . I can hear his familiar and joyous voice. I can see his kind, serene and loving gaze. He came bringing Bibles. His music would echo throughout our whole school. This man gave us hope. He gave us Jesus."

In the Scripture text for today, we read of a man with palsy who wanted to see Jesus. Men brought the man on a litter, and when they couldn't get in the door, they took the roof off and let him down. He met Jesus because these four men cared enough to make a difference.

Because the Maasai saw the love of Jesus in a man's life, many came to know Jesus.

Lord, *let Your love reach out through us. Let Your love and compassion be seen in us. In the name of Jesus, we pray. Amen.*

March 3-8. **Betty Sweeney**, a retired nurse and mother of three grown children, resides in Jersey Shore, Pennsylvania.

That They May Know Him

For God sent not his Son into the world to condemn the world; but that the world through him might be saved (John 3:17).

Scripture: **Mark 2:13-17**
Song: **"More Like the Master"**

In the Scripture for today we find Jesus eating with publicans and sinners. *Why would He do such a thing?* we ask ourselves.

Jesus did not eat with sinners because He felt that their sins did not matter. He ate with them because their condition did matter to God. He didn't need to find out what they were all about because in John 2:25 we read, "He needed not that any should testify of man for he knew what was in man."

We read in the Word of God that Jesus meets the needs of the sin-sick heart. His compassion reaches out to the one who is dying in sin. He is the example for us to follow as we live a life of compassion and love toward our fellowmen.

What can we do today to help the world to know the love of God in a personal way?

Lord, as we witness for You, let the presence of Your Son by the power of the Holy Spirit meet the needs of each of us. May we show forth the gentleness of Your grace as we strive to meet the needs of each troubled heart we know. Let Your love be so prevalent in our lives that all the world will know its Your power. Thank you, Lord Jesus. In thy holy name we pray. Amen.

The Joy of One Lost Soul

I say unto you that likewise joy shall be in heaven over one sinner that repenteth more than over ninety and nine just persons, which need no repentance (Luke 15:7).

Scripture: **Luke 15:1-7**
Song: **"The Ninety and Nine"**

When our children were young we lived in the city. I would often pack a lunch and take the children to meet my husband where he worked, and we would have lunch together. The children thoroughly enjoyed this. One day as we were debarking the 'L' train, my son, who was carrying a lunch pail, caught his hand in the door just as the door closed. I looked up and there was a young man in his early twenties who had spread the door open enough to free my son and the lunch pail. I can still see that young man and his beautiful smile. The kindness of this young man saved my son's life. We felt joy that day!

I believe this is the kind of joy that is referred to in the Scripture verse for today. It is a joy that reaches down deep within us.

When Adam and Eve sinned in the Garden of Eden, there was no hope for mankind, just as it appeared that there was no hope for my son and his lunch pail. That young man intervened; even so Jesus Christ intervened and made a way back to God.

Heavenly Father, *may we never forget the love You show. Help us to constantly be aware that no one but You can bring salvation to the world. In the name of Jesus, we pray. Amen.*

A New Person In Christ

Therefore if any man be in Christ, he is a new creature: old things are passed away; behold, all things are become new (2 Corinthians 5:17).

Scripture: **Mark 2:18-22**
Song: **"There's a New Name Written Down in Glory"**

A child may ask a parent, "Why do I look like this?" The parent answers, "It is just the way God made you." This answer is one that helps us all to feel better about ourselves. When we accept Christ as our Savior and Lord, we are new in Him. He has made us His children. We now belong to Him and can feel the assurance of His presence.

Some people who accept Jesus as Savior think He begins to make over the old flesh. They begin to tag on nice little deeds, and try to be just like the good people in their churches. In the Word of God, we read, "I am crucified with Christ: nevertheless I live; yet not I, but Christ liveth in me: and the life which I now live in the flesh I live by the faith of the son of God, who loved me, and gave himself for me" (Galatians 2:20).

I've learned that we are all made in the image of God. We are all special in His sight.

Lord, I bring all my family, friends, neighbors to you. May you find me faithful in holding them up to you. When someone is hurting, may my hands reach out with your gentleness. Give me a loving heart that knows your forgiveness. May you through me be able to reach some lost person to a new creature in Christ. Thank you, Lord Jesus.

The Lord of the Harvest

The Son of man is Lord also of the sabbath (Mark 2:28).

Scripture: **Mark: 2:23-28**
Song: **"Bringing in the Sheaves"**

Every time I read of Jesus going through the cornfields, I think of my childhood days. For we who have lived on a farm, we know what "planting in corn" means. It was that endless walking of each row, planting where the corn had not come up.

One day my father sent my sister, brothers and me to the cornfield to replant the corn that had not come up. In order to complete the job quickly, every time I came around the end of a row, I threw a cup of corn down over the railroad bank. It wasn't long before the work was completed. Dad was proud of us—that is until he found corn growing on the bank near the cornfield.

I learned a lesson that day. I still remember the disappointment my father felt when he learned that I was the one who threw the corn away.

The disciples were hungry and picked corn. The Pharisees reminded Christ that it was the sabbath. He referred them to the story of David. Jesus reminded the Pharisees that the sabbath was made for man, and not man for the sabbath. Therefore the Son of man is Lord of the sabbath. We worship the Lord of the sabbath.

Lord, open our eyes to Your teachings. May we always depend on You. Help us to desire only to do what You want us to do. In the name of Jesus, we pray. Amen.

Power and Compassion

Trust in the Lord and do good (Psalm 37:3).

Scripture: **Mark 3:1-6**
Song: **"Just a Little Talk with Jesus"**

During my nursing career I have seen heartbreaking events. One night at the closing of the evening shift I saw my vibrant friend, Margie, who had just experienced a stroke, lay before me unable to lift her hand.

I think of the man in our Scripture text. Was he like my friend? What had caused his hand to be withered?

The Scripture tells us that Jesus entered the synagogue and saw the man with the withered hand. He looked around and saw that the Pharisees were waiting to see what He would do. Because Jesus knew the hearts of those looking on, He showed His power and His compassion for the man as He said to him, "Stretch forth thy hand," and the man's hand was made whole.

People in the synagogue watched Jesus. The Pharisees were interested in accusing Him. They left to tell those in power so that they could punish Jesus.

Jesus uses our hands to help those who are sick. The world sees the works of Jesus as we care for one another. In this way, the world can see the power of Christ.

What can we do today to show the power and compassion of Jesus, our Savior?

Lord, *may we be faithful in showing the world Your power and compassion. Help us to follow You. In thy name, we pray. Amen.*

The Crowd Is Coming

Unto thee, O Lord, do I lift up my soul. O my God, I trust in thee: . . Show me thy ways, O Lord; teach me thy paths. Lead me in thy truth (Psalm 25:1, 2, 4, 5).

Scripture: **Mark 3:7-12**
Song: **"To the Work!"**

People came to listen as Jesus taught. They had never heard the Word of God spoken in such a way. Not only His words, but Jesus' actions caused people to wonder who He might be. The crowds kept coming to hear Him.

The people had witnessed Jesus healing the sick, raising the dead, and performing miracles on a daily basis. The word spread quickly among the regions that miracles were happening daily.

We have joined Jesus in His works today. We are His hands, feet, and heart. The world knows of His saving grace by the actions of His disciples. We may tire as Jesus did when He wanted to just rest in the boat on the Sea of Galilee. But there is work to be done. The crowds are coming. Let us help our Savior accomplish the work.

Dear heavenly Father and Lord of all, *direct our path that we may stand firm in You. May our words and actions speak only of Your great love and compassion. Give us strength today to keep serving You even when we feel we are too tired to continue. Help us to look to the life of Christ here on earth as our example to follow. In His holy name, we pray. Amen.*

March 9. Staff

Where Is My Peace?

He said to his disciples, "Why are you so afraid? Do you still have no faith?" (Mark 4:40, *New International Version*).

Scripture: **Mark 4:35-41**
Song: **"Master the Tempest Is Raging"**

The word *peace* entices us! Some of us have lived long enough to know that storms will come in many ways and at the worst times. Storms will come, and we suspect the same thing the disciples suspected when they saw Jesus sleeping in the bow of the boat. We suspect He does not care or is unable to help. Neither is true. The sleeping Jesus arises and in a terse statement, rebukes the storm. We are reminded of Jesus' authority over the wind and waves. Some have not experienced actual deliverance from the storms of life. Where is their "Peace, be still"?

Commentator William Barclay struggled with this passage because his daughter was lost in a sailing accident due to a storm. He asked many times why there was no stilling of the storm for his daughter. He reported that the Lord at least stilled the storm in his heart. In whatever way it comes, Christians have the assurance they will hear, "Peace, be still."

Dear Father, *sometimes we feel as if life is a hurricane. Help us to find peace. Not just the peace that is in the eye of the storm, but also the peace that is in You. Through Christ our Lord, we pray. Amen.*

February 10-16. **J. Michael Shannon** is on the staff at Cincinnati Bible College.

Riding the Storm

Immediately he spoke to them and said, "Take courage! It is I. Don't be afraid" (Mark 6:50b, *New International Version*).

Scripture: **Mark 6:45-51**
Song: **"Tell Me the Story of Jesus"**

The disciples had been in a storm before. They had been in the boat. But something was different this time. This time Jesus was not there. The first time they had this experience Jesus was in the boat. They had learned a mighty lesson that day. This day they would learn something even greater. On the former occasion they marveled that Jesus could command the wind and waves. This time they marveled that he broke the laws of physics and walked on water. Jesus did many miracles. Many of the miracles are like living the parables. When Jesus walked on water, He was proving that He would meet His disciples in whatever situation they found themselves.

As soon as Peter realized it was Jesus on the water, he asked if he could walk on water with Jesus. This is a remarkable request for several reasons. Jumping out of the boat in a storm is like jumping out of an airplane. Peter reasons that it is safer to be with Jesus outside the boat then to be inside the boat without Him. This miracle taught about Jesus' power and His love.

We learn many things in a crisis. Christ will be there for us, and we will ride the storm.

Help us, Father, to remember that in the midst of the storm we must keep a sharp eye on Jesus. In His name, we pray. Amen.

From Torment to Tranquility

He shouted at the top of his voice, "What do you want with me, Jesus, Son of the Most High God? Swear to God that you won't torture me!" (Mark 5:7, *New International Version*)

Scripture: **Mark 5:1-10**
Song: **"How Firm a Foundation"**

What a strange welcoming committee Jesus encountered! Jesus must have felt He was in unfriendly territory. He was in the area of the Decapolis, or Ten Cities, in the area of Gadara. Gentiles dominated it. Keepers of pigs (regarded as unclean) abounded. It was home to demoniacs living among the tombs. One demoniac appealed to Jesus not to torture him. Why did he ask that? Would Jesus actually torment a person? This story is a more magnified version of our story. Here is man wracked by sin and given over to animalistic and harmful behavior. When he sees Jesus, he is tortured by what he could be.

While our problem may not be as severe as his, we are much like this man. We cannot solve our sin problem. Like this man, we can receive from Jesus wholeness, peace and true humanity. When this demoniac was in his right mind, he became a witness to the whole community. When we let Jesus solve our problems, we can become walking sermons on Jesus' love and power.

Lord, if the path to peace leads by way of torment, take us there. We want to follow You. May we come to know peace in You. Through the Prince of Peace, we pray. Amen.

From Amazement to Fear

When they came to Jesus, they saw the man who had been possessed by the legion of demons sitting there, dressed and in his right mind; and they were afraid (Mark 5:15, *New International Version*).

Scripture: **Mark 5:11-20**
Song: **"I Stand Amazed"**

It was a strange sight. They were amazed. The crowd had seen a demoniac cleansed, but that was not the sole source of their amazement. It was also the way it was done that filled them with wonder. The demons asked permission from Jesus to enter pigs, and Jesus granted their request. This was strange then and seems even stranger to us today. When the demons entered the pigs, the pigs were as confused as the man had been. They careened wildly into the lake and were drowned. There must have been some humor in this. What better place for an unclean spirit than in an unclean animal like a pig? (Jews considered pigs to be ritually unclean). Some blamed Jesus for the loss of the pigs, but it was the demons that did it. In the final analysis, a human is worth more than a pig. The people were so amazed that the feeling turned quickly to fear. They asked Jesus to leave their region, and He did. But this remained: a one-time demoniac in his right mind and the amazement.

Lord, may we never lose the sense of wonder. May the amazement we feel draw us closer to You and not farther away. Through Jesus who caused demons to tremble, we pray. Amen.

The Gift of Joy

This, the first of his miraculous signs, Jesus performed at Cana in Galilee. He thus revealed his glory, and his disciples put their faith in him (John 2:11, *New International Version*).

Scripture: **John 2:1-11**
Song: **"Joyful, Joyful We Adore Thee"**

Jesus used an important gathering—a wedding reception—for His first miracle. If we had been Jesus' public relations director, we would surely have chosen a different kind of miracle and a more prominent place. Nevertheless, this was the setting for Jesus' first miracle. Jesus understood how embarrassing it was to run out of refreshment on the biggest day a family will ever experience. After all, a wedding was a community affair that lasted a week. Since Jesus' mother asked for His help, it may have been a relative's or close friend's family.

There is something sweet in the act of a miracle at a country wedding. It sanctifies marriage, and it reveals how much joy would be a part of the Savior's work. The water, colorless and tasteless, drawn from ceremonial washing jars was turned into a kind of divine wine, colorful and effervescent. Well, it may be an unnecessary miracle, and we might not have done it, but aren't you glad He did? He still brings color and effervescence to life.

Sometimes, Father, my life is not so much tragic as it is tedious. Sometimes I handle despair better than drabness. Say the word and bring new vitality to my life, I pray. Through Christ, the joy giver, we pray. Amen.

The Gift of Life

I tell you the truth, whoever hears my word and believes him who sent me has eternal life and will not be condemned; he has crossed over from death to life (John 5:24, *New International Version*).

Scripture: **John 5:19-24**
Song: **"His Name Is Life"**

Death surrounds us and pervades every area of our lives. Everything in this world that lives also dies.

The Bible teaches that God is a God of life. Jesus reminds us that God desires to give us new life—eternal life. Jesus, as the Son of God, gives new life. This new life has both a physical and spiritual dimension.

Often we tell grieving people that death is just a natural part of life. On one level this is true. It is natural in the sense that all living things die.

The Bible teaches that death is an enemy. Thanks be to God, it's a defeated enemy. The promise of Scripture is that God will give His children eternal life. That means that death is simply the transition from one kind of life to another. This is not to discount the grief we feel when a friend or loved one dies. In our grief, we hear the voice of Jesus, speaking for His father, and saying to us "Our God gives life." The question is, "Will we take it?"

Dear Father, *even though death surrounds us, we see that life also surrounds us. We believe that life is more powerful than death. Help us to live in this life that we might also live in the life to come. Through Jesus Christ, our Savior and giver of life, we pray. Amen.*

Authority!

He taught as one who had authority, and not as their teachers of the law (Matthew 7:29, *New International Version*).

Scripture: **Matthew 7:24-29**
Song: **"Wonderful Words of Life"**

There have been many preachers and teachers in the world, but no one ever taught or preached like Jesus. What was unique about Jesus' teaching? His listeners said He taught as one with authority, not like the other rabbis. Other preachers can have the limited authority that comes from knowledge and wisdom. Some have only pretended authority. All can have the derived authority that comes from preaching and teaching the Word of God. Only Jesus had full authority, and it was reflected in His teaching.

The story that preceded this assessment of Jesus is a familiar one. Jesus told of wise and foolish men who were both builders. The foolish man built his house on the sand. Since childhood we know what happened to that house. It went splat. The wise man was the one who heard the word and acted on it. We often miss that part of Jesus' teaching here. It does no good to know something but not act on it. This is what we should always do with teaching from one who has authority. We should listen and do.

Dear Father, how easy it is to just listen. Help us to remember that to listen and do nothing is the same as not listening at all. May we allow You to be Lord of life today. Through the Lord Jesus, we pray. Amen.

Hometown Boy Makes Good

He could there do no mighty work, save that he laid hands upon a few sick folk, and healed them (Mark 6:5, 6).

Scripture: **Mark 6:1-6**
Song: **"All Hail the Power of Jesus' Name"**

The writer Somerset Maugham said of other writers, "We like to see a young man get ahead, but not clear out of sight." People sometimes feel this way about a hometown boy who makes good. They want to see him succeed, but not clear out of sight. It is true that the people at Nazareth rejected Jesus because they thought they knew Him so well! In truth, they did not know Him at all!

Some of us have heard about Jesus and sung about Jesus and read about Jesus for so many years that we think we know Him well. We may thus miss the impact of His divine nature, character, and life. There is an old saying that familiarity breeds contempt. If only we could imagine ourselves learning about Jesus for the first time! How great would be our excitement! Missionaries often work with people who have not known Christ before. They can sometimes see Him through their eyes. It is for the missionaries a rewarding and inspiring experience.

Dear God, help us to appreciate what a wonderful Savior is Jesus our Lord. In His holy name, we pray. Amen.

March 17-23. **Robert Shannon** has been a minister, missionary, and college professor. He and his wife are now enjoying retirement in Valle Crucis, North Carolina.

Now it's Now

When they heard this saying [many] said, Of a truth this is the Prophet. Others said, This is the Christ (John 7:40, 41).

Scripture: **John 7:37-44**
Song: **"Crown Him With Many Crowns"**

Time moves slowly for a little child. In one family parents kept promising their children a trip to Disneyland. To the little girl it seemed a long wait. Finally, they arrived and she saw the outline of Disneyland against the California sky. She exclaimed, "First it was after a while and then it was pretty soon, and now it's now!"

That was the case with the coming of the Messiah. When the prophets first spoke of it, the event was in the far distant future. Then it was in the immediate future. Finally Jesus came, and those who had waited so long could say, "Now, it's now!" Unfortunately, many did not accept the fact that Jesus was the Messiah. They could not understand that the waiting was over. Though the time for the Messiah was obviously right, they did not recognize Him. Though He fulfilled every prophecy concerning the Messiah, they did not recognize Him. Some have had the experience of caring for a loved one whose mind or memory has gone. It is a heart-wrenching thing not to be recognized by those you love. Imagine then how Jesus felt!

Dear God, whatever others may say, we believe that Your Son, the long awaited Messiah, did come into the world in the person of Jesus Christ, and we acknowledge Him. In His name, we pray. Amen.

The Verdict Before the Trial

Look into it and you will find that a prophet does not come out of Galilee. Then each went to his own home (John 7:52, 53, *New International Version*).

Scripture: **John 7:45-52**
Song: **"Jesus Is All the World to Me"**

It is common for people in one place to put down people from a neighboring place. Northern people tell jokes about southern people, and city people tell jokes about country people. People in one state often put down those in the next state. Usually it is all done in fun, but sometimes the jokes are taken seriously. And some of the put-downs are unkind and hurtful.

We see that same sort of thing in today's Scripture. No doubt the Galileans put down the Judeans as patronizing city slickers. Certainly the Judeans put down the Galileans as country bumpkins. Their prejudice against the region so blinded them they would not even look at the evidence. It reminds us of the old saying, "My mind is made up. Don't bother me with the facts." While this was not a formal trial, it is still fair to say that they had decided on the verdict before the trial! If they had only examined the evidence. But they brush aside those who call for fairness, so great is their hatred of Jesus. Do we judge others as unfairly as they judged Jesus?

O Lord, You are just and the true judge of all. Forgive us if we show prejudice or disrespect. Help us to be fair to others and to be faithful to Jesus. In His name holy name, we pray. Amen.

Marks of the Kingdom

And as you go, preach, saying, The kingdom of heaven is at hand (Matthew 10:7).

Scripture: **Matthew 10:5-15**
Song: **"The Banner of the Cross"**

In order to have a kingdom, there must be a territory. "The earth is the Lord's and the fulness thereof" (Psalm 24:1). In order to have a kingdom, there must be a King. Jesus Christ is "the prince of the kings of the earth" (Revelation 1:5). He is the King of kings (Revelation 19:16). In order to have a kingdom, there must be subjects. "Serve the Lord with fear" (Psalm 2:11). Every kingdom has a flag. Ours is the bloodstained banner of the cross. A kingdom must have an army. "And the armies which were in heaven followed him upon white horses, clothed in fine linen, white and clean" (Revelation 19:14). And, of course, the King must have a crown. "On his head were many crowns" (Revelation 19:12). A kingdom must have laws. "The law of the Lord is perfect" (Psalm 19:7). This is the kingdom Jesus came to establish. This is the kingdom to which every believer belongs. There are only two spiritual kingdoms. We have left the kingdom of darkness for the kingdom of God (Colossians 1:13). Someday God's kingdom will conquer and the kingdoms of this world will all be His (Revelation 11:15).

Dear God, *forgive us if we take lightly our privilege to be in Christ's kingdom. Help us to be loyal subjects. We pray through Him. Amen.*

Surprising Examples

Be ye therefore wise as serpents, and harmless as doves (Matthew 10:16).

Scripture: **Matthew 10:16-26**
Song: **"Living for Jesus"**

There are many birds mentioned in the Bible, but we are told to be like the dove. There are many animals mentioned in the Bible. We are instructed to be like the serpent. We are told we are like sheep. We are told we can have strength like eagles (Isaiah 40:31).

We are told to be like doves. The dove is the symbol of innocence and peace. Doves like to be around people. While the dove of the Bible is not exactly the same as our dove in the Western world, it is similar.

There are different kinds of serpents and other animals in different parts of the world. Most animals share a common trait: they try to escape from danger.

When Jesus sent His followers out, they were to avoid danger. They were not to put themselves needlessly in harm's way. Surely we can add that we should not put ourselves in temptation's way. "Lead us not into temptation" is a part of the prayer Jesus taught us. The dove is characterized by innocence; the serpent by wisdom. We are to strive for both qualities.

Dear Father, *we know that there are spiritual dangers in the world. Help us to avoid both temptation and danger. Give us grace to be all that You want us to be. Keep before us always the example of Your Son Jesus. In His holy name, we pray. Amen.*

Recognizing Jesus

He that receiveth you receiveth me; and he that receiveth me receiveth him that sent me (Matthew 10:40).

Scripture: **Matthew 10:37-42**
Song: **"Make Me a Blessing"**

There is story of a shoemaker who dreamed that Christ would visit him the next day. He got up early to be ready. He waited all morning, but the only thing that happened was a beggar came by with wornout shoes. He made him a pair and gave them to him. He waited through the afternoon, but only an old woman came by with a heavy load of firewood. He bought her wood and gave her the food he had prepared for Christ. Night fell, and a lost child came by, crying. He locked the shop and took the child home. When he returned he was sure that Christ had come and he had missed him. He was so sad and thought of ways he would have welcomed his Lord. Then he cried out, "Why did you not come today? And if you did come, why did you come when I was away"? And the Lord answered, "I kept my word. I came to you three times today. I was the beggar, the woman, and the child lost in the street." Jesus said, "Inasmuch as ye have done it unto one of the least of these my brethren, ye have done it unto me . . . Inasmuch as ye did it not to one of the least of these, ye did it not unto me."

Dear Father, *we miss so many opportunities. As You forgive us for the evil we have done, please forgive us for the good we have not done. We pray in Jesus' name. Amen.*

Leave the Light On

And he called unto him the twelve, and began to send them forth by two and two (Mark 6:7).

Scripture: **Mark 6:7-13**
Song: **"So Send I You"**

Long ago streets were lit, not by electric lights, but by gas lamps. There was a man whose job it was to light those lamps every evening. John Ruskin was sitting on a hill overlooking a village at the time the lamplighter began his work. He said the man himself could not be seen, but one could tell where he had left lamps burning!

The twelve apostles whom Jesus sent were like that. Even after they had gone on to another place, one could tell where they had been. We can be like that, too. Whether we go across the street or across the sea, Christ wants to send each one of us out to light a lamp for someone who lives in darkness. Often the light will still be burning even after the life of the lamplighter has ended. It is wonderful to know that there are things that will outlive us, and one of them is our influence. Our mission may not be identical to that of the twelve in today's text, but the motive is the same, and the Master is the same, and the rewards are the same. Often we say to a family member, "Leave the light on!" Jesus, the Light of the world, asks us who reflect Him to leave the Light on!

Dear God, we once walked in darkness, but now we are stepping in the light. Help us to share the light. We pray through Jesus Christ whose life is the light of men. Amen.

Traditions

Howbeit in vain do they worship me, teaching for doctrines the commandments of men (Mark 7:7).

Scripture: **Mark 7:1-8**
Song: **"Turn Your Eyes Upon Jesus"**

Traditions—every family has them. We especially notice traditions during times of celebration—holidays, birthdays, weddings, and parties of all sorts. Searches are made for just the right Christmas tree, the one that reminds you of the tree that sat in the house where you grew up. Or there is that special Thanksgiving recipe for the perfect pumpkin pie, the recipe that Grandma always used. The camping trip you now take with your son makes you feel closer to your dad because you now know how he felt while camping with you.

Traditions bind us together, and we feel comfortable and secure. Traditions give us a sense of true belonging. They help to build a strong family. Traditions give the young and the old something to share together, creating a stronger tie and a deeper understanding of one another.

Remembering and obeying God's commandments is what matters. Having traditions, whether they are old and familiar or something new, cannot become more important than the words of our heavenly Father.

O Father, keep us ever mindful of Your commandments. Help us to worship You. In the name of Jesus, we pray. Amen.

March 24-30. **K.D. Bell** is a Christian writer living in Cincinnati, Ohio.

Inside Out

There is nothing from without a man, that entering into him can defile him: but the things which come out of him, those are they that defile the man (Mark 7:15).

Scripture: **Mark 7:9-15**
Song: **"Let the Words of My Mouth"**

My two-year-old is very independent. She has older siblings whom she tries to emulate. This often leads to many adventures around our home—like the time we had to have a full-house search for the missing guinea pig that was finally discovered hidden in her bedroom. She insists on getting ready to go "bye-bye" all by herself. We find toothpaste "art" adorning bathroom walls, mirrors and doors. Her clothes don't always end up the way she wants, two little human legs rest in one pant leg, pockets on the front are mysteriously on the back, and the beautiful flowers are nowhere to be seen–they're on the inside not the outside.

What would we look like if we wore our "insides" on the outside? What if our inner thoughts were the first thing everyone saw when they looked at us?

When our hearts are full of the joy, peace and understanding of God's word, we reflect true beauty. It isn't what happens to us or around us that matters. Our outsides don't need to be beautiful—our insides do.

Dearest Lord Jesus, *teach me to fill my innermost being with Your teachings and love. When I wear my "inside" on the outside, may I be beautiful and acceptable unto You. In Jesus name, I pray. Amen.*

But It Looks Good on the Outside

For as he thinketh in his heart, so is he (Proverbs 23:7).

Scripture: Mark 7:17-23
Song: "Take My Life and Let It Be"

We have a pear tree in our backyard. In the spring the tree is covered in fragrant white flowers, its limbs stretching farther into the sky than a fruit tree should be allowed to grow. In the summer we are blessed with sweet-tasting fruit, sometimes even more fruit than I know what to do with. I make pear sauce, pear mincemeat, pear halves and even pickled pears. But I think the pears that we like best are the ones we choose, pick and eat straight from the tree. Standing under the tree, we search the boughs for the largest, ripest pear we can find. There are times when the fruit selected turns out to be a lot less appetizing than was first hoped. Sometimes the fruit so golden on the outside is mealy on the inside, or a worm has burrowed in through the tiniest of holes and has grown, fattening itself on the meat of a pear that I for one no longer have any desire to eat.

We may look beautiful on the outside, but the inside of the soul may not hold up under closer scrutiny. Jesus tells us that all sins come from within the hearts of men. To be as God intended us, let us focus on Jesus, and our innermost thoughts can be pure in thought and deed.

Dear Father, *may Your love in me overflow into a world that needs to be molded in Your image. Set me apart to be a living example of Your will—pure and undefiled. In the name of Jesus, amen.*

The Little Things Matter

He that is faithful in that which is least is faithful also in much (Luke 16:10).

Scripture: **Luke 16:10-15**
Song: **"Our Best"**

My grandfather was an interesting man. He stood about five feet ten inches tall, had a tanned complexion and a smile that seemed to perpetually twinkle in his eyes. Like many men of his generation, talking wasn't as important as companionship. Still he had developed his own way of understanding what kind of person you were without asking a battery of questions or spending hours exploring your thoughts. I remember the "dime test." I saw him use it, sometimes multiple times on the same unsuspecting person. In the test, Grandpa would leave loose change, usually a dime (hence the name) lying on the countertop before the guest would arrive. Then he would see if the coin was left untouched by the guest. He learned if you were an honest and trustworthy person or not. He knew that how you respond in ordinary situations shows what kind of person you really are.

Jesus reminds us that little things matter. How we handle the little things shows how we will handle the big things. Do we bend our values to fit the situation? Do we think the situation is so trivial it does not matter? To God it always matters.

Heavenly Father, help us be faithful in little things so that we may prove to be faithful in great things. In Jesus' name, we pray. Amen.

I Want to Be Just Like You

 As ye have therefore received Christ Jesus the Lord, so walk ye in him (Colossians 2:6).

Scripture: **Colossians 2:6-10**
Song: **"Oh, to Be Like Thee"**

I watch my children and my neighbor's children playing together. There is a big age span, ten to two, but they are playing well together mainly because the older girls are accommodating the younger ones. They are swinging and sliding, racing each other, older ones pushing younger ones around the yard in toy cars. There are a few squabbles quickly resolved by the reminder to take turns. I heard one of my older daughters comment to my neighbor, "Look how my little sister does everything your daughter does." "Yes, and look how my oldest daughter does everything you do!" replies my neighbor, and they both laughed.

We often use others as an example of how to live. Sometimes we choose wisely and learn many good lessons. When we believe in Jesus, we have the greatest example to follow. By studying His teachings we can be more like Him. Our faith can be grounded in Him.

The popular question displayed in many settings "What would Jesus do?" should be our constant question. The Bible is where we go to find the answers.

Dearest Lord Jesus, thank You for the Bible so that we may learn to live the Christian life. Teach us to walk in righteousness. Teach us to become more like Jesus everyday. In His name, we pray. Amen.

March 29

A Clean Heart

Create in me a clean heart, O God; and renew a right spirit within me (Psalm 51:10).

Scripture: **Psalms 51:10-17**
Song: **"O for a Heart to Praise My God"**

My house needs a good old-fashioned spring cleaning. I once heard someone say that when her mother used to do the spring cleaning she would clear the room of all its furnishings. The furniture often ended up on the lawn to be cleaned. Drapes and bedding were washed and hung in the sun to air. The walls, windows, and floors were all scrubbed, new paint applied, and when the room was deemed dust free and spotless the furnishings were again arranged in a now fresh and sparkling room. Every room was given the same treatment. That is the kind of cleaning my house needs. The problem is I think I may have to move just to accomplish the task!

Sometimes I think that my spiritual heart needs just that level of work performed on it. I lose sight of the things that God sees as important. I let the clutter of misguided ideas and sins pile up until I'm not sure that anyone looking at me from the outside can tell that this is the place where I invited God to live. How blessed we are that through God's grace and the sacrifice of His Son we can be given a clean heart and a right spirit so that all can see God living in us!

Dear Father, *create in each of us a heart filled with Your praises, a pure heart ready to serve You. In Jesus' name, we pray. Amen.*

Random Acts of Kindness

Give, and it shall be given unto you; good measure, pressed down, and shaken together, and running over, shall men give into your bosom (Luke 6:38).

Scripture: **Luke 6:37-42**
Song: **"Love Divine"**

Years ago a hard-working English woman living in a small African country became widowed with little savings. She found work running a small library at a Christian retreat. She was thankful that God had given her a new place to serve and had provided for her needs. Months went by in contentment until one day an elderly gentleman stopped by and they began to converse. He indicated that he was a widower and wished for some companionship. Soon they were married. When she went to his house for the first time, she was stunned. He had never talked much about material things, but he was very well off indeed. They spent many happy years together, and she thanked God once again for His unexpected blessing.

God promises us that when we put Him first and serve Him we are rewarded in this life and in the next. Second Corinthians 9:6 says, "But this I say, He which soweth sparingly shall reap also sparingly; and he which soweth bountifully shall reap also bountifully."

Dear Father God, *teach us to give freely to others and to trust You to take care of us. Give us the joy that only comes from sharing Your love with others. In Jesus' name, we pray. Amen.*

Safe, Now!

Bless the one who comes in the name of the Lord (Psalm 118:26, *New Living Translation*).

Scripture: **Mark 11:1-11**
Song: **"Hosanna, Loud Hosanna"**

You're treading water at the bottom of a thirty-foot well. In exhaustion and fear, you're almost ready to give up. And then you hear a voice. You see an outline of head and shoulders, peering over the edge of the well, way above you. You hear a *swoosh* and then a rope dangles in front of your weary arms. You're saved!

What is the first word you say?

The hotel room has filled with smoke from the fire raging in the hallway. Then you hear the crash of glass and you see a fireman poke his gloved hand through the broken window. Your rescuer has come!

What is the first word you say?

If you're not thinking "Hosanna!" that's okay. Most of us have never been taught that the word literally means "save" or "save now." It's an expression of praise to God. It is the admission of need from a people looking for a Savior. We need what only Jesus can give: salvation from a fate worse than a bottomless well or a blazing inferno.

Thank You, God, *for sending a Savior. We praise Him for rescuing us from our sin, because we are powerless to save ourselves. In His name, amen.*

March 31. **Mark A. Taylor** is Vice-President of Church Resources at Standard Publishing. He and his wife, Evelyn, have two grown children.

Devotions

𝕸y son, keep my words, and lay up my commandments with thee. Keep my commandments, and live

(Proverbs 7:1, 2).

April

Photo by Julie Riley is of senior editor, Jonathan Underwood, his wife, Kathleen, and their sons Timothy, Benjamin, and Stephen. Their college age son, Joel, was not present for the photo.

My Prayer Notes

_____

_____

_____

_____

_____

_____

_____

_____

_____

_____

_____

_____

_____

_____

_____

_____

_____

_____

_____

_____

_____

_____

Wonderful Peace

He will proclaim peace to the nations. His rule will extend from sea to sea and from the River to the ends of the earth (Zechariah 9:10, *New International Version*).

Scripture: **Zechariah 9:9-12**
Song: **"Wonderful Peace"**

The promise of peace has motivated political leaders through the ages. The prayer for peace has been on the lips of every generation.

We fashion beautiful buildings and intricate diplomacy to create peace, and yet nations still war against each other. We build large armies and display sophisticated weapons to protect peace, and yet terrorists still attack.

And even in the quiet worlds of our everyday existence, conflict rears its head. Co-workers gossip. Neighbors quarrel. Applicants compete. School mates taunt and mock. Husbands and wives break their vows.

We would retreat to the safe confines of our private thoughts, but peace eludes us there, too.

We need the peace that Christ can give. When we trust Him to handle what only He can control, His love will not fail. "He will proclaim peace to the nations," and to our lives, too, when we let Him be the ruler of our hearts.

In our stress, our fears, and our guilt, we need Your peace, heavenly Father. We yield to Your control. Help us to feel the sweet relief that comes from fully trusting You. In the name of Jesus, we pray. Amen.

April 1-6. **Mark A. Taylor** is vice-president of Church Resources at Standard Publishing. He and his wife, Evelyn, have two grown children.

April 2

A Pattern and a Promise

Let every created thing give praise to the LORD, for he issued his command, and they came into being. . . . His orders will never be revoked (Psalm 148:5, 6, *New Living Translation*).

Scripture: **Luke 19:28-40**
Song: **"When Morning Gilds the Skies"**

Today's Bible story reflects a pattern and a promise that we see throughout Scripture. The writers exhort all of nature to praise God. The pastures and the valleys "shout for joy" (Psalm 65:13). Heaven and earth praise Him, along with the seas and everything that moves in the oceans (Psalm 69:34). "The floods clap their hands," and the hills are "joyful together" (Psalm 98:8). The psalmist encourages the sun and moon and stars to praise Him (Psalm 148:3). Because of the Lord's redemption, the prophet urges the mountains and the forests to "break forth into singing" (Isaiah 44:23).

The promise is that God's purposes will always be realized. His will cannot be thwarted forever. His victory is guaranteed. No one can stand in the way of His aim; not anyone—not even you or I.

God has created the earth for His glory. And He has provided a way for earth's people to live with Him forever. We can praise God for His plan and bring Him the greatest glory by accepting it.

We add our praises to the voices of nature, oh God. We acknowledge Your control of all history, and we seek to give You all control of our lives. In the name of Jesus, we pray. Amen.

It's Familiar, It's Frightening

Passion for your house burns within me, so those who insult you are also insulting me (Psalm 69:9, *New Living Translation*).

Scripture: **Mark 11:12-19**
Song: **"More About Jesus"**

We see something familiar in today's Bible story, something we don't like that we've experienced ourselves. Throughout history charlatans interested in personal gain have exploited people who long to worship God. Simon the sorcerer sought a spiritual gift in order to increase his income (Acts 8). Medieval believers paid money to avoid punishment for sin. Contemporary evangelists have used contributions to buy themselves a luxurious lifestyle. Church leaders have traded on their positions to receive personal favors.

Christ's violent reaction against the cheaters in the temple reminds us that God's desire is to know and to be known by us. Christ's anger leads us to evaluate our motives. Why do we teach or sing or work on a committee? How do we react when we don't get recognized, when our assignment is not our first choice?

Christ read the hearts of the temple merchants. He knew they were there to line their pockets, not to help people worship. He knows our hearts, too.

We want to serve You with pure hearts, our Father. Help us to be channels through which others connect with You. In the name of Christ, we pray. Amen.

Relationships Matter

But when you are praying, first forgive anyone you are hold-ing a grudge against, so that your Father in heaven will forgive your sins, too (Mark 11:25, *New Living Translation*).

Scripture: **Mark 11:20-26**
Song: **"We Gather Together"**

Which is most important to a parent: enjoying his kids or seeing his kids enjoy each other?

Which is most important to a teacher: a class that coop-erates or a class that obeys the teacher?

Which is more important to a supervisor: teamwork among employees or respect for the boss?

"Can't we have both?" you ask. And the answer is not only, "Yes, you can," but also, "Yes, you must!" In fact, one enhances and enables the other. Hands and feet work together to achieve the body's goals only when those hands and feet are connected to the head.

So it is with God and us. Jesus lays down this promise: "Ask for anything, and God will grant it." This is followed by, "Before you pray, forgive anyone you've got a grudge against." Does this mean that breaches in our relation-ships with each other can interrupt our relationship with God?

Help us to stay close to You, our Father. Help us to develop healthy relationships with one another. Forgive us if we've let our zeal for Christian causes get in the way of our love for people. Help us to get closer to You by getting closer to each other. We pray in the name of Jesus, our Savior. Amen.

Complete Authority

Jesus came and told his disciples, "I have been given complete authority in heaven and on earth" (Matthew 28:18, *New Living Translation*).

Scripture: **Mark 11:27-33**
Song: **"I Must Tell Jesus"**

A young woman dated a young man who said he didn't believe in God. She was a faithful Christian and was eager to share her convictions with her friend.

At first his questions gave her hope. His constant probing, his objections to the idea of faith, his raising of apparent contradictions in Scripture, his comparison of Christianity to other religions—all these were evidence that she had encountered a bona fide seeker. Or at least that's what she wanted to believe.

Finally, she saw that her friend was not seeking for truth. He didn't want to find faith; he wanted to ruin hers or at least to convince himself that he was right.

In a similar way, the leaders in today's story came to Jesus, not for faith but to justify their lack of it. Every "seeker" who approaches Him this way will not find the truth that only He offers. When we acknowledged Him as the supreme authority, we can find in Him the answers to the questions that trouble us most.

Thank You, Lord, for satisfying our questioning when we accept Your authority. Thank You for showing us how to live. Help us live by Your authority today. We pray this prayer in the name of Jesus, our Lord and Savior. Amen.

Looking Beyond Ourselves

They realized he was pointing at them—they were the wicked farmers in his story (Mark 12:12, *New Living Translation*).

Scripture: **Mark 12:1-12**
Song: **"Nothing Between"**

In today's Scripture, the leaders understood half of the point in the story Jesus told. They were right that the murdering tenant farmers symbolized themselves. But they could not see that the landowner's son represented Jesus. They were too concerned about their own standing with the crowd to ponder the spiritual insight Jesus offered. While saving their lives, they lost them.

Unfortunately, similar tragedies happen today. Whenever we worry more about ourselves than the big issues of life, we are the losers. When we concentrate on our standing in life instead of living a life that permeates the love and compassion of Christ, we are the losers. When we fail to stand for principles of God's Word because we want to climb the ladder of importance, we are the losers. When we worry about our title, our pay, or our reputation more than the example we can be of Christ's servant attitude, we are the losers.

In today's Scripture passage, we learn that by concentrating on ourselves we may lose the opportunity that God is laying at our feet.

***Heavenly Father**, give us grace to love others more than ourselves, to concentrate on Your purposes instead of our lives, and to let Your truth overshadow our egos. In Christ's name, we pray. Amen.*

Acceptable Service

She did what she could. She poured perfume on my body beforehand to prepare for my burial (Mark 14:8, *New International Version*).

Scripture: **Mark 14:1-9**
Song: **"Take My Life, and Let It Be"**

She did what she could. There are many small but noble acts that one can do to glorify God and His Kingdom. I think of an elderly lady who comes each week to the church fellowship hall to put the salt and pepper shakers on the table for the evening fellowship celebration. She does what she can. Another lady at the church comes to the nursery to rock fussy babies to sleep while their parents join a small Bible study group.

We may not preach like Peter or plant churches like Paul. Yet was not the poorest of widows commended for giving her two mites? Why? She did what she could.

What are we doing for the Lord? How are we advancing the Kingdom of God and bringing glory to the King of kings? God asks nothing beyond our ability. Have we done what we can to serve Christ and His Kingdom? Perhaps it's true that most of us will never do great things, but we can do small things in a great way.

Thank You, dear Father, for the opportunity to serve You. Teach us to be Your servants. In the name of Jesus, our Savior, we pray. Amen.

April 7-13. **Dan Nicksich** is the senior minister of First Christian Church in Somerset, PA. He and his wife, Donna, have two sons, Andrew and Derek.

Opportunities

Making the most of every opportunity, because the days are evil (Ephesians 5:16, *New International Version*).

Scripture: **Mark 14:10-16**
Song: **"I Shall Be Like Him"**

Our youngest son asks some interesting questions from the Bible such as "Dad, what does it mean when it says the days are evil?"

I say, "It means that every day brings opportunities for evil as well as for good. What we do is our choice, so the Bible says we are to make the most of every day."

Jesus and two of His disciples used the day to prepare for the Passover feast. Judas watched for an opportunity to betray Jesus. We can use the day for good or for evil.

What opportunities will this day bring? The opportunity to be a Christ-like example on the job? The opportunity to be a godly parent? A loving spouse? A good friend? Or will it be the opportunity to vent some frustration? To fail to forgive?

The choice is ours. Jesus once said, "Seek and you will find." He spoke of seeking God's blessings and opportunities for good. Let us remember that, like the two disciples, we can just as easily seek good as we can evil.

Father, *thank You for each day and the opportunities presented. Help us to choose to use our days for good. Let us not do evil. Our prayer is to show Your love to the world around us. In the name of Jesus, we pray. Amen.*

Dining With Your Betrayer

"This is my body, which is for you; do this in remembrance of me" (1 Corinthians 11:24, *New International Version*).

Scripture: **Mark 14:17-25**
Song: **"According to Thy Gracious Word"**

If someone asked you what you would want to eat for your last meal, what would you tell them? Would you tell them roast goose, dressing, celery, olives, cranberry sauce, apple salad, lobster, creamed peas, french fries, fried chicken, round steak with onion gravy, hot biscuits, orange juice, cherry pie, coconut cake, ice cream and coffee with cream?

It's not the question of what one would eat for the last meal that intrigues me, but rather, with whom one would choose to dine. Some may choose a family member or a close friend. How many would include their betrayer? Jesus included Judas in his special gathering.

Imagine the shock that went through the twelve as they heard Jesus saying, "I tell you the truth, one of you will betray me, one who is eating with me."

Jesus knew the cruel death that awaited Him. He partook of this special meal with the one who would betray Him. God's grace is such that the invitation to His feast is open to us today.

Dear heavenly Father, we thank You for salvation through Your son and for the glorious invitation to partake His feast. May we live in such a way that Your name may be glorified. In the name of Your, who died for the sins of the world, we pray. Amen.

The Foot-Washing Service

After that, he poured water into a basin and began to wash his disciples' feet (John 13:5, *New International Version*).

Scripture: **John 13:1-5**
Song: **"O Master, Let Me Walk With Thee"**

Jesus took on the task of the lowliest servant in order to teach a lesson in humility and service. He went around the table, washing the feet of each apostle.

Some churches do not typically have "foot-washing" services. We believe in following the servant example, not necessarily the specific act. Yet one day, one new Christian showed up at her small group gathering with a pitcher, basin, towels, and an apron. She said she wanted to imitate her Master and wash the feet of those who were gathered. At first it seemed awkward, but this self-effacing, loving act soon touched the hearts of everyone.

The pure heart, motivated simply by love for Christ, will never fail to impact the lives of those who are touched by these unselfish acts of devotion. Living a life that is Christ-like will help to show the world how to live in love for one another.

Jesus' example of the lowly servant image of Jesus, humbly washing the feet of His disciples, can make a significant and lasting impact on us.

Heavenly Father, while it may not seem glorious to be the servant, we know that You call us to be servants. Help us to truly aspire to live up to the example of Jesus. May the world see Christ in us today. In His holy name, we pray. Amen.

Defying Authority

"You call me 'Teacher' and 'Lord,' and rightly so, for that is what I am" (John 13:13, *New International Version*).

Scripture: **John 13:12-20**
Song: **"Jesus Is Lord of All"**

The camp manager couldn't believe his ears. "Who are you to tell me what to do?" Here was a ten-year-old challenging his authority in a Christian camp setting. The young man found out in short order exactly who was in charge. His parents were called, his bags were packed, and he was sent home.

Sometimes I ask children who the authorities are in their lives. The conversation may go something like this:

"Who are the authorities in school?"

"My teachers, the principal."

"Who are the authorities at home?"

"Mom!"

This indicates that children recognize authority and the direction of those in charge.

Jesus said He was rightly called Teacher and Lord. To acknowledge Jesus as Lord is to say He is the ultimate authority in our lives. The things we do and say each and every day reveal just how seriously we take this basic statement of faith, "Jesus is Lord!"

Dear Father, thank You for the Lord of life—Jesus. Help us to deal with that rebellious and defiant spirit that sometimes dwells within us. Teach us, O Father, to live according to Your will. In the name of Jesus we pray. Amen.

By This All Men Will Know

By this all men will know that you are my disciples, if you love one another (John 13:35, *New International Version*).

Scripture: **John 13:31-35**
Song: **"They'll Know We Are Christians by Our Love"**

As he left the Philippines, General Douglas MacArthur vowed, "I shall return." Several years later he made good on his promise.

When it was time for Jesus to leave His apostles, He promised to send the Holy Spirit as a comforter and guide. In lieu of an immediate return, He also left a final wish for His closest friends that they would observe a new command, that of loving one another.

Love is to be the distinguishing mark between His disciples. A familiar chorus captures this same sentiment saying, "They'll know we are Christians by our love."

We have sometimes imagined that strict adherence to a particular doctrine is our distinguishing mark. We dare not lose sight of the fact that for the Christian acts of love are to be both observable and automatic.

Jesus promised to return. As we await His promise, it is our privilege to point others to Him by demonstrating to others what it truly means to be one of His disciples.

Father, my prayer would be that others see Jesus in me. Help me to demonstrate daily that I am truly one of His disciples. With acts of love, words of encouragement, or gifts to help the needy, let me help others see Jesus in me. In His Holy name, I pray. Amen.

Remembering and Anticipating

"For whenever you eat this bread and drink this cup, you proclaim the Lord's death until he comes" (1 Corinthians 11:26, *New International Version*).

Scripture: **1 Corinthians 11:23-28**
Song: **"The Battle Hymn of the Republic"**

The Civil War battlefield at Gettysburg, Pennsylvania, sprang to life through the vivid descriptions of our guide. At one stop on the tour, he pointed to a nearby monument and explained that the name of one of his ancestors was inscribed there along with other casualties of this epic battle. Guiding was his way of both remembering and proclaiming his family heritage.

There are some things we can say of Jesus that can be said only of Him.

He was born of a virgin.

He was both God and man.

He was sinless despite temptation.

More than a name chiseled into granite, His memorial is one observed by the living in conjunction with the Loving One who died and came to life again.

We, too, have the privilege of saying, "I'm proud of the one who died for me." Each Lord's Day, our active participation at His table proclaims to the world our allegiance, our heritage.

Father, we not only look back in remembrance to Christ's sacrifice upon the cross at Calvary, but we also enjoy fellowship with Him as the risen and living Savior. In the name of Christ, we pray. Amen.

At Golgotha

He bearing his cross went forth into a place called the place of a skull, which is called in the Hebrew Golgotha: where they crucified him, and two others with him, on either side one, and Jesus in the midst (John 19:17, 18).

Scripture: **Mark 15:21-32**
Song: **"Were You There?"**

It was Golgotha, "being interpreted, 'the place of a skull,'" where Jesus was led to be crucified. This common place of execution, lined with the skull remains of many who had died there, was where our Lord and Savior gave up His life that we might have everlasting life.

If the religious leaders of the day and others of power had known Jesus' death would not diminish Him or His power but rather bring greater manifestation, I wonder if they would have plotted to give Him a place at Golgotha?

Those who are partakers of salvation rejoice in gratitude. Jesus Christ, the King of glory, chose to lower Himself to experience cruelty, suffering and death at the place of the skull to make eternal life possible for us.

Heavenly Father, we glorify You this day and each day for loving us so much. We are blessed that You allowed Your only begotten Son to be crucified at the place of the skull, the place of death, on our behalf. Thank You for the love that is offered to all mankind in Christ Jesus, our Lord. We praise You for life! In His holy name, we pray. Amen.

April 14-20. **Sallie J. Breaux** ministers with the radio and television ministries of The Hope of Glory Lighthouse in Lafayette, Louisiana.

He Had to Go Alone

And one ran and filled a sponge full of vinegar, and put it on a reed, and gave him to drink, saying, Let alone; let us see whether Elijah will come to take him down (Mark 15:36).

Scripture: **Mark 15:33-41**
Song: **"Jesus Paid It All"**

All alone in the dark is not always a comfortable place to be. In the Scripture passage for today, we see Jesus in the dark, on a cruel, painful cross after being beaten, scourged, pierced in the side, having had thorns thrust into His head. But the greatest burden Jesus was carrying that day was the weight of the sins of the entire world on His shoulders.

The massive darkness that covered the land when Jesus was crucified was of a miraculous nature. Jesus was killed during the celebration of the Passover feast, which took place at the full moon. This vast darkness seems to indicate the magnitude of evil at work in Christ's crucifixion.

What love Jesus has for us to have gone to the cross on our behalf! He suffered such terrible pain and death to reconcile us to God and to save us from the wrath of God. The compassion and love of God through Christ Jesus goes beyond any love we can understand.

***Dear Father**, may we, Your children, be eternally grateful for the shed blood of Your son, Christ Jesus, for the sins of the whole world that includes our sins today. Help us to live lives filled with compassion and love. In His holy name, we pray. Amen.*

Preparation of the Body

Who shall change our vile body, that it may be fashioned like unto His glorious body, according to the working whereby he is able even to subdue all things unto himself (Philippians 3:21).

Scripture: **Mark 15:42-47**
Song: **"He Died for Me"**

The body of our Lord and Savior Jesus Christ was nailed to the cross.

Joseph of Arimathaea, being an honorable and financially able counselor, pleaded with Pilate for the body of Jesus. Joseph purposed to give Jesus a proper and honorable burial. He persuaded Pilate to release the body of Jesus to him.

The Scripture describes the manner in which Joseph of Arimathaea had Jesus' body prepared with the finest linen, finest spices and the finest tomb, which he had purchased for himself.

What an awesome picture of what Christ has done in preparation of the body of Christ to be reconciled to God. He has given us His finest through the cross of Calvary, and we have hope of an even greater glory when one day we live eternally with Him in Heaven.

Thank You, dear Father, for Your Word to us. Thank You for Your love that is a constant reminder of how we should live our daily lives. Teach us, O Lord, that we may live as Christ lived. In His holy and blessed name, we pray. Amen.

Victory Over Death

Buried with him in baptism, wherein also ye are risen with him through the faith of the operation of God, who hath raised him from the dead (Colossians 2:12).

Scripture: **Mark 16:1-8**
Song: **"Christ Arose!"**

Neither death nor the grave could hold Jesus captive because He attained victory over all the works of the devil! Jesus gives victory over death for us. Hallelujah to the Lamb of God!

It was the first day of the week, early in the morning, when Mary Magdalene, Mary and the other women brought additional spices to anoint the body of Jesus. They found the miraculous instead of the natural they were seeking. The stone was rolled away, the body was gone, and the angel of the Lord spoke to them with evangelistic directions: go and tell. The Bible says they quickly ran to tell the other disciples what they had seen.

Jesus had fulfilled what He said He would; He rose from the grave. Today let us quickly spread the word of the risen Savior to all around us. Let us arise to the responsibility of bringing the truth of the risen Lord to the lost and dying of the world. Jesus Christ's work and resurrection live in us today.

Precious Father, thank You for Your Word. Thank You for giving us salvation through Jesus, the Messiah, the Savior, who died and rose again. Thank You for the power of the resurrection. In the name of Jesus Christ, our Lord, we pray. Amen.

The Unexpected Appearance

And it came to pass, that, while they communed together and reasoned, Jesus himself drew near, and went with them (Luke 24:15).

Scripture: **Luke 24:13-27**
Song: **"I Stand Amazed"**

On the day of His resurrection, Jesus appeared to two of His disciples who were on the road to Emmaus. They were in discussion about Jesus' cruel death. The two disciples' conversation expressed sorrow in the death of Jesus and apparent disbelief in what Jesus had spoken concerning His resurrection. Perhaps the suffering of Jesus' crucifixion and Jesus' refusal to defend Himself made His promises of resurrection and power seem unbelievable.

Jesus saw the need to rebuke them for their unbelief and then expounded more fully to them in all the Scriptures the things concerning Himself. How amazing it is that even in the midst of our unbelief Jesus is concerned for our receiving the truth.

We want our conversation of heart to be always open and pleasing to Christ by the power of the Holy Spirit. Paul encourages us in Romans 8:18: "For I reckon that the sufferings of this present time are not worthy to be compared with the glory which shall be revealed in us."

Dear Father, *give us courage to follow You even when our faith falters. Wash away our unbelief. We bring our prayers to You in the name of Jesus Christ, the risen Savior. Amen.*

Recognize the Risen Lord

Believe me that I am in the Father, and the Father in me: or else believe me for the very works' sake (John 14:11).

Scripture: Luke 24:28-35
Song: "Jesus Is the Sweetest Name I Know"

A true experience with Christ causes the soul to yearn for consistent communion and fellowship with Him. Anyone having really recognized the risen Lord is never the same after the experience.

Jesus revealed Himself to the two disciples on the Emmaus road. What an experience this must have been for them once they recognized they were communicating with the risen Lord. From where did He come? When did He appear? Why did He choose these two disciples when many had been at the cross or at the burial site? We are given no answers to these questions in the Bible, only that they said one to another, "Did not our heart burn within us, while he talked with us by the way, and while he opened to us the Scriptures?"

The Lord is risen, He is risen indeed. An open regenerated heart causes us to experience His great love and power each day. Let us today live a life that shows forth the love of Christ.

Heavenly Father, we thank You for our experiences with Your Son and our Savior, Jesus Christ of Nazareth. It is He Who shed His blood for us. Let us share this life-changing testimony with others. Help us to share it with others who do not know Christ. May we all praise His name and shout, "The Lord is risen indeed!" Amen.

Behold My Hands and Feet

But now is Christ risen from the dead, and become the first-fruits of them that slept (1 Corinthians 15:20).

Scripture: **Luke 24:36-49**
Song: **"Christ, the Lord, Is Risen Today"**

How shocked the disciples were when the risen Jesus appeared in the midst of them, bringing peace when they were so troubled and so saddened by His death. He appeared to them in love and concern.

Knowing what was in their hearts and minds and having compassion on their human frailties and fear, Jesus invited the disciples to look at His hands and feet. He said, "Handle me, touch me, see I am real in the flesh."

To further prove His resurrection, Jesus ate with them a piece of a broiled fish and a honeycomb. Once the disciples believed, Jesus was able to further enlighten them in Scripture and understanding of His resurrection.

Jesus continuously manifests Himself to us daily in many ways. We may hear Him as He speaks of peace to our souls as He did to the disciples who walked with Him.

When we allow God to be in charge of our lives, we know that changes will be made in life.

Dear heavenly Father, *help us to live in the glory of knowing that You have given the world salvation through Jesus Christ, our Lord. May we be used to tell the world of His great love. In His holy name, we pray. Amen.*

Faith That Acts

And he said unto her, Daughter, thy faith hath made thee whole; go in peace, and be whole of thy plague (Mark 5:34).

Scripture: **Mark 5:21-34**
Song: **"Faith Is the Victory"**

Hudson Taylor, a famous missionary to China, was on a sailing ship to that country. The vessel passed near some islands where the natives were notorious cannibals. As the ship passed within yards of one of the islands, the winds suddenly died, leaving the ship helplessly adrift. The natives on shore sized up the situation and quickly sent a war party of canoes toward the ship.

The captain asked Taylor to pray for a wind. Taylor agreed to pray for a wind, but only if the captain set the sails to catch the wind when it arose. At first the captain refused. "If you don't set the sails," replied the missionary, "I won't pray." The captain agreed, returned to the deck, and the order was given. Before the sailors finished the job, strong wind began to blow .

The woman who approached Jesus had faith, but she also had to act on that faith. As James said, "Faith without works is dead" (James 2:26).

Dear God, strengthen our feeble and faltering faith. Give us the faith we need to deal with the problems we face each day. But also give us the strength and wisdom to put our faith into action. Amen.

April 21-27. **John Wade** is a professor at Atlanta Christian College and a former editor for Standard Publishing. John and his wife, Barbara, live in Fayetteville, Georgia. They have six children.

When All Else Fails

And he took the damsel by the hand, and said unto her, Talitha cumi; which is, being interpreted, Damsel, (I say unto thee,) arise. And straightway the damsel arose (Mark 5:41, 42).

Scripture: **Mark 5:35-43**
Song: **"Tell It to Jesus"**

Our society grows increasingly complex. We are sometimes called upon to assemble a toy or install a new program in our computers. But when we apply our previously learned skills to the task, we find that we can't get the job done. Then someone gives us some sage advice: "When all else fails, read the instructions."

Jairus, "one of the rulers of the synagogue," had a problem. His daughter was at the point of death and all the efforts of the physicians had failed to help her. Finally he turned to Jesus for help. This must have been a painful step for him because by this time many of the religious leaders had turned against Jesus. Everything else had failed, and so he had to "read the instructions," that is, to call upon Jesus for help.

All of us have or will face problems as serious as the one Jairus faced. Why wait until "all else fails" before calling upon Him? Why not call upon Him first?

Gracious and loving Father, forgive us when we have relied on our own strength and wisdom rather than turning to You. Teach us to come to You for help before, rather than after, "all else fails." In the name of our Savior and Lord, we pray. Amen.

Too Busy to Doubt

Thomas saith unto him, Lord, we know not whither thou goest; and how can we know the way? (John 14:5).

Scripture: **John 14:1-7**
Song: **"I Believe in Miracles"**

There is an old legend about Thomas (and it is only a legend) that tells about his lingering doubts about the resurrection. To overcome his doubts, he tried to speak to some of the other apostles and Christians, hoping that they would strengthen his wavering faith. But they were so busy preaching and teaching across the Roman Empire–Barnabas in Cyprus, Peter in Rome, Paul in Corinth and others at various places–that he could not find any of them to speak to about his lingering doubts.

Then the thought occurred to him that he alone had doubts. All the other followers of Jesus were so busy preaching and teaching that they didn't have time for doubts. Realizing this, Thomas left Jerusalem and traveled to India, where he preached and won converts. While this is only a legend, it does suggest that the best way to overcome doubts is to be actively involved in serving the Lord. When we are busy demonstrating our faith, we have little time for doubts.

We believe, dear God; help our unbelief. Give us the strength to stay busy in our work for You so that we can resist the doubts that can rob us of the wonderful hope we have of someday entering the heavenly house You are preparing for us. In the name of Jesus Christ, our Savior and Lord, we pray. Amen.

Greater Works

Verily, verily, I say unto you, He that believeth on me, the works that I do shall he do also; and greater works than these shall he do; because I go unto my Father (John 14:12).

Scripture: **John 14:8-14**
Song: **"Work, for the Night Is Coming"**

Kale is one of our favorite greens. Here in the South it grows and produces all winter. Then early in the spring, I plow it under. But one year I didn't plow it under, and the whole row went to seed. When I did finally plow it under, I scattered the seeds over the whole garden. Soon the seeds germinated and took over the garden.

Jesus, when He was on earth, was limited in what He could do. Because He was confined to a human body, He could be in only one place at a time. He promised His disciples that the time would come when those who believed on Him would do "greater works than these."

One kale seed can produce only one plant, but that plant, when it matures, can produce thousands of seeds. In the same way, Jesus could only do a limited amount of teaching and making converts. But the countless thousands through His disciples multiplied His efforts. Jesus' works while He was on earth were limited to a small area of land, but today around the world are those who do "greater works" in His name.

O loving Father, we thank You for giving salvation through Your Son. Give us the strength and wisdom to do the "greater works" of reaching the whole world with this hope of salvation. Amen.

Leaving Our Canes and Crutches Behind

But without faith it is impossible to please him: for he that cometh to God must believe that he is, and that he is a rewarder of them that diligently seek him (Hebrews 11:6).

Scripture: **Hebrews 11:1-6**
Song: **"Trusting Jesus"**

Two persons were once viewing a painting that depicted Jesus' healing of the two blind men at Jericho. They agreed that the portrayal of Jesus was outstanding and the expressions on the faces of the two men showed their great joy as a result of their healing. But one of the viewers felt that one of the most significant points in the painting were the two canes lying beside the steps where the two men had sat when Jesus passed by. The artist was showing that when the two men heard Jesus, they had faith to leave behind their canes because they knew they would no longer need them.

Exactly! When we come to Christ in faith, we must be willing to leave behind our canes and crutches–money, power, prestige. How reluctant we are to give up our faith in these in order to have a greater faith in Christ, but that is exactly what He requires.

Gracious God, may we look back across history and through the eyes of faith see how You have rewarded those who have been willing to leave behind their doubts and other canes and crutches and have trusted in You. In the name of Jesus, we pray. Amen.

Faith to Move Mountains

For verily I say unto you, If ye have faith as a grain of mustard seed, ye shall say unto this mountain, Remove hence to yonder place; and it shall remove: and nothing shall be impossible unto you (Matthew 17:20).

Scripture: **Matthew 17:14-20**
Song: **"Faith of Our Fathers"**

Satan used every weapon he had to try to hinder Jesus' ministry, including the powers of the demons. In ways that we don't understand, demons were able to gain control of people and cause them to behave in strange and dangerous ways. Demon possession was rare in Old Testament times, as it was after Pentecost, leading us to think that its frequency during Jesus' ministry was the result of Satan's all-out efforts to destroy it.

Today's Scripture describes a boy possessed by a demon that caused him to fall into fire and into water. The father had come to the disciples for help, but they were unable to do anything. Jesus cast out the demon and chided the disciples for their lack of faith.

Jesus pointed out to His disciples the great power of faith, which can even move mountains. Across the centuries the faith of Christians has accomplished unbelievable things. Today we see that same power of faith to change the lives of lost sinners.

Dear God, we believe; help Thou our unbelief. Strengthen our feeble faith so that through Your power we can accomplish things for Your kingdom that seem impossible. In Jesus name, we pray. Amen.

X's or Crosses?

Take heed to yourselves: If thy brother trespass against thee . . . seven times in a day, and seven times a day turn again to thee, saying, I repent; thou shalt forgive him (Luke 17:3, 4).

Scripture: **Luke 17:1-6**
Song: **"I Would Be Like Jesus"**

When Louis XII came to the throne of France in 1499, he had his advisors prepare a list of those who had plotted against him to keep him from gaining the throne. When the advisors brought him the list, he read it and marked an X by each of the names. When word of his actions got out, those on his list feared for their lives and fled the country or went into hiding.

When Louis heard of their actions, he sent out word that these were not X's but crosses he had placed beside the names. The crosses were to remind him that Christ had died on the cross to forgive sinners. Those who were on the king's list then were invited to come before him, and he forgave them.

We sometimes find it hard to forgive. Perhaps we should write their names on a list and then place a cross beside each name to remind us that Christ forgave us. Even if they offend us seven times in a day or seventy times seven for that matter, Christ tells us to forgive them.

O forgiving Father, teach us to pray carefully and thoughtfully the words "forgive us our trespasses as we forgive those who trespass against us." In the holy name of Jesus, we pray. Amen.

April 28

Outsiders Become Insiders

The woman was a Greek, a Syrophenician by nation; and she besought him that he would cast forth the devil out of her daughter (Mark 7:26).

Scripture: **Mark 7:24-30**
Song: **"The Family of God"**

Since I once served on a church staff, I always watch how people respond to visitors when we visit other churches. After a church service, sometimes when we've lingered not a single person has spoken to us.

At these times, I feel like the Gentile woman who approached Jesus must have felt. Even though I am a Christian, I'm labeled an "outsider" in this church family. I'm sure the Gentile woman felt disapproval in the stares from those who were part of the "in crowd."

When the woman expressed a need, Jesus ministered to her and blessed her. Our Lord no longer walks among us to reach out to outsiders, but they experience the touch of His hand as they clasp ours. They feel the warmth of family fellowship as we draw them into our circle. In God's family, outsiders become insiders.

Lord, thank You that all people can be part of Your family. Help us to notice those around us and invite them to join us. Use us to let those around us know that You accept all people. In the name of Jesus Christ, our Savior, we pray. Amen.

April 28-May 4. **Shirley G. Brosius** is a Christian education specialist and freelance writer from Millersburg, Pennsylvania. She and her husband, Bill, have two sons and three grandchildren.

Be Open and Honest

And they bring unto him one that was deaf, and had an imped-iment in his speech; and they beseech him to put his hand upon him (Mark 7:32).

Scripture: **Mark 7:31-37**
Song: **"Open My Eyes, That I May See"**

As a tailor measured the sleeve length of my son's new sport coat, I commented that I thought he marked the sleeves too short. The man responded with a curt com-ment that I did not understand, and I simply said "OK." Later I asked my son what the tailor had said. To my dis-may the tailor had interpreted my comment as indicating the sleeves were too long and had marked them a half inch shorter than his original measurement.

Honest communication is vital to our physical lives. Jesus' act of restoring the speech-impaired deaf man may be symbolic of establishing communication between God and us, something just as vital to our spiritual lives.

Fortunately, my son was able to rectify my miscommu-nication with the tailor in time to avoid a disaster. God offers opportunities for us to speak with Him through prayer. Christ can help us to correct mistakes as He talks and we listen, as we talk and He listens. We can avoid mistakes such as mine through honest and open commu-nication.

Dear Father and Lord of all, *open our ears to hear You speak by Your Spirit and Your Word. Help us to express true worship to You. In the name of Jesus Christ, our Savior and Lord, we pray. Amen.*

Read the Ingredients

And he charged them, saying, Take heed, beware of the leaven of the Pharisees, and of the leaven of Herod (Mark 8:15).

Scripture: **Mark 8:11-21**
Song: **"Make Me Like You, Lord"**

A store clerk once told me she was excited about belonging to a well-known religious group. She had never understood what comfort her dying grandmother drew from the book of Job until members of this group explained why her grandmother was able to relate to Job's suffering.

The clerk was so impressed with this group's Bible knowledge that she became a member of the group. Their Bible knowledge impressed her. She felt that they better understood the truth.

We may readily identify religious groups as holding different beliefs and teachings, but when people of other faiths come knocking on our door or move into our neighborhood, we may not be as discerning. We may admire their work ethic, their skill as golfers or even their "Bible knowledge," but as we are drawn to personalities, we may also be drawn to the philosophy they hold. Let us be wise and always look for truth and heed Jesus' words of warning, "Beware of their leaven."

Lord, *help us to be discerning in our contacts with others so that we are not drawn away from the truth of Your Word. Fill us with Your Spirit. In Jesus' holy name, we pray. Amen.*

Devotions™

I will bless
the LORD at
all times:
his praise shall
continually
be in my mouth

(Psalm 34:1).

May

*Photo by Julie Riley is of Ronald and
Ruth Davis. Both Ron and Ruth are
editors in Standard's adult educational departments.*

Pray—for the Right Reasons

Lord, trouble not thyself; for I am not worthy that thou shouldest enter under my roof (Luke 7:6).

Scripture: **Luke 7:1-10**
Song: **"Sweet Hour of Prayer"**

I sometimes feel uncomfortable when a call to a prayer meeting stresses coming together to get an answer to a prayer. Prayer meeting is far more than a chance to twist God's arm by collective strength. Rather, we come together to worship and commune with God. In the process, we naturally express our needs. Our dialogue can be much more meaningful than simply reciting a grocery list of our personal and congregational wants.

The centurion had it right. Although he was a man of power, he did not flaunt his strength. Although he was a man of wealth, he saw himself poor in God's sight. The man was keenly aware of his own weakness and unworthiness.

Jesus commended this Gentile for his great faith. And Christ granted his request. We may also expect to receive Christ's approval as we pray in a spirit of humility and trust God's ability to meet our every need.

Lord, although we may have status in the world, we recognize that we are unworthy to stand before You. Thank You for allowing us to approach You in the righteousness of Christ. We know You alone can meet our needs. In Jesus' name, we pray. Amen.

May 1-4. **Shirley G. Brosius** is a Christian education specialist from Millersburg, Pennsylvania. She and her husband, Bill, have two sons and three grandchildren.

Get Plugged Into the Power

And when they had set them in the midst, they asked, By what power, or by what name, have you done this? (Acts 4:7).

Scripture: **Acts 4:5-14**
Song: **"Breathe on Me, Breath of God"**

A museum guide told me that as he showed a group of children an old-fashioned eggbeater, one little girl asked, "Where is the motor?" She was only accustomed to appliances that get plugged in and turned on.

That is actually what the ruler, elders, and scribes asked Peter and John: What or who is your power source? They had heard the powerful preaching and watched the men heal a lame man. They knew that ordinary, uneducated men could not do such things on their own. There must be a source of power.

The power of the Holy Spirit continued to flow as Peter explained that such supernatural power came from the Lord Jesus, the seemingly worthless "stone" that these very "builders" had rejected. The religious leaders had turned their backs on Christ, but Peter now boldly testified that salvation would come by none other. The men couldn't refute Peter's claim. May our lives, too, show such evidence of God's work that others ask, "What is your power source?"

Dear Father and Lord of all, cleanse our hearts and let Your power flow through us. We want to touch people to demonstrate the power of Your love, the power of Your healing touch, and the power of Your forgiveness. In Jesus' holy name, we pray. Amen.

Don't Worry How You Look

For we cannot but speak the things which we have seen and heard (Acts 4:20).

Scripture: **Acts 4:15-22**
Song: **"Make Me a Blessing"**

Blue-footed boobies live on islands mainly off the coasts of central and northern South America. These funny-looking seabirds have a white breast, brown wings, and blue feet that carry a blood supply to warm eggs during nesting. The name "booby" comes from a Spanish word that means "stupid fellow." With odd coloring and an elongated body, the bird looks clumsy on land, even though it skillfully dives to scoop fish from deep or shallow water. The fact that it shows no fear and is easily captured also contributed to its name.

Some might have called Peter and John foolish for not heeding powerful leaders who commanded them not to speak in the name of Jesus. But just as the blue-footed booby cannot change its appearance or its nature, so the disciples, changed by the Holy Spirit, could not stop speaking of Jesus. They simply did not worry about their reputations or what others might call them as they carried the gospel.

Dear Lord and Master of all, *help us to follow You. We want to speak for You and draw others to You just as the disciples did. Help us not to stifle our new nature because of what others may think about us, but help us to enjoy testifying of You in the power of the Holy Spirit. In Jesus' name, we pray. Amen.*

Anything to Report?

And when they had prayed, the place was shaken where they were assembled together; and they were all filled with the Holy Ghost, and they spake the word of God with boldness (Acts 4:31).

Scripture: **Acts 4:23-31**
Song: **"Bringing in the Sheaves"**

My grandson, Daniel, received a half-inch gash on his forehead when he tripped on a pavement outside his other grandparents' home. As his mother cleaned him up and treated his injury, his four-year-old sister Rachel said she was going upstairs. When she returned a while later, her mother asked what she had been doing. "I prayed for Daniel," she said. "Is there anything to report?"

There was good news to report after the disciples prayed for boldness to speak the Word of God. The number of believers multiplied, people were miraculously healed, and an angel opened prison doors. There was bad news, too. Believers were martyred.

We have the privilege of praying to God about our needs. Sometimes we need physical healing. Sometimes we need boldness to witness for Christ. But whatever we pray for and whenever we pray, we can follow Rachel's example. We can look for something to report.

O Lord, thank You for hearing our prayers. Save us from the snare of praying without expecting results. Help us to live in an attitude of anticipation as we watch to see what You do in our daily lives. In Jesus' holy name, we pray. Amen.

Who Is He? Who Are You?

How precious also are thy thoughts unto me, O God! How great is the sum of them! (Psalm 139:17).

Scripture: **Mark 8:27-33**
Song: **"Who Am I?"**

Have you ever been close enough to a celebrity to speak with them and then hesitated to do so? I did when I attended a Home Interior's convention in Indianapolis, Indiana. One day the president of the company, Mary Crowley, walked up the aisle toward the podium. The love that flowed from that group to Mary was like invisible waves moving toward her.

The next day I saw a couple of women talking with Mary. I wanted to approach her and speak, but I felt I had nothing to say to such a lady so I backed away.

Have you ever felt that way about the Lord? Have you ever thought that you are unimportant and that He is so awesome that He wouldn't want you to approach Him?

In Psalm 139 we read that He actually notices us and thinks about us. Does the God of the universe think on significant things? I believe He does. Since He thinks of you and me, we must be valuable in His sight.

Who are we, our Creator God, that You care for us? We are precious to You. We desire a relationship with You. Help us to live in Your light. In Christ's holy name, we pray. Amen.

May 5-11. **Phyllis Qualls Freeman** and her husband, Bill, have three children and four grandchildren.

The Message of the Cross

Let him deny himself, and take up his cross, and follow me (Mark 8:34).

Scripture: **Mark 8:34–9:1**
Song: **"The Old Rugged Cross"**

Arthur Blessitt, a man with a heart after God, wrote the book entitled, *Arthur, A Pilgrim*. The book is about his experiences of transporting a 12-foot cross through many countries around the world. Arthur carried this huge wooden cross into 71 countries across six continents, walking more than 21,000 miles for the purpose of proclaiming a simple message about the love of Jesus. Many people rejoiced, listened and wept as he shared the message of the gospel. Of course, some opposed his message too.

The cross is a symbol of the sacrifice Christ made through His death for our redemption. Everyday we see small gold crosses made into necklaces. Some are smooth and shiny; some are ornate. When we wear them, they help us remember Christ's love for us and the world.

The message of the cross is about suffering and pain. It is the good news of the resurrection. It brings us back into relationship with God, the Father.

Dear heavenly Father, may all who wear a cross around their neck be convinced of its message. Cause those who see the cross to recognize it as a symbol of Your love for mankind and Your desire for a personal relationship with each one of us. Then may we follow closely after You. In the name of Jesus, our Savior, we pray Amen.

Sons and Daughters of God

And will be a Father unto you, and ye shall be my sons and daughters, saith the Lord Almighty (2 Corinthians 6:18).

Scripture: **Mark 9:2-8**
Song: **"The Family of God"**

Have you heard those in the church being called brothers and sisters? We often feel closer to them than we do our blood relatives. We do not choose our natural family, and we do not choose our Christian family. Both our natural family and our Christian family bless us. Some of us are blessed to have a wonderful relationship with our siblings and parents as well as our brothers and sisters in Christ.

A few years ago, my siblings came to my house to spend the entire weekend with my mother to celebrate her 75th birthday. We ate, played games, reminisced and laughed for two days. Mother was ecstatic with her five children all to herself.

Relatives ideally look beyond faults and differences and emphasize the best in each other. We all have weaknesses, whether we are naturally related or in the body of Christ. But because we are in the family of God, we can choose to focus on one another's strengths.

Gracious Father, thank You for letting us be members of Your spiritual family. Whether or not we have peaceful relationships in our natural family, You extend an invitation to us to be loved by the church families. We are so glad we're a part of the family of God. In the name of Jesus, our Savior and Lord, we pray. Amen.

Words of Life

The words that I speak unto you, they are spirit, and they are life (John 6:63).

Scripture: **John 6:60-69**
Song: **"Wonderful Words of Life"**

God breathed into man, and he became a living soul. That breath of life meant that man would live forever.

Second Timothy 3:16 states that every Scripture is God-breathed, given by His inspiration. The word of God is "life" to our spirits.

When my family heard that Dad was to have surgery for lung cancer, we were greatly concerned. We had prayed for him for almost 30 years and felt that God had confirmed to our hearts that he would be saved. Yet he had not accepted Jesus as Lord and Savior of his life.

As I prepared for the ominous trip to be with Dad, the Lord led me to a passage in Numbers 11:23 which said, "Is the Lord's hand waxed short? thou shalt see now whether my word shall come to pass unto thee or not."

Something leaped in my spirit. I knew that God had confirmed His word to my heart. That word seemed alive at that moment.

Dear Almighty God and Lord of all, *we know that You are able to save even when it looks to us as if hope is lost. Help us to live in such a way that the world will see that Your Word is alive and actively working in our lives today. Give us the strength to follow You. We praise You for Your Word, which is spirit and life. We pray in the name of Jesus, our Lord and Savior. Amen*

Desiring to See Jesus

And he (Zaccheus) sought to see Jesus who he was; and could not for the press, because he was little of stature (Luke 19:3).

Scripture: **Luke 19:1-10**
Song: **"Open Our Eyes, Lord"**

Zaccheus desired to see Jesus. Even though there were hindrances, he found a way to see Him. He wanted to see for himself if the reports about Jesus were true.

I think it is quite interesting that this businessman would actually shimmy a tree to get a good look at a rabbi. Would Zaccheus's friends think it odd when they saw him sitting on a limb, searching the crowd to get a glimpse of Jesus? His desire overcame any inhibitions.

I'm glad that we don't have to climb a tree to see Jesus. He is as near as the Word of God or as near as our prayer time. Can it be said of us that we seek to see Him?

How long has it been since we have had a fresh glimpse of Him? Are we willing to push aside every obstacle and set aside our inhibitions to see Him?

Is it easier for us to let obstacles stand in the way of the greatest revelation of our life so we do not feel a responsibility to follow Him? If one "sees" Jesus and is convinced of who He is, then there is a call of responsibility to follow Him.

Loving God, we desire to behold Your face and to gaze upon You. As we seek to see You, we know that You will turn and look upon us with all Your love. We pledge this day to follow You. We want to see Jesus, in whose name we pray. Amen.

Speak and Sing About Him

And that every tongue should confess that Jesus Christ is Lord to the glory of God the Father (Philippians 2:11).

Scripture: **Philippians 2:5-11**
Song: **"I Will Sing of the Mercies of the Lord"**

As a child I became a Christian. It was an awesome experience to me. My father was an unbeliever. He ridiculed my mother's expression of her faith, and when I accepted Christ he made me kneel before him and say a prayer. I remember feeling intimidated because I didn't know how to pray out loud. For many years after that I would only pray silently, although I had forgotten the reason I did so.

One day I asked the Lord to help me be bold in my prayer life and in my witness for Him. The scene of me on my knees before an unbelieving father came back to my mind. I realized that all of those years ago I had assumed a timid spirit because of that incident.

No more, I thought. God has done so much in my life. I will speak His name faithfully. I will pray aloud when it is appropriate.

Great liberation came with this revelation! My spirit soared with praise because of this new freedom.

O Lord, we speak and sing of Your mercy to us. Deliver us from whatever causes us to feel intimidated and hinders our prayer life. We praise You for Your goodness and Your grace. With our tongues we confess that Jesus Christ is Lord. We pray all this in the name of Christ, our Savior. Amen.

Is Jesus Lord and Master?

For the same Lord over all is rich unto all that call upon him (Romans 10:12).

Scripture: **Romans 10:5-13**
Song: **"Jesus Be the Lord of All"**

I used to feel confused about the words "LORD" and "Lord" in Scripture. I knew there must be a reason but no one explained it to me. Why didn't the writer just write it one way? Consistency, that's what I like.

Later, I learned that when the word *Lord* is in all capital letters it refers to Jehovah, speaking of a self-existent God. When the word *Lord* (with only the first letter capitalized) is used, the word means "Adonai" or "Master."

The Old Testament hired servant did a job and was paid for what he did. He then had no more responsibility to the one who hired him, nor did the employer owe him anything other than his wages.

A bondservant, on the other hand, not only had to work for his lord; he also had rights and blessings from the hand of his master. His master offered the bondservant total provision. He was a member of the master's household. The master guided the servant.

Is Christ really our master and our Lord?

O Father, we want You to be the Master of all the affairs of our lives. We will heed Your guidance and honor You as Lord of all. Because we are bondservants, we accept the blessings of total provision you offer to us. In the name of Christ, our Savior, we pray. Amen.

One of Those Days

God is able to make all grace abound to you, so that in all things at all times, having all that you need, you will abound in every good work (2 Corinthians 9:8, *New International Version*).

Scripture: **Mark 9:14-18**
Song: **"Grace to You"**

I love coming home from work. My children are excited to see me, and they come running up to hug me and tell me what they did at school. I kiss my smiling wife, who asks me about my day and tells me about hers.

At least, that's how it is some days. Other days are different. I head home in a bad mood. My wife is working, so I pick up our children from school. They have homework. I help them while trying to figure out what to fix for dinner.

Things aren't always as we want them to be. This must have been true for the apostles also. One day they couldn't heal a boy that had been brought to them. The people around them were arguing and complaining. Then they saw Jesus come over the hill to take over what they couldn't handle. He does the same thing for us. He's right there to welcome us home from a hard day.

Dear God, thank You for being there and for taking over when life is too much for us to handle. Help us to remember that we can leave our problems in Your hands. In the name of Your Son, we pray. Amen.

May 12-18. **Paul Friskney** teaches communication arts at Cincinnati Bible College. He and his wife, Ann, have two children, Hannah and Ben.

In the Wheelbarrow

"'If you can'?" said Jesus. "Everything is possible for him who believes" (Mark 9:23, *New International Version*).

Scripture: **Mark 9:19-27**
Song: **"Faith Is the Victory"**

An old story is told of a daredevil who hooked up a tightrope over a waterfall. He gathered a crowd, and the people watched in amazement as he made his way across the dangerous path. They cheered and cheered when he reached the other side. Then he said, "Do you believe that I can do it again?" The crowd roared their approval. "Do you think I can do it pushing a wheelbarrow?" Again, there were thunderous cheers. "Then, who will get in the wheelbarrow?" Silence.

It's one thing to say you believe something; it's another thing to trust your life to it. The man whose son was demon-possessed wanted to believe Jesus, but Jesus offered what seemed impossible. Could he really trust Jesus to make everything right?

Jesus proved that He could be trusted. In fact, He has proved it many times in many lives. Do you trust Him with every aspect of your life, or are there things that you are holding back from Him? When He has our lives, He can do things with them that no one else can.

Dear Lord, *Your power is so great that it is hard for us to believe it. Help us to move beyond our limited human understanding and to realize that everything is possible for You. Help us to live lives that show that we trust You. In the name of Jesus, we pray. Amen.*

Throw the Switch!

The prayer of a righteous man is powerful and effective
(James 5:16, *New International Version*).

Scripture: **Mark 9:28-32**
Song: **"What a Friend We Have in Jesus"**

The first time my wife and I went to Kosova, we learned some things about flexibility. The electricity wasn't reliable, and nearly every day it would be off for some amount of time. We never knew when, and we never knew for how long. The missionaries with whom we stayed had learned to work around the problem. When the lights went out, they cooked on a wood stove (even in 90-degree heat), lit candles, and opened the windows to make up for the loss of fans.

I learned my lesson too well. A few days after we were back in our cozy house in Ohio, the lights went out unexpectedly. I was undisturbed and began rearranging what I planned to do based on that loss of electrical power. Then my wife came into the room and said, "Aren't you going to go out to the garage and flip the breaker switch on the fuse box?"

When our lives are losing power, we need to stay hooked to God through prayer. When we're connected, we won't need light; we'll be light in a dark world.

Dear Father, thank You for the gift of prayer! We can come to You anytime, knowing that You hear, that You care, and that You have the power to do something. May we always stay connected to You through prayer. In the name of Jesus, we pray, Amen.

Is Your Life a Twister?

I have told you these things, so that in me you may have peace.
In this world you will have trouble. But take heart! I have
overcome the world (John 16:33, *New International Version*).

Scripture: **John 16:25-33**
Song: **"It Is Well With My Soul"**

The movie version of *The Wizard of Oz* has many great
scenes, but one of my favorites is one that passes quickly.
As Dorothy's house is being carried away by the cyclone,
she sees animals, people, and different objects going past.
At one point, an old woman in a rocking chair flies by. In
spite of what is swirling all around her, the old woman
remains calm—just rocking and knitting.

This scene holds a great lesson about life. Many things
will come along in life that we can't understand and even
more that we can't control. How will we respond? Will we
focus on the wind and storm and worry about what's
going to happen to us, as Dorothy did? Or will we, like the
lady in the rocking chair, calmly go on doing what we
know we should no matter what's happening?

Jesus reminded His disciples that peace would come
from Him. That's where we can find it, too.

Dear God, *when life brings things swirling and crashing all around
us, peace can be hard to find. Help us remember that it can't be found
in the world or in ourselves. It only comes from You. Give us Your
peace, which is greater than we can ever understand. In the name of
Jesus Christ, our Savior and Lord, we pray. Amen.*

Two's Company; One's Family

I in them and you in me. May they be brought to complete unity to let the world know that you sent me and have loved them even as you have loved me (John 17:23, *New International Version*).

Scripture: **John 17:20-24**
Song: **"They'll Know We Are Christians by Our Love"**

My grandfather was the oldest of thirteen children. My mom tells of how big family gatherings were. It was like having a town meeting. Still, they were all one family, and they enjoyed the togetherness of family.

Growing up, I only saw that large family occasionally because my parents moved away from their families so that they could go into ministry. Therefore, the church became my extended family. Only later did I realize that I had the relationship with the church that God intended for all of His people. He wants us all to have the same closeness that Jesus and God share. In fact, when we have the kind of unity in the church that we should, we show the world our connection to Christ.

Is the church your family? Do you demonstrate to your community the kind of unity that Christ prayed for and that God desires? If so, what can you do to welcome others into that family?

***Dear Father**, our prayer is the same as Jesus', that we would be unified with each other and with You. We want the world to know of Your love, and we can't show them if we don't love each other. Help those in Your family to be like You. In Christ' name, we pray. Amen.*

Can't Thank You Enough

Jesus asked, "Were not all ten cleansed? Where are the other nine?" (Luke 17:17, *New International Version*).

Scripture: **Luke 17:11-19**
Song: **"Doxology"**

World War I aviator, Eddie Rickenbacker, earned a place in history for his successes in battle. However, one significant moment came in a failure that left him and his crew adrift in a raft for several days. On a Sunday morning, they had a worship service that included thankfulness for survival and prayer for rescue. Then, they settled back to endure another day of slowly dying from thirst and hunger.

Rickenbacker awoke suddenly to realize that a seagull, uncharacteristically far from shore, landed on his hat. He caught the gull, and the meat from it helped relieve their immediate hunger. Other parts of the gull were used for bait. That answered prayer sustained them until they were rescued. Rickenbacker expressed his thankfulness the rest of his life by going to the seashore every week to feed shrimp to the seagulls.

Jesus was troubled by the lack of gratitude from the majority of the lepers. We must be sure that we aren't guilty of the same kind of thoughtlessness

Dear God, thank You for everything You have done, are doing, and will do in our lives. Thank You for making life in You possible through Your Son. In the name of Jesus Christ, our Lord, we pray. Amen.

No Alternative

Jesus answered, "I am the way and the truth and the life. No one comes to the Father except through me" (John 14:6, *New International Version*).

Scripture: **John 6:43-48**
Song: **"Jesus Saves"**

Two words are used much more frequently now than they were in the past: inclusion and tolerance. On one level, these ideas represent concepts that are important parts of Christianity. Christ clearly brought a message of acceptance and forgiveness. He died to show God's love for the whole world and to offer salvation to everyone.

However, sometimes tolerance is stretched in a way that contradicts the message of Christ. It is used to say that it doesn't matter what a person believes. Christians are sometimes attacked as intolerant because they teach that there is good and evil. Good and evil, right and wrong is the concept of Christianity.

Christ clearly proclaims Himself as the way to God. Eternal life comes from belief in Him. True love calls for us to tell others the truth as Jesus did. Do you know someone who needs direction? Are you willing to risk criticism by telling others that Christ is the Way to God?

Dear heavenly Father, we know that You have revealed Your plan of salvation for the world. We accept Your free gift through Jesus Christ. Help us to love others and share Your message with a world that is seeking truth. Help us to show Your love to the world by loving all mankind. In the name of Jesus, our Lord and Savior, we pray. Amen.

May 19

Lord, We Are Able

They replied, "We are able." Then Jesus said to them, "The cup that I drink you will drink; and with the baptism with which I am baptized, you will be baptized (Mark 10:39, *New Revised Standard Version*).

Scripture: **Mark 10:32-40**
Song: **"'Are Ye Able?' Said the Master"**

All was set in place, Jerusalem and the cross—the disciples led by Jesus were on their way. Were the disciples fully aware of His impending betrayal and death? We are not sure.

Among the followers at this telling moment in the life of Christ were James and John. They were somewhat foolish; nonetheless their hearts seemed to be in the right place. They wanted to follow the Lord, no matter where that path would lead. Jesus asked them, "Are you able to drink the cup that I drink?" A king customarily hands the cup to his guests. "The cup" represents the experiences passed to men by God. In this case the cup would be one of extreme sacrifice.

Daily we are handed a cup of service, sometimes even demanding sacrificial service. When that cup comes our way today, may we respond, "Lord, we are able."

Dear heavenly Father, *it is with great honor that we accept the cup of life experiences that You hand us this day. May we be faithful to Your Lordship over our lives today. In Jesus' name, we pray. Amen.*

May 19-25. **Dan Lawson** is Director of Development at Emmanuel School of Religion in Johnson City, Tennessee. He and his wife, Linda, have two children.

The Key to Greatness

"For the Son of man came not to be served but to serve, and to give his life a ransom for many" (Mark 10:45, *New Revised Standard Version*).

Scripture: **Mark 10:41-45**
Song: **"Work, for the Night Is Coming"**

Jesus came to show us love. The Gospel of John records that Jesus came as the "Word" that became flesh and dwelled among us, full of grace and truth.

The church is to continue the ministry of Christ Jesus. He commissioned His followers to go into the world, make disciples, baptize them, and teach them.

Christ came as the teacher, the rabbi. Christ came to fulfill God's will for mankind. We do not come to God by our good deeds, by our keeping of God's law; rather we come to God through the sacrifice of His Son.

Jesus came to save the world and that is our task as well. We live in a world where people from all walks of life are sending out a plea for help. God has given us the lifeguard knowledge to respond to the call for help, as wall as the compassion to save those who are lost. We must be good Samaritans whose natural call it is to serve as He served, and thus obtain the key to greatness.

Gracious Savior of the world, You came to be our suffering servant, and we are indeed grateful. Help us to see our servant role. Give us the compassion necessary to serve with an urgency that reflects the ministry of Your Son. Use us in Your service even today. In the name of Him who gave His life that we might live eternally, we pray. Amen.

Following the Healer

Jesus said to him, "Go; your faith has made you well." Immediately he regained his sight and followed him on the way (Mark 10:52, *New Revised Standard Version*).

Scripture: **Mark 10:46-52**
Song: **"Follow On"**

I once heard a preacher say, "No life is so messed up that God cannot bring order out of chaos." Bartimaeus was a blind man who begged by the roadside in the city of Jericho. When he heard that Jesus was in Jericho, he called out to the Lord, pleading for mercy and for Jesus to restore his sight. Jesus performed the miracle that brought the man's sight back to him. It was the blind man's faith that Jesus said brought about the healing, that brought order out of chaos.

Once Bartimaeus regained his sight, Jesus told him to go his way. Instead Bartimaeus followed Jesus on His way. That is how it must be for us. When Christ brings order out of the chaos in our lives, we cannot help but follow the One who performs the miracle. Once we were lost, now we are found; once we were blind, now we can see. May our faith in Christ make it well with our souls this day.

Father, *You are a God of miracles. We celebrate today Your presence with us. We delight in the miracle of an empty tomb because in some miraculous way it fills all that is empty about us. Bless us as we endeavor to share the joy of Christ with those around us today. In Jesus' name, we pray. Amen.*

Belief Comes From Hearing

"Have you believed because you have seen me? Blessed are those who have not seen and yet have come to believe" (John 20:29, *New Revised Standard Version*).

Scripture: **John 20:24-31**
Song: **"Great Is Thy Faithfulness"**

The population of the world is well over 6,500,000,000 and growing. Today we live in a world filled with people of all walks of life and of all nationalities.

Christ's love is for all people whether one lives in Germany, England, the United States, Afghanistan, Canada, Bangladesh, Egypt, Israel, China, Ethiopia, India, Iran, Jordan, Kuwait, Laos, Libya, Iraq, Japan, Australia, Malaysia, North Korea, Pakistan, Saudi Arabia, Brazil, Turkey, Vietnam, Mexico, Taiwan, or any other place on this earth. Christ Jesus came to save us all.

The gospel message is the message of love and salvation to all the peoples, no matter one's walk in life. We who have heard the message are granted the blessing of telling it to others.

Jesus is the Christ, the Son of the Living God. He came as the Savior of the world. May we be His voice today.

Heavenly Father, we know that Christ has died, that Christ is risen, that Christ will come again. Give us the courage and the opportunity to share that message with others. We know that You have prepared a place for us to live eternally. We pray for compassion and love for all mankind that the world may know Jesus as Savior and Lord. In the name of the Father, the Son, and the Holy Spirit, we pray. Amen.

Depend On Faith

The promise that he would inherit the world did not come to Abraham or to his desendants through the law but through the righteousness of faith (Romans 4:13, *New Revised Standard Version*).

Scripture: **Romans 4:16-22**
Song: **"My Faith Looks Up to Thee"**

Abraham was a man of faith. God made a promise to him when he lived in the ancient city of Ur. God's promise was that if Abraham would pack his family and possessions and move from Ur to a place that God would show him, God would give the land to Abraham and make a great nation out of his descendants.

Probably the most difficult part of God's promise to Abraham related to God making a great nation out of Abraham's descendants. Abraham had no children and was quite old. As he passed from 75 to 99, he knew that he and his wife, Sarah, were far beyond childbearing age. The thought of the two of them being able to even have children would take a tremendous amount of faith on Abraham's part.

God always keeps His promises. Abraham believed that God was a God of His word.

God makes promises to us. He has promised that He is preparing a place for us to live in His presence forever.

Creator of the Universe, we know that You are a God who makes promises and keeps them. Give us the confidence to follow You. Strengthen our faith in You. In Jesus' name, we pray. Amen.

Bound for the Promised Land

By faith he stayed in the land he had been promised (Hebrews 11:9, *New Revised Standard Version*).

Scripture: **Hebrews 11:8-16**
Song: **"May All Who Come Behind Us Find Us Faithful"**

God promised Abraham that if he would move his family from Ur to a land that He would show him, God would give that land to his descendants. So Abraham packed up his family and began his journey, bound for the promised land. He came there, already an old man, with no children of his own. However, he miraculously had descendants, and they were so voluminous that there were enough of them to become a nation. That nation whose roots were founded in the prophet Abraham eventually did inhabit the land of promise. Abraham simply put the family on the track. He bound them for the Promised Land.

Just as Abraham had to begin his journey with a belief that God would be faithful to His promise, so we must rely on our confidence in God's faithfulness. While we have every reason to believe that we will see the land of promise, we must aim those who come after us toward that same land. We will dwell in that land together, eternally in the presence of the God of promise.

Father of promise, thank You for the hope we have for Heaven. We look forward to living in Your presence. It makes our living here on earth worthwhile. May we be faithful to You by sharing the promise of salvation with those who come after us. In Jesus' name. Amen.

Looking Forward to Our Hope

He considered abuse suffered for the Christ to be greater wealth than the treasures of Egypt, for he was looking to the reward (Hebrews 11:26, *New Revised Standard Version*).

Scripture: **Hebrews 11:23-28**
Song: **"My Hope Is Built on Nothing Less"**

A few years ago a young man came to my office at the church. I had never seen him before. He was tall, dark, handsome, muscular, and well-dressed. He appeared to have everything going for him. He got right to the point for his visit by saying, "I have nothing to look forward to. Can you help me?" The problem was that he had everything, yet nothing. He had the gifts that the world can give, but he did not have the gift that only Christ can give. The gift of salvation comes only from Christ Jesus.

Christians are on our way to life, not death. We are on our way to something, not anything. To be void of hope is to be empty. Hopelessness is emptiness.

Christ came to fill that emptiness. Hope depends on Christ and His work. Our hope is not founded on anything that man has done, or can do, for himself. Our hope is not founded on anything that a church has done, or can do, for itself. The hope of the world is in Christ.

O Eternal Father, in the midst of battle, and struggle, and temptation; in the midst of death, and crises, and crowds; in the midst of drugs and addiction, we have something infinitely precious to look forward to, and we thank You. Thank You for Heaven and for life eternal. In Jesus' name, we pray. Amen.

God's Care for You

He hath showed his people the power of his works (Psalm 111:6).

Scripture: **Isaiah 45:1-5**
Song: **"God Will Take Care of You"**

In 586 B.C., the Jews were carried into Babylon by Nebuchadnezzar. Cyrus captured Babylon in 539 B.C. and began liberating God's people. In doing this he was fulfilling the prophecy that even though he was a Gentile he was a type of the Messiah.

A minister's family had serious health problems. The economic burden was crushing. Afterwards he said that the only significant financial aid he received came from a man who was not a Christian.

God can use the actions of unbelievers to take care of His own. Such an act of generosity by a non-Christian may influence him to accept Christ. Sometimes God's providential care comes to us in unexpected ways.

Cyrus let the people of God practice their religion. He made possible their return to Jerusalem and the rebuilding of the temple under the leadership of Ezra and Nehemiah. Although a Gentile, he accomplished God's purpose.

Thank You, Lord, that we have been set free by the sacrifice of Christ. We praise You for liberating us as You did Your children in the days of Cyrus. In Jesus' name, we pray. Amen.

May 26-June 1. **Ross Dampier** is a frequent writer for Devotions. He is a minister emeritus of Central Christian Church in Bristol, Tennessee.

The Plan of God

The Lord by his wisdom hath founded the earth; by his under-standing hath he established the heavens (Proverbs 3:19).

Scripture: **Isaiah 45:7-13**
Song: **"How Great Thou Art"**

A Christian and a skeptic sat under an oak tree that stood beside a pumpkin patch. The skeptic said, "If there was a God who created the world, He would have made a better job of it. He would have put the pumpkins on this huge oak tree and the little acorns on the delicate pumpkin vines." About that time an acorn fell and hit him on the head. The Christian said, "Now aren't you glad that God made things the way He did?"

Isaiah knew that Cyrus would rebuild the city of Jerusalem. He also knew that many people would be unhappy about it. They could not conceive that it would be done "not for price or reward," but because it was the will of God.

We sometimes make the mistake of questioning God. We may think we have a right to some explanation. All the while God's answer is before us. "Where is your faith? I have given you salvation in my Son. I have said I will be with you. I have promised you eternal life."

O Lord, forgive us when we question Your judgments. Let us accept day by day the blessings that You send to us without questioning or complaining. May we accept the things You do for us knowing that they are always a blessing. In Jesus' name, we pray. Amen.

A God Who Shows Himself

But now in Christ Jesus you who once were far away have been brought near through the blood of Christ (Ephesians 2:13, *New International Version*).

Scripture: **Isaiah 45:14-19**
Song: **"To God Be the Glory"**

When I was a very young preacher I delivered a sermon on the text, "Verily thou art a God that hidest thyself" (Isaiah 45:15). I completely missed the point. God is hidden only from those people who deny that He exists or believe only in idols.

For the nation of Israel and for the new Israel of which we are a part, God is not a secret. He has created everything that we see. He remembers His people as He did when He rebuilt the city of Jerusalem. He provides salvation for us in the resurrection of Christ Jesus.

When I was a boy, baseball was not played in a domed stadium. It was played in a ballpark surrounded by a high board fence. The best we could hope for was to find an unoccupied knothole. There came a time when the knothole gang could afford a seat in the bleachers behind left field. It was still a long way from home plate.

Today God provides us with box seats in the drama of salvation, and they are free.

Lord, we know that our ways are not Your ways. Thank you for allowing us to know You better through Jesus Christ. Thank You for providing the hope of life eternal in His resurrection. In His holy name, we pray. Amen.

A Conquering King

The Lord, he it is that doth go before thee; he will be with thee, he will not fail thee, neither forsake thee: fear not, neither be dismayed (Deuteronomy 31:8).

Scripture: **Isaiah 52:7-12**
Song: **"Faith Is the Victory"**

In the year 1307 Robert Bruce was crowned King of Scotland. His enemy, Edward the first of England, defeated him in battle, and he was forced into exile in Northern Ireland. He never gave up. His persistence is illustrated by the story of the exiled king lying in a cave and watching a spider attempt to climb a web to the ceiling. Six times the spider tried and failed, but on the seventh attempt it succeeded. Robert Bruce pondered that lesson. After two years he returned to Scotland and defeated his English enemies at the Battle of Bannockburn in 1314, thus establishing Scottish independence. He never gave up.

When the children of Israel were in exile in Babylon, it must have seemed to them that their God was in exile too. Yet they are told not to despair for the day will come when they will return and their God will be with them, leading the way.

The good news for the Christian is that, even if we feel discouraged, we are winners if we remain true to God.

Lord, we come praying for Your presence so that we can overcome discouragement. Give us a sense of accomplishment and victory through Jesus Christ, in whose name we pray. Amen.

How Can Hope Help?

Zeal for your house consumes me (Psalm 69:9, *New International Version*).

Scripture: **Ezra 1:1-5**
Song: **"Rise Up, O Men of God"**

Barnabas was known as an encourager. What a blessing he was to the early church!

We all need people who are enthusiastic about what we do. As the children of Israel prepared to go back to Jerusalem, they needed plenty of enthusiasm. God was on their side. King Cyrus was sympathetic and helpful. The Israelites had the support of friends and neighbors. But ahead lay a lot of sobering problems for them. In the days to come they would need all the enthusiasm they could get.

In athletics whether a team wins or loses often depends on their mental attitude. That, in turn, will be influenced by the support of the crowd. Home field advantage is not in the imagination. It has everything to do with crowd support.

As Christians, we are assured of the support of a great host of witnesses. We also need the enthusiastic support of fellow Christians, even as they need our enthusiastic support for them.

O Lord God of all, we pray that You will help us to be real encouragers to one another. Give us a positive outlook in all that we do that we may approach the tasks to which You call us with divine enthusiasm. In Jesus' name, we pray. Amen.

Help From Unexpected Places

Remember this: Whoever sows sparingly will also reap sparingly, and whoever sows generously will also reap generously (2 Corinthians 9:6, *New International Version*).

Scripture: **Ezra 1:6–2:2**
Song: **"O God, Our Help in Ages Past"**

I once ministered to a church that had contracted to build a new building. The Sunday after we signed the contract, I preached about being true to the Word of God, and how we work to be true to the Bible.

After the service had started a distinguished-looking man entered. At the close of the service I asked his name. He said he would write me a letter, and he was gone.

Several months later I received his letter. He was a United States Congressman from a distant state. In his letter he told how he had been raised in the Christian Church. He said, "I was so interested in your sermon. It reminded me of sermons I heard when I was growing up. In the church where I now attend they tell me that nobody preaches sermons like that any more. I was delighted to hear that this is not so, and I want to have a part in the construction of your new building." In the letter was a sizeable donation. Help comes from unexpected places.

*Keep us faithful, **Lord,** to the calling unto which You have called us. We desire to continue diligent in the proclamation of Your Word. Lord keep us faithful. In Jesus' name, we pray. Amen.*

Devotions™

Suffer the little children to come unto me, and forbid them not; for of such is the kingdom of God (Mark 10:14).

June

Photo by K. D. Bell is of Honoria Rose Bell. Both mother and daughter are members of Standard Publishing's extended family.

The Joy of Giving

Remember the words of the Lord Jesus, how he said, It is more blessed to give than to receive (Acts 20:35).

Scripture: **Ezra 2:64-70**
Song: **"Give of Your Best to the Master"**

A missionary to Indonesia was showing a visiting friend some of the farm country around the mission. They saw a wife guiding a man pulling a plow. The missionary said that they were Christians. Until recently they had owned a buffalo to pull the plow, but they had sold it and given the money to the Lord's work. The visitor expressed sympathy for these poor people who had been deprived of their only farm animal. The missionary replied, "Oh, they rejoice that they had a buffalo to sell." Remember that Jesus mentioned that "It is more blessed to give . . . ."

The Hebrews fleeing Egypt rejoiced as they gave to build the tabernacle. The Jews returning from exile gave willingly to rebuilding the temple. Thank God for the prosperity that enables us to give to His work.

Make us cheerful givers, O Lord, that our worship may be acceptable to You. Help us to understand that the most essential part of worship is in sacrifice. Bless the offering of a humble and a contrite heart with which we bring the things with which You have prospered us. In Jesus' name, we pray. Amen.

June 1. **Ross Dampier** is a frequent writer for Devotions. He is a minister emeritus of Central Christian Church in Bristol, Tennessee.

Worship Means Commitment

So we say with confidence, "The Lord is my helper, I will not be afraid. What can man do to me?" (Hebrews 13:6, *New International Version*).

Scripture: **Ezra 3:1-5**
Song: **"Come, Now Is the Time to Worship"**

Marriage vows, birth of a child, care of an elderly parent or grandparent, relocation for a new job, acceptance into college, a new mortgage—what do these have in common? Each of them means commitment.

Some are entered into with joy and gladness; others may mean change in lifestyle and expectations. Some are a matter of choice. The choice each of us must make is how we will adjust to our commitments.

Worshiping God was a commitment for the Jews who returned to Israel. Sacrifices that had halted during exile could be renewed. For some people new ventures can be fearful. Unless we are bound to God's strength, and not to our own, we can become virtually immobilized.

Israel's assembly as "one man" (Ezra 3:1) publicly proclaimed her commitment to God, despite surrounding worries. We can accomplish our own commitments when we dedicate to "oneness" with Christ.

Father, remind us of Your strength when we are weak. Give us courage to work and worship. In Christ's name, we pray. Amen.

June 2-8. **Candace Wood** is a Christian educator living in Charlottesville, Virginia. She has two children and three grandchildren.

Worship Brings Gladness

Exalt the LORD our God and worship at his holy mountain, for the LORD our God is holy. Shout for joy to the Lord, all the earth (Psalm 99:9; 100:1, *New International Version*).

Scripture: **Psalm 100:1-5**
Song: **"Shout to the Lord"**

Have you ever been lost? Perhaps your child has been unexpectedly separated from you in an unfamiliar place. If so, the panic and fear you then felt might be flooding your memory even now. On the other hand, think of the joy that filled your heart when your child was found again. A terrible nightmare ended, and you and your child felt safe once again. How glad you were!

How gladly do we worship God? He has given us His Word that we might know how He taught His people to worship Him. When we allow celebration to spill out of a soul that is filled with His Word, it is then that we can worship the God of all truth.

The psalmist speaks of exalting the Lord above all. He speaks of gladness, of rejoicing, of shouting, and of praising Him when we come to worship Him. Let us say with gladness and celebration, "I rejoiced with those who said to me, 'Let us go to the house of the Lord'" (Psalm 122:1).

Dear Lord, thank You for giving us reasons for joy and gladness. May we always remember the pleasing things of life that are blessings from You. And may we spread our joy and gladness to those we meet. In Jesus' name, we pray. Amen.

Worship Through the Ages

But many of the older priests and Levites and family heads, who had seen the former temple, wept aloud when they saw the foundation of this temple being laid, while many others shouted for joy (Ezra 3:12, *New International Version*)

Scripture: **Ezra 3:6-13**
Song: **"Go Light Your World"**

I live in a university town where it is impossible to escape "football fever" each fall of the year. Competition between two of the state's leading universities is legendary. A home game means untold teasing between fans of the teams about how badly each is going to suffer defeat. In most cases this is mutually given and received in a good-natured manner.

When we look at the world, we see many different ways in which we do things, and we often feel that our way is the best. But let us remember that God has created a world of diversity—people with different talents and interests and ways to express worship for God. With our diversity we worship Him.

How good that we can cheer for whichever college team we prefer and still be friends. But more important is the manner in which we allow our differences to be used to bring the world to Christ.

Our Creator and Father, *thank You for all the differences You have made in Your creation, both in the earth itself and in Your children. Help us to use our own uniqueness in ways that will honor You and build Your church. In the name of our Savior, Jesus Christ. Amen.*

Worship Refuses Discouragement

Let us encourage one another—and all the more as you see the Day approaching (Hebrews 10:25, *New International Version*).

Scripture: **Ezra 4:1-5**
Song: **"God Will Make a Way"**

When was the last time you felt that the little things in life caused you to feel discouraged? It is not often the life-changing events that cause us to feel discouraged, but the little day-to-day irritations that seem to cause us to be discouraged with daily living. Life is filled with difficult events that make or break us.

We are instructed by the Word of God to encourage one another. When we feel that those around us see and feel the discouragement we are experiencing, we are lifted to continue to serve the Lord.

While here on earth, Jesus must have felt discouraged especially when the recipient of a miracle didn't bother to thank Him or when a lesson's meaning escaped His hearers. His example to us is that He always went to His Father. Jesus remained faithful to His purpose of bringing salvation to mankind. Focus on His Father never wavered. And He achieved His purpose.

Let us take Jesus' focus and sense of mission as a personal call to encourage others.

Dear heavenly Father and Lord of all, *help us in times of discouragement to remember that You can see where we cannot. We look to You for the strength to live this day in confidence. Thank You for Jesus, our Savior, in whose name we pray. Amen.*

Worship Withstands Trials

We are hard pressed on every side, but not crushed; perplexed, but not in despair; persecuted, but not abandoned; struck down, but not destroyed (2 Corinthians 4:8, 9, *New International Version*).

Scripture: **Ezra 4:6-16**
Song: **"Crucified With Christ"**

Have you stood in a den of lions recently? Met any colossal giants? Ever seen a place to minister but found yourself hiding in the fish department instead? Been chased into a wilderness by a life-threatening mob?

Many hazards that interfere in our lives seem to be of such magnitude. All week we may be surrounded by events that require all of our time and effort. So in a thoughtful moment on Sunday morning, we name several people who need a friend, we resolve to be one, only to be overwhelmed first thing Monday morning with obligations or unexpected pressures that snatch our time. Before we realize it, the week passes and our good deeds go undone.

When we are pressed down, trodden upon, defeated, anxious, weak, and insufficient for the tasks at hand, let's consider following the faith of a Daniel, a David, or a Moses.

Father, thank You for each day, even those of adversity. Teach us to use our trials to grow our faith. We love You for standing with us in the lion's den, in the fish's mouth, and when we are confronting and crossing unknown barriers. In Christ's name, amen.

June 7

Worship Demands Perseverance

Blessed is the man who perseveres under trial, because when he has stood the test, he will receive the crown of life that God has promised to those who love him (James 1:12, *New International Version*).

Scripture: **Ezra 4:17-24**
Song: **"In His Time"**

If you were to chart outstanding events in your life, what would the list include? A wedding, a birth, a new house, or the discovery of precious family heirlooms?

Some events may not be at the top of our list of cherished memories, but they may be life-changing in their impact. Their value cannot be diminished, for many times they serve to redirect our priorities.

Today's Scripture describes how work on the temple was forced to a standstill. The distressed Jews must have worried. Were more persecutions imminent? How long-lasting might they be? Would they ever be able to worship in the temple again?

When we experience dry spells in our lives, times when we feel unsure, unloved, and alone, we risk emphasizing those negative emotions. God is with us always, not just in the best or the worst of times, but also when nothing seems to be happening.

Precious Lord, *thank You for sustaining us even during the times when life is "ordinary" and we do not sense any measurable growth or fervor for Your kingdom. Allow us to rest in Your shadow as we are nurtured by Your protection. In Jesus' name, we pray. Amen.*

Worship Promises Fulfillment

We tell you the good news: What God promised our fathers he has fulfilled for us, their children, by raising up Jesus (Acts 13:32, *New International Version*).

Scripture: **Isaiah 44:24-28**
Song: **"Standing on the Promises"**

Suppose you could sit on the sidelines and witness God's perspective of events happening and time passing. He speaks the world into existence. He communes with people and deals with nations. He sends His precious Son to become a sacrifice for the mankind that He loves so dearly. He entrusts His Spirit to comfort and assist us.

One theme runs true throughout God's attention to His creation: His promises are faithful and unchanging.

In a culture that demands immediate satisfaction, we sometimes lose sight of this truth. When we inconvenience ourselves to perform even the smallest service for Him, we feel entitled to special reward.

Let's revisit God's perspective to remind ourselves that He is not slow in His promises (2 Peter 3:8-9) just because we don't always see immediate results. He has and will fulfill all His promises so that we can experience the joy of His fellowship. Make your worship an anticipation of that fulfillment.

Dear Lord God, *thank You for fulfilling Your promises to us. We are grateful for Your unending love despite our selfish desires. Work in our hearts and lives to make our worship more faithful to You. In the name of our Savior, we pray. Amen.*

Keep Building

I tell you that you are Peter, and on this rock I will build my church, and the gates of Hades will not overcome it (Matthew 16:18, *New International Version*).

Scripture: **Haggai 1:1-6**
Song: **"The Church's One Foundation"**

The rebuilding of the house of the Lord was a landmark experience in the lives of the Israelites in the time of Haggai. And building the church of God is an ongoing task for twenty-first century Christians.

The church of God, of course, is much more than stones or bricks and steel or wooden beams. As Paul teaches the Ephesians, the church is the body of Christ, and as Christians we are members of His body.

However, as a part of Christ's body, the church, we are admonished to do some building. For example, Paul urged the Corinthian Christians, who were fascinated with spiritual gifts, to excel in gifts that build up the church (see 1 Corinthians 14:12). Paul urged the Thessalonians to "encourage one another and build each other up." And he committed the Ephesian elders to God and to the word of His grace, "which can build you up."

*We thank You, **dear God,** that as Your children we are Your temples and that Your Spirit dwells in us. Help us to honor You by living holy lives so that we may be fit dwelling places for Your Spirit. In the name of Christ, our Savior, we pray. Amen.*

June 9-15. **Ron Henderson** is retired after 40 years of teaching English at the college level. He and his wife, Gerri, have two children and ten grandchildren.

God Is With Us

And the Lord stirred up the spirit . . . of the whole remnant of the people (Haggai 1:14, *New International Version*).

Scripture: **Haggai 1:7-15**
Song: **"Spirit of the Living God"**

Have you been discouraged? Have you ever wandered aimlessly, without purpose, without direction or enthusiasm?

At our school we have a "Spirit Coordinator." Her task is to involve students and faculty in support of the athletic programs. In sports, it's commonplace to speak of the home field or home court advantage. Why? Because athletes can actually elevate the level of their performance when they know that many people are pulling for them. And this is true not only in athletics but also in almost any sort of human endeavor. Imagine being a key leader in your home congregation without anyone pulling for you. Now imagine being such a leader who has the whole-hearted support of the entire congregation. It makes a difference.

How did the Lord "stir the spirit" of the leaders? The Lord said, "I am with you." Can you imagine anything more spirit-stirring than that promise?

We praise You, dear Lord, for Your encouragement through Your Holy Spirit. Help us in times of discouragement to allow You to stir our spirits so that we can be a source of strength for others and so that we can be effective in the work You have called us to do. In the name of Christ, our Savior, we pray. Amen.

Be Strong

**Be strong and courageous. . . . for the Lord your God goes with
you; he will never leave you nor for forsake you** (Deuteronomy
31:6, *New International Version*).

Scripture: **Haggai 2:1-9**
Song **"Just a Closer Walk with Thee"**

When God stirred the spirits of the people, they gladly
set to work rebuilding the house of God. About a month
later God directed Haggai to speak again to the leaders
and to all the remnant of the people. The reason? It seems
that some were beginning to lose heart. For those who
knew the house of God in its former glory, the structure
they were now working on seemed like nothing. And so
the people are instructed to take heart, to be strong. It's
one thing to get "psyched up" and dive into a project; it
may be another thing to find courage to stay at it when the
results are not quite what was expected.

We often hear the colloquial expressions of encouragement: "Hang in there!" "Keep your chin up!" or "You can
make it!" A rallying cry in the Old Testament is "Be strong
and courageous." The challenge of the Christian walk is to
find courage to press on.

In today's Scripture God says to the people, in effect,
"Be strong; take courage; for I am with you."

*We are weak, O Lord, but You are strong. Perhaps, like the Apostle
Paul, we can boast all the more gladly about our weaknesses so that
Christ's power may restore us. Give us the strength we need to use this
day to Your glory. In the name of Christ, we pray. Amen.*

We Persevere

We also rejoice in our sufferings, because we know that suffering produces perseverance (Romans 5:3, *New International Version*).

Scripture: **Ezra 5:1-5**
Song: **"Jesus, I My Cross Have Taken"**

God stirred the spirits of the people, and they set to work rebuilding the house of the Lord. God was with them. At a point of discouragement, God urged them to be strong, to take courage. He was with them. When the work was in danger of being brought to a stop by Tattenai, governor of Trans-Euphrates, and his associates, "the eye of their God was watching over the elders of the Jews, and they were not stopped" (Ezra 5:5, *New International Version*). The Israelites persevered; the rebuilding continued.

There seem to be levels of resources called upon in this process. It's important to be "psyched up," to have enthusiasm for the work at hand. It's important, if enthusiasm should fail, to be strong, to have courage. It is also important that courage be backed up by perseverance when opposition mounts.

The Apostle Paul reminded the Corinthians that he knew something about trials and opposition. He records a catalogue of the difficulties he faced: imprisonment, floggings, shipwreck, hunger, thirst, and much more. When opposition mounts, we, like Paul, must press on.

Thank You, dear God, *for the assurance that "Greater is He that is in me than he that is in the world." Day by day we depend upon Your sustaining power. In Christ's name, we pray. Amen.*

Servants of God

We are servants of the God of heaven and earth (Ezra 5:11, *New International Version*).

Scripture: **Ezra 5:6-12**
Song: **"O Master, Let Me Walk With Thee"**

The Israelites who were rebuilding the Temple, on being challenged by the secular authorities, affirmed with confidence that "we are servants of the God of heaven and earth." Interesting. When was the last time you heard someone say, "I am a servant of God"? People usually identify themselves by occupation or profession by saying, I'm a teacher; a lawyer; an accountant; an electrician; a computer programmer. In the church, we might hear some say, I am the minister; an elder; the treasurer; the youth minister. Ideally, any of these people should be able to say, "I am a servant of God."

Jesus set the example. Paul reminds us in Philippians 2:7 that in His incarnation, Jesus "took the very nature of a servant." Jesus "came not to be served but to serve." And He taught His disciples that "whoever would be great among you must be your servant." Paul and Peter and James and Jude, in the opening lines of their epistles, claim for themselves the title "servant of Christ," or "servant of God." Today, let's be servants of God.

We thank You, O Lord, that we have been called to be Your servants. Give us courage and understanding this day to serve You in all we do. Teach us to follow Your leading and be happy to say, "I am a faithful servant of the Lord." In the name of Christ, we pray. Amen.

Pressing On

Not that I have already obtained all this, or have already been made perfect, but I press on to take hold of that for which Christ Jesus took hold of me (Philippians 3:12, *New International Version*).

Scripture: **Ezra 5:13-17**
Song: **"Higher Ground"**

Ezra tells of the time when Sheshbazzar came and laid the foundations of the house of God in Jerusalem. And he says, "From that day to the present it has been under construction but is not yet finished." The rebuilding of the house of the Lord was not smooth sailing. There were bumps along the way; there was even a period of time when the task was abandoned. But it was renewed, the people pressed on, and the task was brought to completion. And on the appropriate day, the people celebrated their accomplishment.

Any honest scrutiny of our lives will convince us that we are not quite the people we ought to be; we do not reflect the glory of God as fully as we would like. But we can take the approach of the apostle Paul, who was determined to press on toward the goal, knowing that "our light and momentary troubles are achieving for us an eternal glory" (2 Corinthians 4:17).

O God, our help in ages past, Our hope for years to come, Our shelter from the stormy blast, And our eternal home! We praise You for Your goodness to us when we falter. Sustain us by Your love and power. In the name of Your Son, Jesus, we pray. Amen.

From This Day

For there is no difference between Jew and Gentile—the same Lord is Lord of all and richly blesses all who call on him (Romans 10:12, *New International Version*).

Scripture: **Haggai 2:13-23**
Song: **"This Is the Day"**

For many years prior to the rebuilding of the house of the Lord, the people of Israel had been punished for their sins. God had "struck all the work of [their] hands with blight, mildew and hail"(Haggai 2:17). But brighter days were coming, and the turning point was a particular day–the twenty-fourth day of the ninth month. "From this day on," says the Lord, "I will bless you."

No doubt all of us can identify some "this days" in our lives; some days marked by blessings that continue to the present time, blessings for which we are grateful.

Years ago, on a particular day which I can no longer document, one of my teachers dropped the word to me that an English professor at our college would soon be leaving. He advised me to prepare to take the position. I took his advice, and more than forty years later I look back and realize that through the agency of my teacher, God blessed my life—from that day—in ways that I could not have anticipated

Dear Father, *many events in my life show me that You have been leading me all along the way. I know that all blessings come from You. Let me be, this day, a blessing to someone as I walk the path that You desire for me to walk. In the name of Jesus, my Savior, I pray. Amen.*

No Great Thing for God

The Lord says, "This seems unbelievable to you–a remnant, small, discouraged as you are–but it is no great thing for me" (Zechariah 8:6, *The Living Bible*).

Scripture: **Zechariah 8:1-6**
Song: **"God Will Take Care of You"**

The young couple and their three toddlers were moving 750 miles to their first pastorate. Waiting for the promised funds for moving expenses, they were told, "We'll reimburse you when you arrive." Then an unexpected check from an expired insurance policy and a 5-dollar stay at a USO with free breakfast gave them enough money for the trip.

Twenty-eight specialists told the gospel songwriter there was no cure for his condition. But after 19 years, a series of events, including a friend's unplanned trip to Guatemala where he "just happened" to meet a doctor who knew of a medicine, led to a complete healing of the "incurable" disease.

What problems are we facing today? Are they financial, physical, or spiritual? Are they, as the children of Israel, captivity? It may seem unbelievable to you but it's no great thing for God. He has the answer for you!

Dear Father and Lord of all, *whatever we're facing today, help us to take it to the foot of the cross and leave it there. We pray this prayer in the name of Jesus, our Savior and Lord. Amen.*

June 16-22. **Donna Clark Goodrich** is a wife, mother, and grandmother, freelance writer, editor, proofreader, and seminar leader from Mesa, Arizona.

We Can Go Home Again

This is what the LORD Almighty says: "I will bring [my people] back to live in Jerusalem" (Zechariah 8:8, *New International Version*).

Scripture: **Zechariah 8:7-12**
Song: **"Lord, I'm Coming Home"**

There are times I disagree with Thomas Wolfe's statement; "You can't go home again." I love going back to Michigan, especially in the fall when the leaves change. I enjoy driving by the schools I attended, houses I lived in, places I worked.

In another sense, however, I agree with him because it's not the same. My parents are gone; one house has been torn down. But in some ways, it's better now. I take my husband and three children with me. I see school friends, and time has a way of erasing hurtful memories.

The children of Israel were back home, but it wasn't the same. Before there had been no prosperity, nothing but division and strife. Now God told them your "seed shall be prosperous; the vine shall give her fruit, and the ground shall give her increase."

Have you wandered away from home but long to return? You have only to take the first step. Your Father is waiting for you with open arms.

O Lord, perhaps some of us have not only moved from place to place and left family and friends, houses and jobs, but maybe some of us have left our Christian upbringing. Thank You for Your Promise that You are waiting for us. In the name of Jesus, we pray. Amen.

The Street Where You Live

These are the things that ye shall do; Speak ye every man the truth to his neighbor . . . and let none of you imagine evil in your hearts against his neighbor (Zechariah 8:16, 17).

Scripture: **Zechariah 8:13-17**
Song: **"Make Me a Blessing"**

I complained to my family about our new neighbor. "I wish Jean had never moved on this street." Jean's husband worked out-of-town during the week and she was forever asking me to take her somewhere. With five children, her list of errands was never-ending.

On this particular evening, I had just driven 20 miles and was getting ready to go to a revival meeting. My neighbor asked me to take her back those same 20 miles to visit her five-year-old daughter in the hospital. I couldn't refuse.

"I hope you didn't have plans for tonight," Jean sounded almost apologetic.

When I said I was going to church, she replied, "We went to church where we used to live." Then she added wistfully, "But since we moved here, no one's asked us."

Is there a family in your neighborhood that you wished were not there? Here's the answer: show them love and let them see Christ in your daily life. Introduce them to God and watch your neighborhood change.

***Lord**, You've told us to show mercy and compassion to the widow and the fatherless, the stranger. Help us to show love to our neighbors that they may see You. In the name of Christ, we pray. Amen.*

Wise Men Still Seek Him

And when they had found him [Jesus], they said unto him, All men seek for thee (Mark 1:37).

Scripture: **Zechariah 8:18-23**
Song: **"Turn Your Eyes Upon Jesus"**

We live in a day when there are more resources for Christians than ever before. On almost any given week-end you can pick up the religious section of a big-city newspaper and see listings of special services, concerts, and workshops. Religious presses release hundreds of new books every year, and most cities offer Christian radio and TV programming.

A lady in our Bible study group who had been going through a struggle confessed one morning, "I've read books that deal with my problem, I've watched videos, I've called in to Christian radio talk shows, I've gone to retreats. But this week I realized that the answer is in Jesus Christ!"

We can be thankful for anything that helps us in our walk with God. But in and of themselves they are not the solution. They merely point us to the Source of satisfaction. Jesus has said, "I am the way and the truth and the life." He alone is the final answer.

Lord, we are thankful for Christian authors and singers, for those who give of their time to travel around the country speaking the truth. But, Lord, let us never use them as a substitute for studying Your Word and following Your leading. Whatever we're struggling with today, let us look to You alone. In the name of Jesus, our Savior, we pray. Amen.

Praise Him in the Temple

Lord, here in your Temple we meditate upon your kindness and your love (Psalm 48:9, *The Living Bible.*).

Scripture: **Psalm 48:1-8**
Song: **"Praise Him! Praise Him!"**

There was always singing in my home. My mother loved to sing, and she taught us all the hymns of the church. We would sing the hymns as we worked. We never needed a hymnbook because these hymns were embedded in our minds and hearts. Just thinking of these hymns easily brings me to the foot of Jesus. Perhaps this is what the Lord meant when He reminded us to know His Word and to meditate upon it day and night.

As I entered the church this past Easter morning, I longed for the opportunity to once again sing the hymns that so easily bring me to the throne to worship Him. But no! Soon the pulsing sound of drums filled the sanctuary and I said out loud, "Not today."

Just then I glanced at an elderly lady in a wheelchair joyously waving her crippled arms and tapping her toes. I smiled, put my hands together, and began to sing: "Celebrate Jesus, Celebrate."

God is still the same today, and He is worthy to be praised. Let us go into the temple to worship Him!

Almighty God and Father of all, *help us to worship You in spirit and truth. Teach us to worship and praise You in the church, in the home, and at work. In the name of Jesus, we pray. Amen.*

A Lifelong Guide

For this God is our God for ever and ever: he will be our guide even unto death (Psalm 48:14).

Scripture: **Psalm 48:9-14**
Song: **"All the Way My Savior Leads Me"**

I was reading Adam Clarke's comments on the verse for today: "For this God who did all these wonderful things is our God. He is our portion, and He has taken us for His people. He will be our guide through all the difficulties of life unto death. He will never leave us."

What a wonderful promise. This God—not just any god, not the unknown gods of the Romans, but the one and only true God—led me as a young person when I made decisions that affected the rest of my life.

The true and living God led my husband and me as my husband served two years in the U.S. Army. Our God guided us as we worked our way through the seminary. Our God led us as we raised our children into adulthood. The true and living God led us through days of financial struggle and a number of serious medical crises.

The good news is, no matter what we may face in the days to come, the true and living God will still be our Guide—even unto death!

Lord, there are days that we have so many decisions to make, it's hard to know what to do. You've been there for us in the past, and You've promised that You'll be there in the days to come. We will follow You. In the name of Jesus, we pray. Amen.

Determined To Stay True

My heart is fixed, O God, my heart is fixed: I will sing and give praise (Psalm 57:7).

Scripture: **Psalm 57:7-11**
Song: **"Now I Belong to Jesus"**

Some writers have suggested that the word "fixed" in the above verse actually means "determined."

I remember as a young teen telling a friend that I was always going to be a Christian. She replied, "You can't say what you'll do when you get older. You don't know what will happen." But, having seen too much in our family of what sin could do, I sang along with the others in our youth group, "I am determined, I've made up my mind. I will serve the Lord."

Can we make up our minds to serve the Lord no matter what comes our way? Look at David and all that happened to him. He met up with first a bear, then a lion, and finally a giant. The father of his best friend tried to kill him, but still he said his heart was "fixed." It would have been so easy to give up, but he just kept praising God.

When our determination begins to waver, let's do as David did; let's give thanks! It will help every time so let's just make up our minds!

Heavenly Father, we use determination in so many parts of our lives—in our education, in our work, in our family. Teach us to use that same determination to stay true to You, no matter what. And if things get hard, help us to remember all the good things You've done for us and to praise You. In the name of Jesus, we pray. Amen.

Search the Document of Life

Thy word is a lamp to my feet and a light to my path (Psalm 119:105, *Revised Standard Version*).

Scripture: **Ezra 6:1-5**
Song: **"Wonderful Words of Life"**

My grandparents came to America from Germany. They brought with them a wonderful sense of values and a love for teaching children to obey. I was blessed with a loving father who was a fair and strict disciplinarian.

When my father died, I was given his baptismal certificate. I was thrilled to receive the document that is over eighty years old, and I will treasure it for the rest of my life. I was especially delighted that it is written in German. "Let the children come to me . . ." is written on it in German. The document was filed away for many years. It was an interesting discovery to read this record of my father's baptism.

We have a record. It is the Bible. We can search it for knowledge and instruction on how to live. By so doing, we can show the world how the Word of God can change the world and save the souls of all who come to Him.

Dear heavenly Father and Lord of all, thank You for documents that record important events in our lives. May we search through the most important record of all, Your Word, which brings us closer to You, that Your church may continue to follow Your teachings. In the name of Jesus, our Savior, we pray. Amen.

June 23-29. **B.J. Bassett** is a writer, conference presenter, and Christian education director. She and her husband have four children and two grandsons.

I Work for the Master

Let it be carried out with diligence (Ezra 6:12, *New International Version*).

Scripture: **Ezra 6:6-12**
Song: **"Give of Your Best to the Master"**

Sometimes people in the work force may call in sick when they are simply emotionally exhausted, rather than being physically ill. Sometimes, out of duty, one may go to work when it would be best for all concerned if that person rested at home for a day.

As believers we are witnesses to others. Whether at the top of the corporate ladder or at the bottom, we learn to use our God-given talents to do our job to the best of our abilities—not only in the workplace, but also in our leisure time. As believers, we serve the Master with diligence—showing others right from wrong. In this way, we exhibit Christian characteristics at the work place, at home, on the ball fields and in our communities.

Out of His great love for us, God allowed His only Son to suffer and die for our sins. Because of His great love, our hearts and souls want only to give Him the best in our homes with our families, in the work place, and in our communities. Today let us live a joyful life at work, home, and community.

Dear heavenly Father, thank You for the opportunity to work for You. Teach us to be the examples that the world needs to see Your great love. We want to serve You diligently in everything we do. In the name of Jesus, our Savior, we pray. Amen.

The Winner!

Then the people of Israel—the priests, the Levites and the rest of the exiles—celebrated the dedication of the house of God with joy (Ezra 6:16, *New International Version*).

Scripture: **Ezra 6:13-18**
Song: **"Victory in Jesus"**

There are many reasons to celebrate. Anniversaries, birthdays, graduations, promotions, and the birth of a new baby are just some of the reasons to celebrate. When my little brother learned to walk, we celebrated. After toddling to the open arms of one of us, we'd hold his arm high in the air and shout, "The winner!"

I celebrate my achievements by doing jigsaw puzzles. I love jigsaw puzzles and look forward to finishing a project so I can pour out onto my dining room table all those little pieces that I can have fun putting together.

Another reason to celebrate is waking up in the morning knowing God loves us. And it doesn't stop there. Like the Israelites, we celebrate with joy because we know that a mansion is being built for us in glory. For some of us, on the day we arrive in Heaven we'll run into the open arms of Jesus and shout, "The winner!" What a victory! What a celebration that will be!

Dear heavenly Father and Lord of all, our hearts are full of joy knowing You love us. We can hardly wait until we see the mansion You are building for us in glory. On that day we'll run into Your open arms and celebrate with You. In the name of Jesus, Lord and Savior of all, we pray. Amen.

Sing to the Lord a New Song

O sing to the Lord a new song (Psalm 96:1, *Revised Standard Version*).

Scripture: **Psalm 96:1-6**
Song: **"I Will Celebrate"**

A few years ago I wanted the church where I worship to have a children's choir. I knew I wasn't able to do it myself. So after talking with the church leadership, I learned about a young couple who had recently begun attending this congregation. They had expressed a desire to be involved in a children's choir.

Today the children's choir, called "New Song," is much more than I envisioned. It is more like a music academy. They have Bible stories, crafts, and music theory. They have adopted grandparents from the congregation, and they sponsor a child through Compassion International.

The choir is an outreach ministry. Any elementary child in the community can be a member of the choir. They have been asked to sing at a local shopping center and an elementary school. Their recent fund-raiser was for the community's Pregnancy Care Center.

What I was unable to do, God did–through the vision and talents of others.

Dear heavenly Father, thank You for giving us visions and thank You for still being a God of miracles. Thank You that Your children can praise You with a new song. May we always give You the honor, praise and glory for anything good You do through us. In the name of Jesus, our Lord and Savior, we pray. Amen.

Daddy's Coming

Therefore keep watch, because you do not know the day or the hour (Matthew 25:13, *New International Version*).

Scripture: **Psalm 96:7-13**
Song: **"Jesus is Coming Again"**

Judy did not make friends easily with her brash personality. It wasn't until I had known Judy for many years that I learned something sad that had happened when she was a little girl.

She told me that her parents were divorced when she was a little girl. She lived with her mother. Her daddy would often promise to come and get her on Saturdays. She looked forward to Saturdays only to be disappointed. She would get cleaned up and put on a pretty dress. Then she'd skip outside and sit on the curb in front of her house. She sat on that curb waiting. Her father did not come. She felt abandoned.

We have a heavenly Father who keeps His promises. He is coming again because His Word says, "For as the lightning comes from the east and shines as far as the west, so will be the coming of the Son of man" (Matthew 24:27). We know that He will never abandon us. He does what He says He will do. Rejoice; our Father is coming!

O heavenly Father and Lord of all, what a joy it is to be able to read Your Word and know that You keep Your promises. We are not abandoned, and we have the assurance of Your return. While we wait for that glorious day, may we serve You with joy. In Christ's holy name, we pray. Amen.

Tears of Joy—Jesus Saves

If you confess with your lips that Jesus is Lord and believe in your heart that God raised him from the dead, you will be saved (Romans 10:9, *Revised Standard Version*).

Scripture: **Psalms 98:1-6**
Song: **"Wonderful Grace of Jesus"**

I am thrilled when my family expresses love for the Lord. Recently my husband and I received e-mail from our daughter. It brought tears of joy. It read as follows:

Hi Mom and Dad:

I have great news! On Wednesday night, the boys and I were snuggling in front of the fire reading books. Every night we have been reading the devotional that you gave Ben. The devotional for Wednesday was about the Passover. We talked about Jesus being the pure Passover Lamb for us and that He died for our sins. For the first time, I saw the glimmer of comprehension in Ben's eyes. I shared several Scripture verses with him about what to do to be saved. Ben said the prayer at the end of the devotional time, and his prayer was beautiful. When he looked up, he had tears in his eyes. Isn't it incredible that God used that devotional time to be the catalyst for Ben's understanding of salvation.

I love you both, Mellie.

Dear Lord, *thank You for Your grace and love. Thank You for sending Your Son to die on the cross to pay the price for us. May we confess our sins, repent, and believe that Your Son died and rose again so we can spend eternity with You. Amen.*

Worship at His Footstool

Extol the LORD our God; worship at his footstool! Holy is he!
(Psalm 99:5, *Revised Standard Version*).

Scripture: **Psalm 99:1-5**
Song: **"We Exalt Thee"**

While shopping for a greeting card the other day, I
found the perfect one. On the front of it is a picture of
Jesus and a small child. Jesus is sitting on a rock. His long
white tunic, made of a coarse fabric, shows signs of wear
and is discolored from walking along the dirt road. His
outer robe is a russet color, and His feet are clad in san-
dals. Lovingly, He is gazing down at a small child who
stands at His side. The child's little arms and folded hands
rest in the Master's lap. Jesus has His arm around the
child. There is light around the Master and light on the
curly headed child as he looks up into the face of his
loving Lord.

The picture on the front of the card tells the story which
is recorded in Psalm 99. No matter how old we are, God
wants His children to worship Him at His footstool.

*Dear heavenly Father, You are holy and worthy of praise. What a
privilege to be Your child. May we always worship You at Your footstool. Thank You for Your Word and its instruction. And thank You for
artists who inspire us by using their God-given talents. In the name of
Jesus, our Savior, we pray. Amen.*

Devotions™

𝕴 will meditate in thy precepts, and have respect unto thy ways. I will delight myself in thy statutes: I will not forget thy word (Psalm 119:15, 16).

July

Photo of missionary Jody Hesler in Bakcheserai, Ukraine taken by Andrew Wood.

Confessing Our Sin

If we confess our sins, he is faithful and just to forgive us our sins, and to cleanse us from all unrighteousness (1 John 1:9).

Scripture: **Nehemiah 1:5-11**
Song: **"I Need Thee Every Hour"**

Confession has a power that few allow themselves to experience. By admitting to God our shortcomings, we can rise above them. It is easy to believe that we control our destinies. Confession reminds us that we are helpless without God. It is easy to treat God as a grandfather who grants our wishes. Confession reminds us that God has provided for what we need most, our forgiveness. Confession keeps our perspective clear.

Nehemiah shows us something about confession. His confession was heartfelt, unconditional, and specific (verses 5-7). He prayed not only for himself, but also for his country (verses 6, 7). His confession was coupled with repentance; he expected to restore relationship with God by renewing obedience to Him (verses 9, 10).

Read the rest of Nehemiah's story. See how his confession preceded his effectiveness for God. Ponder how confession could revolutionize your spiritual life.

As we list our specific sins today, O God, we pray for Your forgiveness, we long to be close to You, and we recommit ourselves to obedience. In Jesus' holy name, we pray. Amen.

June 30-July 6. **Mark A. Taylor** serves as vice-president of church resources at Standard Publishing.

Training for Service

Behold, I send you forth as sheep in the midst of wolves: be ye therefore wise as serpents, and harmless as doves (Matthew 10:16).

Scripture: **Nehemiah 2:1-5**
Song: **"Seek Ye First"**

The facilities manager for our congregation learned his job by working for several companies. As he managed large staffs in the food service industry, he learned to motivate, delegate, and negotiate so that workers do their jobs efficiently. Then he decided to use his skills in the local church. Now, with half the salary and twice the satisfaction, he's managing staff to make the church building a productive tool for God.

The abilities he taps and the tasks he performs are not much different from those in his previous "secular" work. The world taught him most of the skills and knowledge he uses to serve God so capably today. God wants His people to work through the world's systems to bring Him glory and to spread the gospel.

Because of Nehemiah's relationship with the king, he was the perfect person to tackle the big job God needed him to do. The challenge for each Christian is to decide how God wants to use what we know and do best.

Thank You, God, *for all that You've allowed us to learn and do. Help us to see how You can use those experiences and skills for Your special purposes in the weeks ahead. In Jesus' name, we pray. Amen.*

Walking in Faith

Thy word is a lamp unto my feet, and a light unto my path (Psalm 119:105).

Scripture: **Nehemiah 2:6-10**
Song: **"My Faith Looks up to Thee"**

Picture driving through a fog so thick that you can barely see the car in front of you. The edge of the road is hidden. Streetlights are swallowed in the murk. Your car's headlights illumine just the next few feet.

You've made the trip many times before, so you know what to look for. You've allowed more time to get there. You can see only as far as you'll go in the next few seconds. But you have to get there. You keep going.

Nehemiah had prepared well. He had the king's blessing, the king's army, and the king's orders for safe passage and necessary materials. He had done all he could. Yet he knew that the mission would succeed only with God's blessing. He could not see the challenges ahead of him. He could not guarantee the outcome.

Like the driver in the fog, like Nehemiah taking up his task, we will face paths whose turns are unknown and whose way seems treacherous. Then we will have the exhilarating experience of truly trusting God and actually walking by faith.

Forgive us, Father, when us forget that Your presence and help are the reason we go safely. Help us to pursue the task You have for us, even if we can't see how the mission will turn out. In Jesus' holy name, we pray. Amen.

Assessing Reality

And you cannot be my disciple if you do not carry your own cross and follow me. But don't begin until you count the cost (Luke 14:27, 28, *New Living Translation*).

Scripture: **Nehemiah 2:11-15**
Song: "I Am Thine, O Lord"

Every good general consults his spies before going to battle. He must know the enemy's location and strength before committing his own troops.

Every good businessman examines a company's books before deciding to buy it. He must know the assets and liabilities before spending a fortune to acquire it.

Every good leader investigates the size of the task before him so he can decide wisely how to proceed. Nehemiah knew he could not gather the resources to rebuild the walls of Jerusalem until he saw with his own eyes how badly they were destroyed.

But there's more here than a lesson in leadership. Centuries after Nehemiah, Jesus told the crowds they should not consider becoming His disciple unless they were willing to love Him more than anything (Luke 14:25-33). Before rushing to follow Jesus, we must decide that we're willing to pay the price of discipleship. Like a leader, like Nehemiah, when we do this, we set the stage for our success—our spiritual success.

Heavenly Father*, help us to see what following You may require of us. Help us to pay whatever price You demand in order to do Your will. In the name of Jesus, we pray. Amen.*

July 5

Assuming Leadership

They replied at once, "Good! Let's rebuild the wall!" So they began the good work (Nehemiah 2:18, *New Living Translation*).

Scripture: **Nehemiah 2:16-20**
Song: **"Where He Leads Me, I Will Follow"**

It is interesting that the officials responded so well to Nehemiah's idea, yet they had not suggested it.

It wasn't that they didn't notice the walls were ruined. It wasn't that they thought rebuilding the walls was a bad idea. As soon as Nehemiah told them his plan and how God had blessed it, they said, "Let's go!"

The difference between these officials and Nehemiah was the difference between those who are called leaders and those who actually lead. Possessed by his vision and strengthened by his complete dependence on God, Nehemiah acted boldly. Humble enough to ask for help and walk by faith, Nehemiah could not be dissuaded. The only thing keeping the walls from being rebuilt was a leader like Nehemiah.

All around us are tasks we know God would like to accomplish. Workers are ready, but they need a godly leader who will show them the way. Is there a place in your world where you could be that leader?

***Dear God**, help us to see where You want us to lead. Give us strength to accept the leadership task You have in store for us. And if You are not calling us to lead, give us grace to follow the leader You put in our lives. In Jesus' name, we pray. Amen.*

Celebrating the Relationship

Many sacrifices were offered on that joyous day, for God had given the people cause for great joy. The women and children also participated in the celebration, and the joy of the people of Jerusalem could be heard far away (Nehemiah 12:43, *New Living Translation*).

Scripture: **Isaiah 26:1-6**
Song: **"I Will Celebrate"**

Our culture is driven by fun-seeking. We fill our homes with gadgets to show movies, record TV programs, and play games. We seek more dangerous new experiences. We flock to amusement parks for the illusion of risk.

But no fun is as fulfilling as the joy God's people felt after they rebuilt the Jerusalem wall. Their dedication ceremony followed festivals marked by reading the law of Moses, confessing their sins, and praising God for His faithfulness through the ages. This is hardly the stuff of an amusement park ad, yet it inspired a joy that comes only from connecting with God. The people not only entered a rebuilt city but also enjoyed a restored relationship. They experienced spiritual renewal from rediscovering God's truth and recommitting to His ways.

Joy is available to everyone who seeks God today.

Heavenly Father, *multiply my joy as I desire to know Your will and do it. Help me see that a relationship with You provides peace and joy no earthly experience can equal. In Jesus' holy name, we pray. Amen.*

Revenge Is the Lord's and the Work Is Ours

Do not take revenge, my friends, but leave room for God's wrath (Romans 12:19, *New International Version*).

Scripture: **Nehemiah 4:1-6**
Song: **"Onward, Christian Soldiers"**

We all have had, and will face, opposition. How will we respond to those who, out of self-serving motives, try to keep us down? The Jews living in Jerusalem during the time of Ezra and Nehemiah responded to opposition in a remarkable way.

Sanballat and Tobiah mocked the Jews. They ridiculed them saying that the Jews were too weak and didn't have the resources or ability to rebuild the walls of Jerusalem. It would be natural for the Jews to seek revenge.

God's people gave their anger and revenge to the Lord. They chose to pray. They went to work, putting their energy toward building the walls. When we seek revenge we shift our focus from the positive things we need to do. Let us follow their example and let God be responsible for revenge while we attend to the work God gave us.

Lord, whenever we are despised, help us to turn our hurt over to You and allow You to accomplish Your justice with those who are self-serving. Help us to focus on You. Amen.

July 7-13. **Glen Elliott** and his wife, Jolene, live in Tucson, Arizona, where he serves as executive pastor of Pantano Christian Church.

Fear—the Enemy's Weapon

Fear of man will prove to be a snare, but whoever trusts in the LORD is kept safe (Proverbs 29:25, *New International Version*).

Scripture: **Nehemiah 4:7-14**
Song: **"Trust and Obey"**

When America faced fighting war in two theaters, President Roosevelt reminded the nation of a profound truth. He said, "The only thing to fear, is fear itself."

This was the same message Nehemiah gave to Israel as they faced the daunting task of rebuilding the walls of Jerusalem and creating security. The workers were tired. The rubble was immense. Rumors of attack were circulating among the people. Fear was growing.

So Nehemiah took charge. He posted a 24-hour guard and spoke to the people. He reminded them to trust God and fight for the good of the people of God.

Fear clouds our thinking and robs us of strength. Fear is usually the greatest thing that we must overcome, greater than the challenge itself. In Alcoholics Anonymous circles fear serves as an acronym—Future Events Appearing Real. We often expend a great deal of energy on future events that rarely come true. Fear is meant only to strengthen and awaken us to action, but it destroys us when we continue to live in its shadow.

Dear God, help us to arrest the fear in our hearts and enable us to respond to our challenges and difficulties by trusting You. We ask Your Holy Spirit to help us clear our minds and choose right actions. In the name of Christ, our Savior, we pray. Amen.

Be Ready!

Let us not be like others, who are asleep, but let us be alert and self-controlled (1 Thessalonians 5:6, *New International Version*).

Scripture: **Nehemiah 4:15-23**
Song: **"Will Jesus Find Us Watching?"**

While a missionary in Ukraine, I discovered many similarities between the Boy Scouts of America and the Pioneers of the former Soviet Union. Both organizations share the same motto—"Be prepared!" This is the same command Jesus gave His disciples.

Some 400 years before Christ, Israel needed to rebuild the walls of Jerusalem. They were in danger of attack by the enemy. Nehemiah had the builders carry weapons while they worked. Others were stationed as guards. Nehemiah instructed the people to join together when they heard the sound of the trumpet so they could fight in strength. The leaders never took off their clothes or weapons. The goal was to maintain constant readiness.

Let us be prepared every day for the attacks of Satan. He is looking for the time we might let "our guard" down. Our weapons to overcome the Evil One are God's Word, the power of the Holy Spirit, prayer, and the support of other Christians. Let's be ready.

Dear God, help us this day to be alert to the schemes of the Evil One and to let Your Holy Spirit and Your Word guide our lives. Help us to remember to rely on our fellow Christians in overcoming temptation to sin. In the name of Jesus, we pray. Amen.

Finishing Well!

Let us not become weary in doing good, for at the proper time we will reap a harvest if we do not give up (Galatians 6:9, *New International Version*).

Scripture: **Nehemiah 6:1-9**
Song: **"Anywhere with Jesus"**

So often we see someone who is near to completing a project, a life dream, task or milestone, only to become distracted or discouraged and fall short of success.

Nehemiah led the people to rebuild the walls of Jerusalem, and the work was almost finished. The enemies of the Jews tried to lure him away from the safety of Jerusalem. They wanted to harm Nehemiah and thus demoralize the people. When that failed they discredited him.

But Nehemiah is an example of a remarkably secure and wise person. We can learn several things from Nehemiah. First, stay focused on finishing that which God has called you to do. Second, don't let the jealousy and the slander of others distract you. Third, say "no" to the things that are not pertinent to finishing the task. And finally, ask the Lord for strength to carry on.

Let's remain faithful to the task God has given. Let's finish well!

O God, You call us to make a difference in the lives of those around us. Help us to be wise to the schemes of the Evil One, who wants to distract us. We repeat Nehemiah's prayer, "Now strengthen my hands," in order to finish well. In Christ's name, we pray. Amen.

God is More Than Able!

Now to him who is able to do immeasurably more than all we ask or imagine, according to his power that is at work within us, to him be glory in the church and in Christ Jesus throughout all generations, for ever and ever! (Ephesians 3:20, 21, *New International Version*)

Scripture: **Nehemiah 6:10-19**
Song: **"A Mighty Fortress Is Our God"**

For more than 70 years the Communist regime of the Soviet Union persecuted, tortured, and martyred hundreds of thousands of Christians. This political oppressor seemed powerful and unwavering. In 1991, the former Soviet Union collapsed. Not a shot was fired. While many will suggest the fall was due to political, economic, and military reasons, we can also see this as a miracle. Many millions of prayers went before God on behalf of our persecuted brethren. God heard them all!

Nehemiah and the people of God rebuilt the walls of Jerusalem in just 52 days. This massive project was completed some 400 years before Christ. Further, the task was carried out under constant threat from the enemies that encircled Jerusalem.

Nehemiah records that the enemy nations surrounding Jerusalem realized that this work had been done with God's help. God is able to do the "unbelievable."

God, we give You honor and glory for Your greatness and power. We are confident that You still do the miraculous and rule over the entire world. May the nations see You. In Jesus' name, we pray. Amen.

Let the Celebration Begin!

Is any one of you in trouble? He should pray. Is anyone happy? Let him sing songs of praise (James 5:13, *New International Version*).

Scripture: **Nehemiah 12:27-31b**
Song: **"All Creatures of Our God and King"**

It's not easy to be a parent. My teens are quick to ask for help with school projects or car problems. But occasionally they forget to offer words of appreciation or fail to understand all the time, energy, and resources that I've invested in them. While I want to serve them unconditionally, it's also important for them to learn to give honor to those upon whom they depend. In this sense, God is not much different.

The walls of Jerusalem were completed. It had been no easy task. Numerous times Nehemiah and the people petitioned God for help. Now was the time to celebrate with music and song to give honor and praise to God who provided for Jerusalem's security.

In times of trouble we naturally ask God's help. But are we just as quick to give Him the praise that He's due? In James 5:13 we are reminded not only to ask for help in times of trouble but to also sing songs of praise in the midst of our happiness.

Dear God, we are deeply grateful for all that You provide. You give us all that we need. You help us in times of trouble. Thank You for being generous and gracious. Forgive us when we fail to honor You as You deserve. In the name of Jesus, our Savior, we pray. Amen.

Joy and True Worship

Therefore, I urge you, brothers, in view of God's mercy, to offer your bodies as living sacrifices, holy and pleasing to God—this is your spiritual act of worship (Romans 12:1, *New International Version*).

Scripture: **Nehemiah 12:43-47**
Song: **"Take My Life, and Let It Be"**

The people of God were overwhelmed with joy. They were grateful for the security of Jerusalem provided by the walls. They met for a great celebration. There were two choirs. All the people joined in. The sound of rejoicing was so loud that it could be heard far away.

There was more to this celebration than the expression of joy. They offered sacrifices and praised God. They gave sacrificially to re-establish the system of worship.

What comes to your mind when you think of worship? Worship begins as a daily habit of remembering how good and great God is. In true worship we can't help but be filled with joy and gratitude. Our joy and gratitude flow over into how we live for Jesus throughout our day. True worship is to live for Jesus every moment. True worship is to live holy lives, to please God, and to give of ourselves sacrificially. As you complete this reading, prepare yourself to truly worship all day long.

Dear God, we give You praise. We thank You for all You've given us. Now help us to worship You with our entire lives this whole day. We desire to keep You the focus of our thoughts, actions, and words and thereby give glory to You. In the name of Jesus, we pray. Amen.

Going Home

The Israelites settled in their own towns (Nehemiah 7:73, *New International Version*).

Scripture: **Nehemiah 7:66–8:1**
Song: **"When We All Get to Heaven"**

I peered out of the truck windows, looking for familiar landmarks. My grandparents' home had been on a farm nearby, so I had precious memories of Sunday afternoon visits here. I remember running through fields with cousins, aunts and uncles together, and grandma cooking. Memories flooded my mind as I pointed out sights.

Israel had been away from its home for 70 years, but a remnant of 42,360 people was allowed to return. Many changes had taken place in the homeland, but those who had once lived there looked around anxiously for landmarks as they drew near home. There wasn't much left, but just being home brought joy.

The word *home* can bring many memories to our minds, but the promise of a heavenly home brings a picture to which nothing else can compare. God is preparing that home for us, a home where we'll live with Him forever.

Thank you, Father, for Your Son who died on the cross for our sins. We praise You for salvation and eternal life through Him. In Jesus' name, we pray. Amen.

July 14-20. **Helen F. Curtis** and her husband, Jim, live in Elizabethton, Tennessee, and have been involved in ministry for over 38 years. They have three children and seven grandchildren.

With the Lord's Help

My help comes from the Lord, the Maker of heaven and earth (Psalm 121:2, *New International Version*).

Scripture: **Nehemiah 8:2-6**
Song: **"To God Be the Glory"**

Ezra stands before the people, who have returned from captivity, to read the word of God to them. They can see the rebuilt walls of Jerusalem around them and know that the enemies are outside those walls. Hard work and hard times lie ahead, but God has been with them. His protecting hand had brought them home. It is time to praise God, and Ezra offers that praise to Him. The people bow facedown and worship the Lord.

Israel's help had come from the Lord. His abiding presence had been with them. Captivity had been difficult, but He was there.

A dear friend lost his life helping a farmer. Corn was leaking through the silo door, so he offered to repair it. As he worked alone, the door came open. He was buried alive under the corn. Though in shock his wife was able to say, "God is holding my hand. It is only with His help that I can get through this tragedy."

God's reassuring presence is our help and strength in time of need. Let us give Him praise.

Dear Father, we praise You for Your abiding presence. We bow in Your presence today to give You thanks and to give You praise. In the name of Jesus, we pray. Amen.

A New Beginning

If we confess our sins, he is faithful and just and will forgive us our sins and purify us from all unrighteousness (1 John 1:9, *New International Version*).

Scripture: **Nehemiah 8:7-12**
Song: **"Whiter than Snow"**

At last a toy I can enjoy with my grandchildren! No fast moving figures. No buttons to push. I simply use the pencil attached to the frame and draw on the board. If I make a mistake or want to start all over, I slide a button from one end of the board to the other and my frame is a clean slate. Mistakes can be wiped clean any time.

Ezra read the Book of the Law of God as all the people stood before him. As Ezra read, their sins were plainly pointed out. They saw how horribly they had sinned and how they'd forsaken God's commands. Grief filled their hearts, and they began to weep and mourn.

As the people mourned, Ezra and the Levites encouraged them. It was time to repent of those sins of the past and time to start with a brand new slate. Thoughts of a new beginning filled their hearts with joy. Our heavenly Father offers us a new beginning. Repenting of our sins brings forgiveness and a new start.

Thank You, Father, for being loving and forgiving. Thank You for Your Son, who gave Himself as the sacrifice for our sins. Forgive us where we have failed You. Help us today to begin anew with a clean slate, washed clean by Jesus' blood. In His holy name, we pray. Amen.

Sharing Experiences

And their joy was very great (Nehemiah 8:17, *New International Version*).

Scripture: **Nehemiah 8:13-18**
Song: **"Praise Him! Praise Him!"**

The children of Israel had been freed from bondage in Egypt. To remind them of this freedom, the Feast of Tabernacles was to be observed yearly. Living in booths of branches, they remembered God's care.

Ezra read to the Israelites about this feast, and they entered into it with great enthusiasm. They knew the pain of living in bondage, and they understood the pain behind what had happened in Egypt. Having been in bondage, they could celebrate this feast in a way that others had never celebrated.

The words *breast cancer* were not the words I wanted to hear. Nor did I want the mastectomy that followed. A friend who had experienced the same thing came to visit. She was ready and willing to answer questions that plagued me. Having been through the same surgery, she understood and helped me in a special way.

Understanding increases significantly through experience. Using this understanding, we can reach out to others with love and compassion during those times that are hard and rejoice with them during times of joy.

Thank You, Father, for those You send into our lives to help us during the hard times as well as the good. In Jesus' name, we pray. Amen.

Learning His Word

Teach me, O Lord, to follow your decrees; then I will keep them to the end (Psalm 119:33, *New International Version*).

Scripture: **Psalm 119:33-40**
Song: **"Work for the Night Is Coming"**

God specifically instructed His people about His decrees. In Deuteronomy He said, "Impress them on your children. Talk about them when you sit at home and when you walk along the road, when you lie down and when you get up" (6:7). He also said, "Learn them and be sure to follow them" (5:1). Learning God's commands was important, but obedience must follow.

When my granddaughter visits, I often hear her tiny voice saying, "Can I help?" She loves to help in the kitchen, and I give her an easy task. She concentrates hard as she works, wanting to get it just right. Learning simple tasks can start very early. Instructions may be repeated many times; but seeing the joy when the task is mastered is worth it. Teaching is followed by action.

Constant instruction in God's word is important in our lives, but learning is to be followed by doing. The psalmist wanted to be taught God's decrees, and he was going to keep them to the end. Let us learn God's commands and practice what we learn.

Dear Father, *thank You for Your Word. We pray we will apply it daily. We want to be doers of the word and not hearers only. In Jesus' holy name, we pray. Amen.*

Gathering Wisdom

I have hidden your word in my heart that I might not sin against you (Psalm 119:11 *New International Version*).

Scripture: **Psalm 119:97-104**
Song: **"Wonderful Words of Life"**

Children love going on field trips and my seven-year-old Will was no exception. After one trip, I asked him about it. His eyes lit up, and words tumbled out as he eagerly told me things he had learned at the bat house. "A brown bat can eat over 1,200 mosquitoes an hour," he said. He continued to tell me about how they sleep and about their radar. His interest in this small creature had been kindled; he wanted to learn more about it.

The psalmist's interest in the Word of God had been kindled. The things he had learned from his study were bringing results that he could see. He found he had more wisdom than his enemies did, more insight than his teachers did, and more understanding than his elders did. The desire to obey the law had been kindled and kept him on the right path.

A study of God's Word brings results in our lives. His letters to us give us help and guidance. It is here we go to find His message and words of love. Let's go to His word each day and search for His truth for our lives.

Father, we thank You for Your Word that feeds us daily and causes us to grow in You. May we meditate on it daily and grow in You. In the precious name of Jesus, we pray. Amen.

Following His Lead

Direct my footsteps according to your word (Psalm 119:133, *New International Version*).

Scripture: **Psalm 119:129-136**
Song: **"Where He Leads Me"**

One of my favorite childhood games was "Follow the Leader." Laughter would erupt from my playmates and me as we followed our leader through whatever path he chose to lead us. Each leader tried to find new ways of leading his followers. Swinging on the monkey bars, hopping on one foot, turning somersaults, all brought on giggles as we tried to follow our leader's footsteps.

Who is the leader of your life? Who directs the way you go? We want to make sure the one we follow is going the right direction. The psalmist asked God to teach him His decrees and to direct his footsteps by His word. When we seek direction for our lives, we want to go to God for that direction. A study of His Word brings the course we need to follow as He shows us the way of righteousness.

"I am the LORD your God, who teaches you what is best for you, who directs you in the way you should go" (Isaiah 48:17). What better direction can we receive than from God Himself?

Father in Heaven, we give You praise for the guidance You give us from Your Word, a guide for our lives. Help us to search that guide daily for the way we should go. In Jesus' name, we pray. Amen.

Being Honest With Ourselves

If we confess our sins, he is faithful and just and will forgive us our sins and purify us from all unrighteousness (1 John 1:9, *New International Version*).

Scripture: **Nehemiah 9:1-5**
Song: **"Dear Lord, and Father of Mankind"**

After years of captivity in Babylon, for Israel to see Jerusalem come back to life and be surrounded by a protective wall was thrilling. It was time to celebrate and to thank God for His grace and mercy. But the fact remained that Israel had seriously violated God's law.

How can humans have a relationship with God? He is God; we are human. He is holy; we are sinners. Awareness of God's presence also makes us aware of our sins, as when Isaiah "saw the Lord" (Isaiah 6:1).

Confession of sin is being honest with ourselves, recognizing that we are less than perfect, that there are areas of our lives that need improvement and revision.

Since sin is an affront to God, we confess our sin to Him. We admit to Him that we have done wrong or have failed to do what is right. Then we learn what grace really means—God's forgiving our sin. Then we experience true freedom from the burden of guilt.

Dear Father, we rejoice that You are the God of unlimited grace and forgiveness. We pray in Jesus' name. Amen.

July 21-27. **Dr. Henry Webb**, a minister and retired college professor, and his wife, Emerald, serve Christ and His church in Johnson City, Tennessee.

The Majesty of Creation

The heavens declare the glory of God; the skies proclaim the work of his hands (Psalm 19:1, *New International Version*).

Scripture: **Nehemiah 9:6-12**
Song: "Doxology"

Explosions happen when a container cannot confine forces released by its contents. This can happen with bombs and even with people. We can get so "full" of a subject that it just "has to spill out."

Have you ever been so filled with joy that you simply had to explode somehow? We grope for words adequate to convey the feelings of joy or praise we hold within.

Israel was contemplating the magnitude and majesty of God's creation. The vast universe in which we live and the minute precision in which it operates reflect "the glory of God," who designed it all. To pause and reflect on this compels us to say with Israel: "Blessed be your glorious name, and may it be exalted above all blessing and praise" (Nehemiah 9:5).

Look about at the marvelous world in which we live. Thank and praise the great creative God who designed and provided it for our well-being and enjoyment.

If this creation is so bountiful and beautiful, in spite of the sin that is here, what must Heaven be like?

Blessed be Your name, **O God**, *Heaven and earth are full of witness to Your glory. Help me to reflect Your glory in my life. In Jesus' name, we pray. Amen.*

God's "Burial Ground"

He does not treat us as our sins deserve or repay us according to our iniquities (Psalm 103:10, *New International Version*).

Scripture: **Nehemiah 9:16-21**
Song: **"It Is No Secret"**

Sometimes we may refer to "the good old days." We hold fond memories of times past; but few want to return to those good old days. They had their problems, too.

Such was the case with God's people, Israel. There were some things in Israel's past which were less than admirable. However, it was comforting for Israel to realize that God buries some things because He is "a forgiving God, gracious and compassionate, slow to anger and abounding in love" (Nehemiah 9:17).

God does not hold the past over our heads to becloud our future. It is tragic if we allow past failures to destroy future possibilities. As Paul affirmed (Philippians 3:13, 14), there comes a time to move on. The past is irretrievably gone. All that we have is the future. It is ours to make of it largely what we will.

God can forgive our sins, bury the past, and fill the future with blessings. That is just what He wants to do.

Heavenly Father, because You hold the future in your hands, I commit myself into Your keeping. Help me to look forward in faith to the life you hold before me. In Jesus' name we pray. Amen.

God-likeness Is Not Easy

Blessed are the merciful, for they will be shown mercy (Matthew 5:7, *New International Version*).

Scripture: **Nehemiah 9:26-31**
Song: **"Calvary Covers It All"**

It's hard to forgive. I don't like to do it. It is much easier to be bitter than it is to be loving.

There are limits to almost everything in life. We all must find the borders that limit our conduct and attitudes. Probing for these limits, Peter asked Jesus, "How many times shall I forgive my brother when he sins against me? Up to seven times?" (Matthew 18:21). Peter was unprepared for Jesus' answer: "Seventy-seven times." There are no limits to extending forgiveness.

Isn't that unreasonable? But how many times have I asked God to forgive me? Night after night, year after year, I close each day praying for God's forgiveness of that day's sins. He has never said: "Enough! I've forgiven you before, and you sinned again."

Thank God, His forgiving is without limit. Jesus' reply to Peter actually reflected His Father's grace and mercy. What challenges me is that Jesus expects that, as a child of God, I do likewise, easy or not. Since I ask this of God, He also asks it of me. Fair enough!

Father in Heaven, *forgive our resentments, prejudices, animosities, and grudges that accumulate in our hearts. Remind us who desperately need Your mercy that it is our place to extend it to others. In Jesus' name, we pray. Amen.*

Commitment Means Advance

Be faithful, even to the point of death, and I will give you the crown of life (Revelation 2:10, *New International Version*).

Scripture: Nehemiah 9:32-38
Song: "Higher Ground"

Today's text records a momentous event. The people of Israel made a solemn commitment to live faithfully according to God's Law. They set a goal for themselves.

Commitments are milestones that mark progress in life. They become goals to be achieved, aspirations to be realized, and victories to be won. But commitments challenge us, place demands on us, carry a price.

We make many kinds of commitments. Some involve financial arrangements; others are of a more spiritual nature. All commitments involve integrity of character. There are times when honoring a commitment is inconvenient or difficult. God honors the person "who keeps his oath even when it hurts" (Psalm 15:4).

Israel was not faithful to its commitment. More correctly, some were faithful while others were not. All humans do not perform in the same manner. But all are better for trying. Sometimes our achievements are meager because we fail to set higher goals.

Father in Heaven, open my eyes to what You would have me to be. Give me the courage to strive for my highest ideals, and the wisdom and strength to achieve them. In Jesus' name, I pray. Amen.

The Whole Will of God

For I have not hesitated to proclaim to you the whole will of God (Acts 20:27, *New International Version*).

Scripture: **Nehemiah 10:28-34**
Song: **"I Would Be True"**

It's nice to pick a garment off the rack. We select the one that appeals to us and leave the others. Many people enjoy eating at a cafeteria, selecting from among the array of dishes offered what is pleasing and rejecting what does not suit. We like to pick and choose.

It is tempting to approach God in the same way. We are confronted with a number of commands in doing God's will. Some are quite acceptable to us; others are down-right inconvenient. Too often we obey God's will in ways we like and ignore what we don't like. This is a very human tendency and nobody is immune from it. Unchecked, it can lead to self-righteous attitudes.

We can avoid this peril. By conscientious and diligent reading of the Bible we are able to confront "the whole will of God." The parts of God's will that challenge us are what make us grow spiritually. Is regular prayer a challenge? Make provision in your life to do it! Is tithing a challenge? Find a way to do it! When we do, we find that the doing makes it easier. This is how we grow spiritually.

Father in Heaven, help me to have the courage to live according to Your will. May my life reflect, to a fuller extent, Your will for me today. In Jesus' name, I pray. Amen.

Blessings of Faithful Worship

Let us not give up meeting together, as some are in the habit of doing, but let us encourage one another—and all the more as you see the Day approaching (Hebrews 10:25, *New International Version*).

Scripture: **Nehemiah 10:35-39**
Song: **"I Love Thy Church, O God"**

The temple was an important building to the people of Israel—not for its structural majesty—but for what was done there. There the people presented their sacrifices, brought their tithes, presented their offerings to the Lord. There they raised their voices in praise, sought forgiveness, and made peace with their God. The temple itself was a mere building, but its influence touched the lives of thousands of people. That was its real worth.

Our country has many beautiful church buildings. But the real beauty is not in buildings but in the people. As Israel pledged its support for the temple, we must resolve to support Christ's church. Through His church Christ touches millions of lives in positive ways. Without the church, our communities could become jungles. Our support of Christ's work blesses both us and all those who are touched by Him.

God who is worthy of the praise of all mankind, use me to touch others so that they may be more aware of Your love, Your majesty, and Your grace. Help me to be Your servant. In Jesus' name I pray. Amen.

Who's the King of the Mountain?

Pride goes before destruction, a haughty spirit before a fall (Proverbs 16:18, *New International Version*).

Scripture: **Obadiah 1-9**
Song: **"How Great Thou Art"**

Two brothers were playing "King of the Mountain." In a heated toss, the younger brother fell off, smashing Mom's prized planter. Dad rushed out and sentenced the younger brother to an hour of labor. The older brother taunted, "Who's king of the mountain now?"

"I am!" Dad replied and pronounced another sentence.

Jacob and Esau were brothers at birth and enemies as adults. The battle raged on for generations to come. "Jacob versus Esau" became "Israel versus Edom."

The nation of Israel had disobeyed and was paying the price for rebellion. Edom stood in self-pride, enjoying Israel's demise. The country prided itself on fortifications, wealth, and wise men. "Who's king of the mountain now?" might have been their taunt.

"I Am!" God's responded with righteous judgment.

What about us? Do we watch with pleasure when our brothers stumble and fall? Who is king of our mountain?

Almighty God, we acknowledge You as Creator of everything. We submit to You. In Jesus' name. Amen.

July 28-August 3. **Pam Coffey** is a minister's wife and mother to twin sons. She lives in Arcadia, Indiana.

What Did I Do?

For whoever exalts himself will be humbled, and whoever humbles himself will be exalted (Matthew 23:12, *New International Version*).

Scripture: **Obadiah 10-16**
Song: **"Reach Out and Touch"**

The scene of the two brothers playing "King of the Mountain" continues. As the older brother heard his judgment, he turned to his father: "What did I do?"

His father replied, "You didn't help your brother when he fell and was hurt. You even seemed to enjoy it."

Edom may have cried out to God, "What did I do?" The answers came immediately. Although Israel was a brother nation, Edom stood by while strangers invaded Israel's land and carried off its people and treasures. Edom delighted in Israel's misfortune.

Sadly for Edom, its delight was premature. What goes around comes around. God told Edom, "Whatever you have done will be done to you. Israel's grief will be for a short time, but yours will go on and on."

Do we stand by while God's people are being ransacked and destroyed? Do we look down on those who have fallen under hard times? If our brother is hurting do we rush in to share God's love and grace, or do we walk to the other side?

Heavenly Father, please forgive us. May we be Your hands and feet to all Your children. In Jesus' name. Amen.

You Can Go Home

But on Mount Zion will be deliverance; it will be holy, and the house of Jacob will possess its inheritance (Obadiah 1:17, *New International Version*).

Scripture: **Obadiah 17-21**
Song: **"Lord, I'm Coming Home"**

"You can go home now." To those who have been displaced and ravaged by war, those must be some of the sweetest words one could ever hear.

The Israelites had been enslaved but would be brought back to the comfort of home. Not only would they enjoy what was once theirs, their area would be expanded.

Obadiah predicted that deliverance would come from Mt. Zion—the holy hill of Jerusalem. Who is that ultimate deliverer? Jesus Christ.

From a remnant of Jews brought back from captivity, Jesus came to our earth. He embodied Himself among His chosen people and lived under Roman rule. Then He slowly climbed another hill in Jerusalem and died an excruciating death.

Yet He will return and rule, saying to His people, "You can come home now."

Israel's deliverer, our deliverer, is coming again. Will we be able to taste the sweet blessings of coming home to Him? The choice is ours. What will you choose?

Lord Jesus, thank You for enduring the cross so that we might live. We eagerly await the day when we will be home with You. Maranatha!

You Are Mine

But now, this is what the LORD says—he who created you, O Jacob, he who formed you, O Israel: "Fear not, for I have redeemed you; I have summoned you by name; you are mine" (Isaiah 43:1, *New International Version*).

Scripture: **Isaiah 43:1-7**
Song: **"Amazing Grace"**

Do you remember being caught doing something wrong by someone you deeply loved? Being found out was bad enough; but the worst part was the distance you felt between you and that person. The world was bleak and gray and each day seemed endless. Then you received assurance of that person's love. The world grew brighter, colors returned, and the day grew brighter.

In Isaiah 42, Israel was described as blind and deaf. God's anger was being poured out. Just when it seemed as though despair were the only reality, God blessed Israel with a reminder of His love. He had called them by name and put His stamp on them. God promised He would bring His chosen ones from afar and gather them together at His table. That's grace—amazing grace.

Have you ever felt estranged from God? Does there seem to be a wall of separation between you? God is calling each of us. May we all cross that bridge of grace in Jesus Christ and experience the joy of reunion with Him.

Gracious Father, *thank You for loving us. Thank You for Your amazing grace. In Jesus' name. Amen.*

Devotions™

𝕰vening, and
morning,
and at noon,
will I pray

(Psalm 55:17).

August

*Photo of Theresa Hayes, editor
at Standard Publishing taken
by Julie Riley.*

August 1

No Other God

I, even I, am the Lord, and apart from me there is no savior (Isaiah 43:11, *New International Version*).

Scripture: **Isaiah 43:8-13**
Song: **"O God, Our Help in Ages Past"**

The neighboring cries to the Israelites were deafening. "Have I got a god for you!" "This god will make you prosperous." "Let me craft one up—it will be just what you're looking for. This god's for you."

The children of Israel were probably getting emotional whiplash as they turned from one voice to another. They dug themselves deep into a pit of lies, far away from the voice of God, until He shouted, "Stop!"

He got their attention. Then He reached down, pulled them up from the miry clay, and reminded them, "I, even I, am the Lord; apart from me, there is no savior."

Generations have come and gone since Isaiah was written, yet those voices still remain. "Try this for a positive self image." "This plan will make you rich." "Experience new sensations of enjoyment."

Are you getting emotional whiplash? Look up to God—our solid rock and Savior. He is the only way.

You are the one true God, O Lord. We know there is no other. Please forgive us when we turn from You. You alone are worthy of our praise. In the name of Jesus, we pray. Amen.

August 1- 3. **Pam Coffey** is a minister's wife and mother to twin sons. She lives in Arcadia, Indiana.

Water for a Thirsty Land

For I will pour water on the thirsty land, and streams on the dry ground; I will pour out my Spirit on your offspring, and my blessing on your descendants (Isaiah 44:3, *New International Version*).

Scripture: **Isaiah 44:1-8**
Song: **"There Shall Be Showers of Blessing"**

It had been a dry season. Then the rains came. The parched earth soaked up the moisture, and the yards and fields turned to a beautiful luscious green.

With the rain came a bonus. As the showers mixed with sunshine, beautiful rainbows painted the sky. It was a delight to see them and also to see people stop in their tracks and look up in awe. It was almost as though God were saying, "Remember me? I'm still in control."

Israel was going through a spiritual desert, but God promised to pour out refreshing streams through His Spirit. Those who were barren as the parched ground would be watered by God's grace. With His promise, however, came a reminder: "I am the first and I am the last; apart from me there is no God" (Isaiah 44:6).

Have you ever felt parched within? Remember that God is still in control. Claim the promise that if we hunger and thirst after God's righteousness, we will be filled.

***Thank You**, God, for Your Holy Spirit who refreshes us with Your presence. Thank You for Your love. In Jesus' holy name, we pray. Amen.*

Supreme Comfort

As a mother comforts her child, so will I comfort you; and you will be comforted over Jerusalem (Isaiah 66:13, *New International Version*).

Scripture: **Isaiah 66:10-14**
Song: **"The Family of God"**

From the very beginning of time God has enacted and lived out a very special covenant relationship with the people of Israel. He has birthed them, loved them, nurtured them, mourned over them, disciplined them, and promised them an indescribable future with Him.

How could such a mighty God shoulder a group of people in such a personal way? God is pictured not only as the only true God, but also as a loving mother who cradles a hurting child. It makes me want to rush up to the people in Isaiah's time and say, "Do you realize just how special you are to be called children of God?"

The good news is that we all can be called children of God. We can be adopted through Jesus Christ.

Thank God that, through Jesus Christ, we have been redeemed. No matter who we are, we can be adopted, forgiven, marked with God's seal, and promised a future with Him in His glory.

Share God's good news with somebody today.

Hallelujah! Praise You, Jesus! You have paid the price so that we could be part of Your family. May we live out our gratitude and share Your love with excitement and joy. In Your holy name, we pray. Amen.

Stormy Weather

It will be a dark and gloomy day, a black and cloudy day (Joel 2:2, *Today's English Version*).

Scripture: **Joel 2:1-11**
Song: **"Lead, Kindly Light"**

"Dark and gloomy, black and cloudy"—just the kind of day to dampen our spirits unless we are in the midst of a drought and desperately need rain.

Of course, Joel is talking about an incredible swarm of locusts, not nourishing rain. Most of us are not familiar with an approaching swarm of locusts, but we have heard hair-raising stories from old-timers about them.

Our days of darkness and gloom aren't that fearful, but they do depress our spirits. How do we get through days when we can't see clearly and may live in dread of what lies ahead—the result of a biopsy, possible loss of a job, the loss of a friend who will be moving away soon?

Tough times and stormy weather come to all of us. At times we may say with Joel, "Who can endure it?" These are the times when we walk by faith—times when we don't know what lies ahead, but we know who walks with us in the gloom.

Lord, we often bring gloom on ourselves. Help us learn through these experiences that test our faith, and help us walk through them, knowing You are beside us. In Jesus' name, we pray. Amen.

August 4-10. **Wanda M. Trawick** serves as Director of Christian Education at the Watauga Avenue Presbyterian Church in Johnson City, Tennessee.

August 5

Headed for the Barn

Return to the LORD your God, for he is gracious and compassionate, slow to anger, and abounding in love. (Joel 2:13, *New International Version*).

Scripture: Joel 2:12-17
Song: "Just as I Am"

It was a beautiful day, and I was enjoying a canter through the fields on my horse, Marali. We were going at a fairly fast pace alongside a one-lane dirt road. Suddenly, we came upon a big pile of trash someone had dumped in the weeds. Marali shied abruptly, and I went sailing off. Before I could get back up, off she went, galloping at full speed toward the barn. Other riders saw her and tried to catch her, but no one could.

Have you ever been on a horse that was headed back to the barn? Ever tried to catch one? What was back in the barn? Home was back in the barn—where sweet feed, sweet hay, and cool, fresh water awaited her. It was where she could lose the burden of rider, saddle, and bridle. In short, where the load would be lifted.

When we return to God, we are like a horse headed back to the barn. God is our home, where all the load of sin is lifted and where we are nourished in His care.

Heavenly Father, we come to You, not in fear, but in shame for falling so short of Your glory. Thank You for opening Your arms to us as we hurry to Your forgiving embrace. Let us show kindness and love to all around us. In the holy name of Jesus, we pray. Amen.

Watching Over Bambi

Animals, don't be afraid. The pastures are green; the trees bear their fruit, and there are plenty of figs and grapes (Joel 2:22, *Today's English Version*).

Scripture: **Joel 2:18-22**
Song: **"This is My Father's World"**

Nineteenth-century British author, Anna Sewell, wrote only one book in her lifetime, but *Black Beauty* became an instant children's classic. The story is about a horse who both witnessed and suffered terrible abuse at the hands of human owners.

Some of the owners and handlers were cruel out of ignorance, some out of pure meanness. The horses in the novel suffered as a consequence of human sin, just as Bambi and the forest animals suffered in the fire caused by human carelessness. In the end of the stories about Black Beauty and Bambi, the horse is restored to his original kind owner, and the young deer eventually becomes a great stag in the rejuvenated forest.

Plants and animals suffer when humans allow greed and ignorance to take over. When we recognize our mistakes, we return to God's plan for taking care of the earth, and restoration of the earth begins to take place.

Father, thank You for the "friendly beasts" we have known and loved. Thank You for plants and animals that provide our daily food. Thank You for the beauty of the earth around us, and help us do no harm to the planet You have given us to be our home. In Jesus' name, we pray. Amen.

Good News, Bad News— Which Affects Us Most?

Be glad, ye children of Zion, rejoice at what the LORD your God has done for you (Joel 2:23, *Today's English Version*).

Scripture: **Joel 2:23-29**
Song: **"This Is the Day"**

When I went to the mailbox that morning and found the grade slip from the graduate school I attended, my heart skipped several beats. If the grade were an "A," I would have finished my degree with a 4.0 average. Sure enough, it was an "A," and the glow of pleasure I experienced lasted all of an hour.

When I went to bed that night, I thought about it and realized that, if I had not gotten the "A," my chagrin and disappointment would still have been with me—not for just a day, but for weeks.

Why do some of us focus more on bad times than good times? May we allow the good feeling to emerge when the sunlight breaks through the clouds. What happened yesterday is over and done with. Today rejoice in the new things God has in store for you.

Father, don't let us become so overwhelmed with times of mourning, times of failure, and times of turmoil that we don't recognize and appreciate fully the times of rejoicing, the times of success, and the times of peace that You give us. In Jesus' name, we pray. Amen.

I Know That My Redeemer Lives

Then, Israel, you will know that I am the LORD your God (Joel 3:17, *Today's English Version*).

Scripture: **Joel 3:16-21**
Song: **"He Lives"**

Think back over the times you have known the Lord was with you. What the Lord promised Israel was that his handiwork would be so evident that they would know He was the Lord their God.

Most of us don't have constant experiences that enable us always to say with complete honesty, "I know he lives and is here with me right now." But we do have "mountain-top" experiences from time to time that we look back on and say, as did Job, "I know that my redeemer lives" (Job 19:25).

Sometimes we experience moments when "I think" or "I hope" or even "I believe" can't express the fullness of our relationship with God. Sometimes we just want to raise a clenched fist and say, "Yes! I know!"

Have you ever felt that way? If not, your time is coming. That day will come when you will know that your Redeemer lives. Hope for that moment, expect it, watch for it and don't miss it!

O Lord, our Redeemer, we know that You are our God and are always with us. In moments when we find it hard to believe, help us to have a faith that is steady and sure. In the name of Jesus, we pray. Amen.

Here I Stand

Then Peter stood up with the other eleven apostles and in a loud voice began to speak to the crowd (Acts 2:14, *Today's English Version*).

Scripture: **Acts 2:14-23**
Song: **"Stand Up, Stand Up for Jesus"**

When I was nine, my older sister and I were riding our bicycles on a gravel road when her bike slid in the rocks, resulting in a terrible-looking knee wound. My mother and I were allowed in the doctor's office to lend our support while the deep scrape was cleansed and bandaged. I watched with interest until the doctor approached her with the biggest needle and hypodermic syringe I had ever seen. I disappeared behind a folding screen and huddled on the floor with my eyes shut.

Thirty years later I stood at her bedside in a hospital room, waiting for her to take her last breath as she lay dying of cancer. Something in me wanted to cry out, "Look, I'm still here, and I am still on my feet! "

It took thirty years of experience and maturity to enable me to stand in a critical situation. It took only 50 days for a cowardly, denying Peter to stand up in front of a huge crowd and proclaim the One he had denied.

What enabled him to do it? The Holy Spirit.

Thank You, Father, that Your Holy Spirit stands beside us and holds us up in situations in which we cannot stand alone. In Jesus' holy name, we pray. Amen.

From Unwanted to Legendary

This Jesus, whom you crucified, is the one that God has made Lord and Messiah (Acts 2:36, *Today's English Version*).

Scripture: **Acts 2:29-36**
Song: **"Praise Him, Praise Him"**

His name was Pal—a beautiful dog with a bad habit. He could not stop chasing motorcycles. The frustrated owner took Pal to an obedience school. The dog's owner decided he really didn't want the dog and gave him to the trainer to pay the bill.

That was in the 1940's. He trainer's name was Rudd Weatherwax, who trained dog "actors." Pal, the dog rejected by his owner, became the first Lassie of the classic movie, "Lassie Come Home." Pal's descendants continued to play Lassie in movies and television for over 50 years.

Pal failed to meet his owner's expectations, just as Jesus failed to meet the Messianic expectations of His countrymen. Both were rejected. Pal's trainer made him a movie legend. God made His Son Lord and Messiah. Rejection doesn't have to be the end of the story for any of us.

Thank You, Lord, that You can use those who are rejected by men. We thank You that You take us to Your heart when others reject us. Thank You that You take our weaknesses and failures and turn them into triumphs. We pray in Jesus' holy name. Amen.

Responsibility

God will give to each person according to what he has done (Romans 2:6, *New International Version*).

Scripture: **Malachi 2:1-9**
Song: **"Footprints of Jesus"**

Once every four years, we American citizens have the privilege and responsibility of electing the President of the United States. We expect him to be a person of integrity and to abide by the truth in all circumstances. He is our leader.

Sometimes presidents let us down. And, if they do, the whole country suffers. God had chosen the tribe of Levi to be responsible for the care of the Tabernacle and the Testimony (Numbers 1:53). They had not been faithful to the teaching of the Testimony. So the entire nation was suffering the rebuke of the Lord.

In the church we must be careful in the leaders we select to guide us. James reminds us that "we who teach will be judged more strictly" (James 3:1). We need to follow Jesus, "the way and the truth and the life" (John 14:6).

Dear Lord, bless all who lead our country. May the Holy Spirit guide those who have responsibility as leaders of the church. In Jesus' holy name, we pray. Amen.

August 11-17. **Don Cox** has served as Pastor/Counselor at Central Christian Church in Mesa, Arizona, since retiring from Beaverton, Oregon, Christian Church.

On Being Refined

Create in me a pure heart, O God, and renew a steadfast spirit within me (Psalm 51:10, *New International Version*).

Scripture: **Malachi 3:1-5**
Song: **"Take My Life and Let It Be"**

When I grew up in Wilmington, California, oil derricks dotted the landscape. When workers struck oil, the derricks were taken down and oil pumps installed. The crude oil was delivered to the refinery. In the refinery anything unwanted was removed. Out of the refinery came gasoline and other synthetics for our daily use. The crude was useless; the refined, valuable.

Articles in the Tabernacle and the Temple were made of pure gold. Pure gold is refined by fire so that there is nothing left except gold—pure gold. Only that which was "pure" was good enough for God's Temple. Jesus reminded: "Blessed are the pure in heart, for they will see God" (Matthew 5:8). It has been said, "God cared enough to give the very best"—the One without sin—the pure One.

God allows us to face trials of many kinds, so that we "may be mature and complete, not lacking anything," (James 1:2-4) Through all these experiences of life He is refining us for our benefit and His glory.

Lord, help me look at the daily things in my life as a refining process. Thank You for what You do in my life. In the name of Jesus, the pure One, I pray. Amen.

Time to Turn Around

Come to me, all you who are weary and burdened, and I will give you rest (Matthew 11:28, *New International Version*).

Scripture: **Malachi 3:6-12**
Song: **"I Surrender All"**

Some years ago four young preachers from the Northwest traveled by car from Oregon to Buffalo, New York, to attend a convention. We decided we would drive all night, see the city all day, and return the next night, taking turns driving and sleeping. One volunteered to drive first, and the others went to sleep. After a while we stopped. The driver explained that he thought he had made a wrong turn somewhere. According to the map, we had traveled 70 miles in the wrong direction.

Israel was headed in the wrong direction—away from God. "You have turned away from my decrees and have not kept them. Return to me, and I will return to you" (verse 7). Most of us are familiar with the question: "Will a man rob God?" They were being dishonest about the tithe. But is the tithe all that God wants? The whole world is His already. God wanted them! They were His people, but they had drifted away. He called them back to himself.

Father, help me to return to You and remain in You. In Jesus' name, I pray. Amen.

God's Treasured Possession

Give, and it will be given to you. A good measure, pressed down, shaken together and running over (Luke 6:38, *New International Version*).

Scripture: **Malachi 3:13-18**
Song: **"I'd Rather Have Jesus"**

Israel had been through some rough times. There were the Assyrians and the Babylonians. The temple had been sacked. The silver and gold had been plundered. The walls of the city had been torn down and the temple destroyed. The walls had been repaired and the temple had been rebuilt, but it wasn't the same.

So Israel complained. It seemed that the ones who had plundered the city and destroyed the temple had gotten away with it. The evildoers had prospered and seemed to have everything, but God's people were destitute. Some were saying, "It is futile to serve God."

It was a bad attitude; but not everyone felt that way. The positive thinkers began to talk to each other. God listened to them and created "a scroll of remembrance" on which was written, "They will be mine, . . . in the day when I make up my treasured possession" (verse 17).

As the father in the parable of the prodigal son, God wants us. Jesus prayed, "Father, I want those you have given me to be with me where I am, and to see my glory" (John 17:24).

Father, I give myself to you that I may be your treasured possession. In Jesus' name, I pray. Amen.

The Day Is Coming

Repent, then, and turn to God, so that your sins may be wiped out (Acts 3:19, *New International Version*).

Scripture: **Malachi 4:1-6**
Song: **"I Have Decided"**

"Surely the day is coming." But what kind of a day will it be? It will be a day of contrasts. It is a day of judgment by fire. Anything that will not endure the fire will be burned; "not a root or a branch will be left" (verse 1). It is also a joyous day when "the sun of righteousness will rise with healing" (verse 2).

The contrast is deliberate: "That great and dreadful day of the LORD" (verse 5). How can it be both "great" and "dreadful"? It depends upon whether we revere God's name and keep His Word. We make the choice.

A man in our Bible study requested prayer for his son. Several DUIs had landed the son in prison. He now admits he has been an alcoholic for 20 years. He knows he can't beat his addiction alone. He has called out to God and is enrolled in a 12-step program. For him "the day" arrived; he had to make a choice. He chose right.

"We must all appear before the judgment seat of Christ, that each one may receive what is due him" (2 Corinthians 5:10). That will be a "great day" for those who belong to Christ.

Dear Father, *I long to draw close to you. Help me to eagerly anticipate that great day when I see you face to face. In Jesus' name, we pray. Amen.*

The Guarantee

Having believed, you were marked in him with a seal, the promised Holy Spirit (Ephesians 1:13, *New International Version*).

Scripture: **Psalm 89:19-29**
Song: **"Blessed Assurance"**

The Metropolitan Insurance Company guarantees its reliability and strength by the picture of the rock of Gibraltar. Chevrolet promotes the sturdiness of its truck proclaiming it is "like a rock!" Look at a dollar bill. It is a Federal Reserve Note, good for legal tender, guaranteed by the United States of America, signed by the Treasurer of the United States and the Secretary of the Treasury. Look at the other side. "In God we trust." How is that for a guarantee? The dollar is good around the world.

"In God we trust." What are the benefits of such a trust? They are listed in this passage. His hand will sustain me. His arm will strengthen me. He will crush my foes. He will maintain His love for me forever. He will give me the right and privilege to call out to Him: "You are my Father," "'My God," "The Rock," "My Savior," and His covenant with me will never fail!

Jesus' words are reassuring: "On this rock I will build my church, and the gates of Hades will not overcome it" (Matthew 16:18, *New International Version*).

Thank You, God, *for all Your guarantees. Help me to trust in You alone. You are my Rock. In Jesus' name, I pray. Amen.*

Getting to Know God

Whoever does not love does not know God, because God is love (1 John 4:8, *New International Version***).**

Scripture: **Psalm 89:30-37**
Song: **"How Great Thou Art"**

Philip Yancey's book, *Disappointment With God*, spoke to me because I had similar problems in trying to fathom the actions of God in the world and in my life. I am still trying to know Him better. I can relate to the vision Isaiah had and then wrote: "The LORD has spoken: 'I reared children and brought them up, but they have rebelled against me. The ox knows his master, the donkey his owner's manger, but Israel does not know, my people do not understand'" (Isaiah 1: 2, 3).

David did not write this psalm. It was written about David and how God was able to use him to accomplish His purpose. As a result, we can learn more about God.

I discovered several things in this passage. God is just. He will punish us when we disobey. But He will not stop loving us because of our disobedience because "God is love." God can always be trusted. He will never betray His faithfulness. He will never violate His covenant or alter what He has said. He will always be true. He affirms His holiness. We are to be holy as God is holy. His holiness is to rub off on us as we get close to Him.

O God, I praise You. I long to know You more. May I draw closer each day. In Jesus' name, I pray. Amen.

The Mind Reader

But Jesus would not entrust himself to them, for he knew all men. He did not need man's testimony about man, for he knew what was in a man (John 2:24, 25, *New International Version*).

Scripture: **Daniel 1:18–2:6**
Song: **"No One Understands Like Jesus"**

Early in a relationship people wonder how they can understand their partner's unspoken messages. However, check in on the same couple forty years later, and you'll find that they seem to read minds. They sit together for hours without speaking but are in constant communication. A sigh, a smile, a twinkle in the eye convey more information from their hearts.

King Nebuchadnezzar wanted to be understood. What he needed was a true friend and advisor, the kind who would know and understand his inmost thoughts.

Only God provides the answers the king sought, just as only God can provide the fulfillment we seek in our relationships. If we seek our fulfillment in Him, we will find Him to be our best friend.

Dear Friend, *thank You for loving us. Help us not to expect others to fill the void that only You can fill. Teach us to know You better, so that we may be better friends to You. In Christ's name, we pray. Amen.*

August 18-24. **Andrew Wood**, a former missionary to Ukraine, teaches at Cincinnati Bible College.

Blessed Are the Peacemakers

Blessed are the peacemakers, for they will be called sons of God (Matthew 5:9, *New International Version*).

Scripture: **Daniel 2:7-16**
Song: **"Help Somebody Today"**

A couple of years ago, violent riots broke out in Cincinnati, Ohio, after the shooting of an African-American man by a Caucasian police officer. The mayor imposed a curfew, brought in extra police from outside the city, and called on religious and community leaders to use their influence to stop the violence. On one occasion a narrow line of ministers and priests were all that separated an angry band of rioters from baton-wielding police. The intervention of the clergy helped calm the situation and saved many people from injury.

In today's text, Daniel provides just such a voice of reason. He could have tried simply to save his own life; instead, he intervened tactfully in a dangerous situation to try to save others. He didn't stop to consider whether or not the wise men of Babylon were worthy of being rescued. He simply saw that someone needed help, and he was prepared to give it.

The role of peacemaker is to find a way to help.

Lord Jesus, may Your peace overflow in the lives of Your people. Give us opportunities, wisdom, and courage to act as peacemakers in situations of conflict we encounter today. In Your holy name, we pray. Amen.

Sharing Our Burdens

Therefore confess your sins to each other and pray for each other so that you may be healed. The prayer of a righteous man is powerful and effective (James 5:16, *New International Version*).

Scripture: **Daniel 2:17-23**
Song: **"I Am Praying for You"**

Our first house was a "fixer-upper." The floors needed refinishing, the rooms needed painting, light fixtures needed replacing. I relished the satisfaction of doing everything myself. In fact, we didn't invite our friends until the renovation was done. Showing the house at that point was not as satisfying as I hoped. They had not seen the house in its original condition.

We are sometimes tempted to hide our problems and act as if we "have it all together." We're surprised when a "perfect" Christian marriage ends in divorce or a young person falls into drug addiction. When our friends conquer their problems, we are deprived of seeing the change and rejoicing with them.

When Daniel had a big problem, he turned to his friends. As a result, the faith of several people was strengthened. Is there a hidden burden you've been carrying for too long? Share it with a friend today.

Sustainer of life, *give us the humility to share our needs with others so that You may be publicly glorified through our weaknesses. In the name of Christ our Savior, we pray. Amen.*

The Mystery of Life

Can you fathom the mysteries of God? Can you probe the limits of the Almighty? (Job 11:7, *New International Version*).

Scripture: **Daniel 2:24-28**
Song: **"How Great Thou Art!"**

I read my first mystery novel as a teenager. I remember eagerly following the twists and turns of the plot, trying to identify the killer. Not until the last few pages of the book was the criminal revealed. My mouth literally dropped open when I discovered that the least likely character of the book, one who seemed to have an iron-clad alibi, was actually the culprit!

God's plan in this world has more surprises than even the greatest mystery novelists could devise. When mankind falls into sin, it appears all is lost until God Himself makes a surprise appearance in the world in the form of an infant in a manger. When the Messiah is crucified, once again it appears all is lost, but God snatches victory from the jaws of death. Today God's plan continues to unfold in the world, as some unlikely people come to faith in Him.

God who reveals mysteries will one day bring our stories to a surprising and victorious climax in Christ.

Author of life, *may the outcome of Your work in us astonish the world and bring glory to You. In the name of Your Son, our Savior, we pray. Amen.*

Swaying Towers

Therefore everyone who hears these words of mine and puts them into practice is like a wise man who built his house on the rock (*Matthew 7:24, New International Version*).

Scripture: **Daniel 2:29-35**
Song: **"The Church's One Foundation"**

A beautiful marble tower rises to the sky in the city of Pisa, Italy. Under normal circumstances, it might be known as "The Marble Tower of Pisa," or "The Majestic Tower of Pisa." Instead, we know it as "The Leaning Tower of Pisa." Soon after the tower was completed, it became obvious that the foundation was unstable. Year by year, the tower began to lean to one side. To this day, the best methods devised have only been able to slow its movement, not stop it. Thus, despite the beauty of this monument, our attention is drawn to its fatal flaw.

The statue in Nebuchadnezzar's dream was built on an unstable foundation—a mixture of iron and clay. When the stone struck the statue in the weak place, the structure was destroyed. No matter how strong the head, when the feet are weak, the statue can't stand.

Let's demolish the leaning towers in our lives and build on the solid rock of Jesus Christ.

Great Architect, help us to demolish the unstable towers of in our lives. In the name of Jesus, we pray. Amen.

The Strongest Kingdom

Of the increase of his government and peace there will be no end (Isaiah 9:7).

Scripture: **Daniel 2:36-45**
Song: **"Lead on, O King Eternal"**

The collapse of the Soviet Union in 1991 came as a surprise, even to those who lived there. It was obvious the country had its problems, but no one expected this superpower to be stripped of its empire and fragmented into separate countries virtually overnight. Imagine the despair of people who believed in the communist system and invested their life's energy and resources into it!

Like the Soviet Union at the height of its power, the kingdom of Babylon appeared strong and secure, yet God revealed to the king that it would be replaced by a series of inferior kingdoms. Ultimately, no government will be able to withstand the Kingdom of God.

At times when all seems secure in our lives, we would do well to remind ourselves that "this too shall pass." Let us remember God during both the successful and trouble-free times of our lives, lest He send us reminders of the frailty of our own "kingdoms."

King of kings, reign over our lives today. We praise You for the blessings You have brought to our lives. Thank You for allowing us to be citizens of Your everlasting government. In the name of Jesus, our Savior and Lord, we pray. Amen.

The Last Word

But the Lord is in his holy temple; let all the earth be silent before him (Habakkuk 2:20, *New International Version*).

Scripture: **Revelation 21:1-7**
Song: **"Be Still, My Soul"**

We live in a world full of argument and debate. Presidential candidates debate the issues for months during a campaign. Every piece of legislation issued by our Congress is debated for hours before being signed into law. Ultimately, however, someone has the last word—a President is elected and implements his platform; Congressional debate ends, and laws go into effect.

According to Scripture, Someone will have the last word in all of human history. One day, God will step into this bickering world and say in effect, "Enough! I will have the last word." In a world of confusion and chaos, we can find strength in knowing that the last word has not yet been spoken. When it is, the entire universe will fall silent before our infinite God.

Almighty Father and Creator of the universe, in the name of Jesus we are bold enough to approach Your throne. You are all powerful, all knowing and infinite. We are Your servants. No words are enough to praise You adequately. We fall silent in worship before You. In the holy name of Jesus, our Lord and Savior, we pray. Amen.

August 25

Your People Will Be Delivered

There will be a time of distress such as has not happened from the beginning of nations until then. But at that time your people—everyone whose name is found written in the book—will be delivered (Daniel 12:1, *New International Version*).

Scripture: **Daniel 12:1-7**
Song: **"No One Understands Like Jesus"**

Edson was unhappy. He was crushed by poverty and had lost hope. One day he asked me if I knew what it was like to be poor, and I had to confess that I had little personal experience with his kind of poverty.

He explained it like this: "When you are poor it is like you are living far in a forest and find you have to go to town to stay alive. You do not own a car or a bicycle, and you have no money for bus fare. Since it is too far to walk you decide to hitchhike. But once you get out to the road you discover that all the cars are going in the wrong direction. That is what it is like to be poor."

The distress of poverty, persecution, and suffering is made worse when it seems that no one cares. Jesus cares! Don't give up.

Eternal Father, Strong to Save, *we pray for the oppressed and persecuted. We pray through our Deliverer, Jesus. Amen.*

August 25-31. **Dr. David Grubbs** is the president of Cincinnati Bible College and Seminary in Cincinnati, Ohio. For years, he and his wife, Eva, served as medical missionaries to Zimbabwe.

The Mystery Is Solved

Many will be purified, made spotless and refined, but the wicked will continue to be wicked. None of the wicked will understand, but those who are wise will understand (Daniel 12:10, *New International Version*).

Scripture: **Daniel 12:8-12**
Song: **"Standing on the Promises"**

What does a witch doctor's doctor do when the witch doctor dies? He goes to the funeral.

It was a crowded funeral service with hundreds of people attending. Some had traveled a long time to get there. The witch doctor was actually a spirit medium. He became rich and famous and powerful because he convinced people that he could speak beyond the grave. But now he was dead and being buried.

His tomb was a small cave, and during the funeral some men sealed the opening of the cave with cement. The purpose of that was to keep animals and enemies from getting to his now helpless body.

"Multitudes who sleep in the dust of the earth will awake: some to everlasting life, others to shame and everlasting contempt" (Daniel 12:2).

I left the funeral feeling sad for my patient, the spirit medium. I was happy not to be so rich and famous.

Dear Father, *thank You for giving us a new and meaningful life. In the name of Christ, we pray. Amen.*

An Open Door

I know your deeds. See, I have placed before you an open door that no one can shut (Revelation 3:8, *New International Version*).

Scripture: **Revelation 3:7-13**
Song: **"It's Just Like His Great Love"**

The 12-year old child was discovered locked in a closet. Her mother had put her there. Later, in the home of a loving couple, she regained her health.

For the rest of her life, the most beautiful sight she will enjoy will be an open door, which no one can shut.

The Bible uses the open door as a symbol of opportunity, providing freedom from obstacles that would keep one from achieving his goal in life. Jesus says, "I know you don't have the strength to keep the door open. I also know about your faithfulness. See, the door is open, and I'll keep it open for you. Trust me."

Sometimes it seems that bad people are in control and God's people have no influence or power. During such times our faith may weaken and doubt creeps into our lives. Let us stand firm in Christ. We dare not weaken. Remember, Jesus is holding the door open, and no one can close it again. He is waiting for us to walk with Him.

Lord, Jesus, *thank You for opening the door. With the door open the view is great. We want to walk with You into the future. In the name of Jesus, our Savior, we pray. Amen.*

Victory over Brokenness

But thanks be to God! He gives us the victory through our Lord Jesus Christ (1 Corinthians 15:57, *New International Version*).

Scripture: **1 Corinthians 15:50-56**
Song: **"When All My Labors and Trials Are O'er"**

Njodzi was 14 years old when we first met him. He had spent the last ten years in a special institution for children with severe handicaps. He could not walk but rolled across the floor to get from one place to another. Speech was difficult. He had never been to school.

Because he could not control his frustration and anger, the institution sent him to Mashoko Christian Hospital. That is where we met him.

We soon learned that he understood and spoke three languages. He had a wonderful sense of humor and loved to play pranks on his caregivers, and he wanted to go to church.

Later, he said, "Chiremba (doctor), I believe in Jesus and I want to be baptized."

Njodzi was locked in a broken body that held him prisoner. While there is no hope of his being released on earth, he will one day enjoy singing and dancing with the saints in Heaven.

Dear Father, we look forward to the day when these broken earthly bodies are exchanged for heavenly ones. Until then, may we serve You with all our heart, soul, mind, and strength. In Christ, we pray. Amen.

Never Again Hungry

Never again will they hunger; Never again will they thirst. The sun will not beat upon them, nor any scorching heat (Revelation 7:16, *New International Version*).

Scripture: **Revelation 7:9-17**
Song: **"There Shall Be Showers of Blessing"**

By the third year of the drought conditions were tragic. Grass was a memory. Trees had been cut down so cattle and sheep could eat the leaves. Along the dusty roads were bleached skeletons of farm animals, and in the forests the bones of elephants and antelopes.

Most families in rural Africa were malnourished. Others ate as few as three or four times a week. As the sun scorched down, no relief was in sight. Instead of rain there were dust storms killing people by filling their lungs with dirt. When the rain finally came, people stood outside with their faces turned toward the sky, enjoying the water. It was a time of rejoicing.

The Bible pictures the joy of Heaven to be something like that. After the scorching sun of our life on earth and the hunger and thirst for a better place, we will enjoy the fullness and rest that Jesus gives.

Dear Lord, we live in such abundance that severe drought and starvation are unreal to us. Help us to see this life for what it is and to look with anticipation to Your eternal rest. In the name of Christ, our Savior, we pray. Amen.

For the Healing of the Nations

On each side of the river stood the tree of life, bearing twelve crops of fruit, yielding its fruit every month. And the leaves of the tree are for the healing of the nations (Revelation 22:2, *New International Version*).

Scripture: **Revelation 22:1-7**
Song: **"Jesus Saves"**

Clara was admitted to the hospital when she was six. Her father had recently died, and her mother was a patient with tuberculosis. Clara had tuberculosis. She also suffered from AIDS, as did her mother.

When the AIDS epidemic swept over Africa, it came as a surprise. The number of cases increased monthly. It came like a mighty tidal wave and soon swept over the entire continent. As the wave of death hit, the storm continued to beat upon the continent for years.

Africa needs healing. So does France, England, Mexico, Israel, the United States and all the other nations of the earth. Disease, drug addiction, poverty, violence and ignorance are on every hand.

The healing of the nations is simple: Jesus. He is the Great Physician who provides the leaves for healing.

Heavenly Father, *thank You for removing the guard from the tree of life. Thank You for Jesus who came to heal the nations. Give us the missionary zeal to make Him known to all peoples. In His holy name, we pray. Amen.*

I Don't Know You

But he replied, "I tell you the truth, I don't know you"
(Matthew 25:12, *New International Version*).

Scripture: **Matthew 25:31-40**
Song: **"Jesus Loves Me"**

She called me collect and woke me from a deep sleep. She needed help, and I had once told her to phone me for that help. Unfortunately, the telephone operator mispronounced her name. I was certain that I didn't know her. Later, when I realized my mistake, I returned her call and was able to give her the promised help.

She was in tears. "You said you didn't know me, and I did not know what I would do." She could not understand why I would refuse to acknowledge her.

Jesus told a story about ten young women who were to honor the bridegroom. They had been invited to celebrate his wedding at a party. Five of them made sure that they were ready for his arrival. However, five of them who were not prepared and were made to stay outside and when they arrived too late He said, "I tell you the truth, I don't know you."

We want to make sure that we are prepared for Jesus to say to us, "I know you. You are my children."

Heavenly Father, we are happy to be identified by wearing Your name. Forgive us when we are not prepared to honor or to celebrate You. In the holy name of Jesus, we pray. Amen.

Devotions™

> ## One generation shall praise thy works to another, and shall declare thy mighty acts
>
> (Psalm 145:4).

September

Photo by K. D. Bell is of her twin daughters Chloe and Cleo at West Virginia's Blackwater State Park. They are members of the Standard Publishing extended family.

Knowledge of God's Glory

We do not preach ourselves, but Jesus Christ as Lord, and ourselves as your servants for Jesus' sake (2 Corinthians 4:5, *New International Version*).

Scripture: **2 Corinthians 4:5-10**
Song: **"Glory to His Name"**

Paul writes of light and earthen vessels. In the story of Gideon in Judges 7, we see his faith as he took three hundred men to fight the Midianites. The Bible describes the Midianites as a large, well-equipped army. Gideon divided his men into three groups and equipped each man with a trumpet and a pitcher with a torch inside so that the light could not be seen. When Gideon's men reached the outskirts of the enemy's camp, they blew the trumpets and broke the clay pitchers, revealing the light of torches. When the Midianites saw the light from the torches and heard that rag-tag army shout, "A sword for the Lord and for Gideon!" they ran for their lives.

The gospel of Jesus Christ liberates by giving us the knowledge of the glory of God through Jesus Christ. For the light to shine in our lives, these earthen vessels need to be broken. These vessels are broken when we submit ourselves fully to the Lord. Let's serve Him today!

Dear Father, *thank You for revealing Yourself in Your Son Jesus. You have brought Light into this world and new life to all that come to You. Glory to Your name, we pray. Amen.*

September 1-7. **Dr. Willard Walls,** the European coordinator for CMF International, and his wife, Ruth, are church planters in England.

A Common Spirit of Faith

We know that the one who raised the Lord Jesus will also raise us with Jesus and present us to God with you in his presence (2 Corinthians 4:14, *New International Version*).

Scripture: **2 Corinthians 4:11-15**
Song: **"Draw Me Nearer"**

The apostle Paul chronicled in his writings many of his experiences in ministry. Shipwreck, imprisonment, persecution, and stoning were some of the terrible things he experienced for the sake of Christ. In this we see that death held no fear for Paul. Death is not the end. Yes, it will be our final experience in this earthly life, but as long as we are alive we live and speak of our faith so that the grace of God can be seen. How can we do this? We are joined to Christ Jesus, and His Spirit energizes us.

"We know that the one who raised the Lord Jesus will also raise us with Jesus and present us to God together with you" (verse 14).

On the Easter just before he died, D. William Sangster printed a note to his daughter. He had been leading a renewal movement in the British Isles after World War II. Then his ministry, except for prayer, was ended by a disease that progressively paralyzed his body, even his vocal chords. He wrote: "How terrible to wake up on Easter and have no voice to shout, "He is risen!"

Father in Heaven, thank You that while our bodies grow older and weaker we are renewed inwardly. In Christ's name we pray. Amen.

Our Example

We put no stumbling block in anyone's path, so that our ministry will not be discredited (2 Corinthians 6:3, *New International Version*).

Scripture: **2 Corinthians 6:3-10**
Song: **"Blest Be the Tie That Binds"**

The collection of things, which characterized Paul's ministry and ours, can be placed in three categories: physical, mental, and spiritual.

The apostle says that we ought to be careful about our personal behavior. Don't give offense or do anything that might be an obstacle to anyone. He isn't talking about hurting someone's feelings. That's nearly impossible. The preacher, Dr. Harry Ironside, mentioned some church folk he had to deal with: if you don't shake hands with them, they feel you intended to slight them. If you do shake hands with them, you hurt their arthritis. If you stop to speak with them, you are interrupting. But if you do not, you are a little snooty. If you write them a letter, they know you are after their money. If you do not write, then you are neglecting them. If you stop to visit, you hinder them from their work, but if you do not visit, it shows you have no interest in them. But we can live in such a way that we are living testimonies to the gospel.

Lord God, only through Your power can we live in such a way to cause no one to stumble. May we glorify and honor Your name and become a clear and unobstructed profession of faith for others to see Your love and grace. In the name of Christ, we pray. Amen.

Suffer for Being a Christian

So then, those who suffer according to God's will should commit themselves to their faithful Creator and continue to do good (1 Peter 4:19, *New International Version*).

Scripture: **1 Peter 4:12-19**
Song: **"Fill Me Now"**

Suffering is not a word that we take on easily. On September 11, 2001, when two hijacked planes struck the towers of the World Trade Center, the world watched in horror. What followed were scenes and stories of personal and family suffering.

Peter writing of suffering reminds us that it is not strange to suffer. Suffering because of our faith is not accidental; it is the Christian experience. The Lord said of Saul when he was chosen to be an apostle, "Go and do what I say. For Paul is my chosen instrument to take my message to the nations and before kings, as well as to the people of Israel. And I will show him how much he must suffer for me" (Acts 9:15,16, *The Living Bible*).

In suffering we develop and prepare for the coming of the Lord. "If children, then heirs; heirs of God, and joint-heirs with Christ; if so be that we suffer with him, that we may be also glorified together" (Romans 8:17).

Father, we know of the sufferings of the great saints of the past. We know of the sufferings of the Lord while He was on earth. But our suffering seems to overwhelm us. Lord, it is our prayer that You strengthen us during our sufferings and grant us forgiveness when we question Your sovereignty. In Christ's name, we pray. Amen.

A Servant of Faith

Consider it pure joy, my brothers, when you face trials, of many kinds, because you know that the testing of your faith develops perseverance (James 1:2-3, *New International Version*).

Scripture: **James 1:1-8**
Song: **"Hiding in Thee"**

Suffering is not unique to the Christian; however, the way we respond to suffering is personal. Is James saying that we ought to be joyful in the depth of our trials and sufferings of life? I don't think so. We will experience all kinds of emotions in our sufferings. That's because we are human. James is telling us that sufferings don't come without purpose; they are not an end in themselves. Paul writes, "We know that all things work together for good to them that love God" (Romans 8:28). The joy that James talks about is the result of the suffering. What is God doing in my life? The attitude of the Christian is one that acknowledges that God is in control of my life.

In the Boston Marathon, there is a legendary obstacle called Heartbreak Hill. It's the longest, steepest hill in the race. Heartbreak Hill tests runners to the very core of their determination and their strength. There are Heartbreak Hills in life. At times we face Heartbreak Hill.

Our Father, we acknowledge that in Your purpose we don't always understand what is happening to us. Nonetheless, we give thanks for the words of James that suffering will develop patience and endurance in our Christian journey. In Jesus' name, we pray. Amen.

A Promised Crown

Blessed is the man who perseveres under trial, because when he has stood the test, he will receive the crown of life that God has promised those who love him (James 1:12, *New International Version*).

Scripture: **James 1:9-12**
Song: **"Be Still, My Soul"**

James states that a crown of life is the final result when one endures life's trials. Testing can bring us closer to the Lord or make us more distant. Testing can produce patience and wisdom. Victor Frankl said, "A weak faith is weakened by predicaments and catastrophes whereas a strong faith is strengthened by them." Someone has said that life gives the test first and then the lesson.

A five-year-old ring bearer was worried as he looked down the long aisle of the church where his aunt was to be married the following day. His grandmother said, "I'll give a prize to the one who does the best job tomorrow."

On the wedding day the little ring bearer performed without a hitch. When his grandmother told him he had won the prize, he was both excited and relieved. "I was pretty sure I had it," he admitted, "until Aunt Dana came in wearing that white dress and the horn was blowing. Then I started thinking—she might win!"

O Lord, we acknowledge that You love us and have in Your heart the best for us. We find it difficult at times to have the right attitude toward the trials that test us. Help us, O Lord, to gain wisdom and insight from the experiences of life. In Jesus' name, we pray. Amen.

Created by the Word of Truth

Every good and perfect gift is from above, coming down from the Father of the heavenly lights, who does not change like shifting shadows (James 1:17, *International Standard Version*).

Scripture: **James 1:13-18**
Song: **"Jesus Shall Reign"**

The word *temptation* can be used in two different ways. James first uses the word meaning a testing under trial. In today's Scripture, he uses a second sense, which is the temptation to do evil. Now God does not tempt us with evil. God is holy and there is no evil in Him.

We are prone to blame God for the consequences of decisions that we make. This has been the case since creation (Genesis 3:12, 13). James writes that when we are tempted to do evil, it is our own sinful desires that draw us away from the light of God.

A family in Haiti cowered at home during the February 1998 solar eclipse and was found dead the next day. Suffocation was suspected because the family had plugged all openings to their home to block out the sun. Seemingly, thousands of Haitians hold the superstition that an eclipse will blind or kill them. As tragic as this event was, how much more so is it tragic that millions of people are still afraid of the Light of Life, Jesus Christ.

Lord of light and God of all, we acknowledge our sin and repent of the wrong we have done. Thank You for Your forgiving love and grace. In the name of Christ, our Savior, we pray. Amen.

Live With the End in Mind

The good man brings good things out of the good stored up in his heart, and the evil man brings evil things out of the evil stored up in his heart (Luke 6:45, *New International Version*).

Scripture: Luke 6:43-49
Song: "Give of Your Best to the Master"

Today a thriving self-help industry offers guidance to thousands of searching people who willingly fork over large amounts of money in order to live fulfilled lives. The discerning reader finds at least some of the common self-help principles consistent with Biblical teachings, as in this passage from Luke.

Jesus commonly taught using agricultural and architectural metaphors. He said that good fruit comes only from good fruit trees and that a good house rests on a solid foundation. Good actions come from a good heart, just as evil actions spew from an evil heart. Good people wisely build the foundation of their lives on God's Word, and evil people build foolishly on other foundations. When we live with the end in mind—producing good fruit and living in a house built on a solid foundation—we live with a good heart and with our house built upon God's Word.

Dear Lord, *we see Your shining perfection, and our dull imperfection makes us ashamed. When we witness Your goodness and mercy, our sinfulness makes us feel condemned. Please purify us. Amen!*

September 8-14. **John Ketchen** teaches educational psychology and is the Director of Distance Learning at Johnson Bible College in Knoxville, Tennessee.

Progression Towards Action

**Do not merely listen to the word, and so deceive yourselves.
Do what it says** (James 1:22, *New International Version*).

Scripture: **James 1:19-25**
Song: **"Onward, Christian Soldiers"**

How frequently we hear or utter the following words to children or even our spouses, "Did you hear what I said?" or "Listen to me." When we speak, we want people, whether child, spouse, co-worker, or anyone else for that matter, to listen. When we ask or tell someone something, we really want confirmation. But we also want the individual to take action, to do what we ask.

James writes that God wants the same from His children. Hearing involves nothing more than passive physiological movement of sound waves in our ears. But listening, on the other hand, demands conscious attention to what someone says. James says that when we listen to God's Word, anger subsides, and moral filth loses its appeal and control over us. Certainly listening produces significant results in our Christian lives, but real progress occurs when we act upon our listening to God's Word. Personal reflection through listening to God's Word encourages our reaction to His perfection by our responsibly wearing the name of Christ.

Dear Lord, we confess that we often hear Your Word but we fail to live out Your Word in our lives. We confess our struggles as listeners. Help us to listen to You, and apply it. Help us to act upon Your Word in our lives. In the name of Christ, our Savior, we pray. Amen.

Religion 101

Religion that God our Father accepts as pure and faultless is this: to look after orphans and widows in their distress and to keep oneself from being polluted by the world (James 1:27, *New International Version*).

Scripture: **James 1:26–2:4**
Song: **"Make Me a Channel of Blessing"**

What exactly is religion, especially pure religion? Everyone and every world religion answer the question a little differently. Some say that true religion results from rationality, from logical thinking and reasoning concerning God and His Word. Others suggest that religion in its purest form comes from intuition, from simply feeling and believing with little concern for thought. We want to know how God sees religion and what He expects of us. James describes pure religion. He says simply that pure and faultless religion concerns caring for others and living a pure life.

James develops the theme of action-based Christian living built upon the foundation of listening to God's Word. True religion involves action—helping others and living pure lives. Christians care for orphans, widows, and the less fortunate. Christians treat all people equally. Pure religion means living out God's Word in our world.

Dear Father, we walk the thin line between being in this world and being of this world. Sometimes we feel the pull to do things this world promotes and values, but also we feel the greater filling of Your Spirit in our lives. In the name of Jesus, we pray. Amen.

September 11

Live Mercifully Toward Others

Speak and act as those who are going to be judged by the law that gives freedom, because judgment without mercy will be shown to anyone who has not been merciful (James 2:12, 13, *New International Version*).

Scripture: **James 2:5-13**
Song: **"I Would Be True"**

James further develops the theme of favoritism introduced in James 1:1. Christians act mercifully toward others—without favoritism. The logic about why Christians practice mercy flows in two directions. First, God loves the poor. He blesses them, as Jesus expressed in the beatitudes. He honors them. The command to love our neighbor should stand at the top of every Christian's "to do list." Second, we condemn ourselves when we fail to show mercy. When Christians want God to show mercy towards us, but lack mercy toward others, we fail to practice what we want God to show towards us.

Jesus taught, "I desire mercy, not sacrifice" (Matthew 9: 13). Our human nature feels we must sacrifice—earn—God's love and mercy, but Jesus desires mercy. Among other things, He wants His followers to treat others as they desire God to treat them. Mercy towards others stands at the center of Christian living.

Dear Father and Lord of all, *we confess our tendency to associate with others who think and act like ourselves. Sometimes we fail to understand how You love all people in this world. Help us to see through Your eyes. In the name of Jesus, we pray. Amen.*

Dead Faith

Show me your faith without deeds, and I will show you my faith by what I do (James 2:18, *New International Version*).

Scripture: **James 2:14-18**
Song: **"Stand Up, Stand Up for Jesus"**

The movie *Dead Man Walking* designates a condemned man walking to the execution chamber—a play on words. Perhaps the play on words also describes the Christian who claims faith yet fails to demonstrate that faith. James suggests that actions follow faith in Christ. A true man or woman of faith is recognized by the way he/she lives. Every good teacher tells the class that behavior comes from an attitude of the heart. Even psychologists suggest that behavior follows attitude.

We find this teaching throughout Scripture. Jesus taught, "out of the overflow of the heart the mouth speaks" (Matthew 12:34). Paul described both the fruit of the Spirit and the fruit of sinful nature. James describes the principle. Christ-like behavior flows from faith in Christ. When we fail to demonstrate our faith in Christ by our actions, we need a spiritual doctor's appointment lest we become merely dead men/women walking, claiming faith without appropriate deeds.

Dear Lord, please examine our actions and behavior. If You find us failing to show our faith in how we live, please show us our illness, our sick faith. Please show us how to express our faith. Please prod us to live out our confessed faith. In the name of Christ, we pray. Amen.

September 13

Are We There Yet?

As you know, we consider blessed those who have persevered (James 5:11, *New International Version*).

Scripture: **James 5:7-12**
Song: **"Faith Is the Victory"**

When we begin our trip to grandparents' house, we hear our children say, "Are we there yet?" "No." "When will we be there?" "In a little while. Be patient." Excited children want to feel grandpa's hugs and eat grandma's chocolate cake. Children naturally show their excitement and impatience about coming events. In fact, part of maturing includes learning patience.

Adults sometimes show impatience. Our patience wears thin when we fail to get what we want when we want it. The early Christians also wanted instant gratification but in a different way and for different reasons than we want today. They faced suffering and wanted Christ to return quickly. James encourages those early Christians to be patient about Christ's coming. "Are we there yet?" "No." "When will we be there?" "In a little while. Be patient." Christ will return! Let us patiently live so He will find us watching and waiting.

Dear Father and Lord of all, our patience sometimes wears thin about relationships, the economy, health, the condition of the world, and so many other temporary and earthly things. Teach us patience about these earthly things. And help us to wait and live with anticipation and excitement for Jesus' triumphant return. In the name of Jesus, our Lord and Savior, we pray. Amen.

Appropriate Prayer

The prayer of a righteous man is powerful and effective (James 5:16, *New International Version*).

Scripture: **James 5:13-20**
Song: **"Sweet Hour of Prayer"**

Remember September 11, 2001? God worked for good in many different ways. We witnessed heroism not seen in many years. We saw patriotism recalled from the mothballs and dust of time. Multitudes gave money, material supplies, blood, and encouragement to help suffering people. Individuals unknown to families attended funerals for firemen because there weren't enough firemen to attend funerals of fallen comrades. President Bush and members of Congress called on Americans to pray. In one voice, we prayed to God expressing our sorrow and indignation.

Why do we so often become complacent about praying without ceasing? James suggests Christians pray appropriately. An appropriate prayer exists for every situation—for those experiencing trouble, joy, sickness, and even sinfulness. God answered Elijah's prayer about the weather. God grants the privilege of coming to Him in prayer as a son or daughter crawls in a father's arms for a sweet conversation. What a blessed privilege!

Dear Father and Lord of all, *we know You listen to us. We believe that You can answer every prayer we utter. Please teach us to pray as Jesus prayed—not our will but Your will be done. Please help us pray as righteous people. In the name of our Savior, we pray. Amen.*

Seven Plus One

Search for it as for hidden treasure (Proverbs 2:4).

Scripture: **Proverbs 2:1-5**
Song: **"Work, for the Night is Coming"**

I love getting the newest issue of *National Geographic* and finding in it a beautiful map! A recent edition included a fantastic map called "Treasures of the World Lost and Found."

Proverbs 2:1-5 describes the search for wisdom. The search for treasure requires effort. The number seven in the Bible expresses completeness, perfection, or intensity. In these verses the total intensity of a search for wisdom is described not with the number seven, but with seven plus one more. Eight efforts to discover the treasure! They are: (1) accept words; (2) store up commands; (3) turn the ear; (4) apply the heart; (5) call for insight; (6) cry for understanding; (7) look for; (8) search for.

If all eight actions are applied, one discovers the ultimate treasure, the fear and knowledge of God.

If one's life is based on the fear and understanding of God and that is the ultimate treasure, then one really gladly pays a high price in the search. How hard will you and I search for God today?

***Heavenly Father**, please move in our spirits. We want to follow You in all that we do. In the name of Jesus, we pray. Amen.*

September 15-21. **David Reece** is a college professor at Johnson Bible College and ministers at Blount Christian Church. He and his wife, Cindy, have one daughter, Sarah.

It's Not Hide and Seek

For the Lord gives wisdom, and from his mouth come knowledge and understanding (Proverbs 2:6).

Scripture: **Proverbs 2:6-11**
Song: **"Open My Eyes, That I May See"**

Sarah squealed and wiggled as she hid under the dining room table. She was playing "Hide and Seek" with her cousins, and she couldn't wait to be found. She was so excited that she gave her hiding spot away. It wasn't hard at all to find her eager face!

God doesn't hide from us—He wants to be found. He wants His people to have knowledge and understanding. He encourages us to search for the treasure, which is He, and then He provides a means for finding the treasure. His Word is the source of wisdom, and God willingly reveals Himself through it.

When a child reveals her hiding place, she jumps up and dashes for home base. When God makes Himself known, He enables those who find Him to walk blamelessly, be protected by discretion, walk on every good path, and be guarded by understanding. They find that wisdom and knowledge are pleasant to their souls. God provides victory for the upright.

We can know Him today. He's waiting to be found.

Dear Father, *thank You for allowing us to find You. We are deeply grateful that You want to be found so much that You have revealed Yourself to us. We revel in Your presence. In the name of Christ, our Savior, we pray. Amen.*

New Batteries

Christ will shine on you (Ephesians 5:14, *New International Version*).

Scriptures: **Ephesians 5:11-17**
Song: **"Heavenly Sunlight"**

If you want to experience real darkness, go spelunking. There you can sense total blackness, and it can be terrifying. On a recent caving trip I dropped to a lower chamber to explore a new passageway. I got turned around and confused about which way to go. Then my flashlight flickered, dimmed, and died! In the space of one minute I was transformed from a confident explorer into a panic-stricken human mole.

This situation is not limited to caving. Many people feel dark confusion when their normally bright confidence fades because of tragedy, loss, distress, or sin. They sense the darkness creeping over them and know they have lost the light.

Rummaging around in my backpack, I found a pack of fresh, new batteries. I popped them into my 4D cell; variable beam mag light and the cave became as bright as day. New batteries made all the difference.

We may not be crawling around in a literal cave, but we sometimes find ourselves in spiritual darkness. Let's remember to let Christ shine in us.

Dear Father and Lord of all, please remind us that when darkness spreads around us, we can still walk in the light with You. In the name of Jesus, our Savior, we pray. Amen.

The Umbrella Prayer

And we pray this in order that you may live a life worthy of the Lord (Colossians 1:10a, *New International Version*).

Scripture: **Colossians 1:9-14**
Song: **"Sweet Hour of Prayer"**

Umbrellas serve as good metaphors for comprehensive coverage. So we have umbrella insurance policies, which cover many types of liability and situations in one. There is an umbrella prayer in the Bible. "And we pray this in order that you may live a life worthy of the Lord and may please him in every way" (Colossians 1:10a, *New International Version*). Some people say that prayer is the least we can do, but prayer is the most we can do.

In this passage the umbrella prayer covers: enabling believers to be fruitful, to be knowledgeable about God, to be strengthened with all power, and to be thankful. Often we don't know what to pray for when friends or family come to mind. The Holy Spirit intercedes for us when we don't know how to pray, and besides, God knows what we need before we ask. Therefore, we can pray this umbrella prayer and not fret about being too specific. We can ask for God to fill us with the knowledge of His will through all spiritual wisdom. That way, God will enable all of us to live a life in the Lord.

Heavenly Father, *we know that sometimes our prayers are general and open-ended. That's because we don't know how to pray. Teach us to pray. And in the meantime, please accept our umbrella prayers. In the name of Jesus, we pray. Amen.*

September 19

He "Busted" My Lip

If anyone is never at fault in what he says, he is a perfect man (James 3:2, *New International Version*).

Scripture: **James 3:1-6**
Song: **"Wonderful Words of Life"**

Sunday morning I preached about controlling the tongue. Later that week while mowing my yard, I was mumbling negatively about a Christian brother. It wasn't serious, just a passing comment about some trivial trait. I bent low under a tree branch causing my hand to slide off the self-propelling lever on the mower. The lever flew up and smacked my lip. I shut the mower off and ran to the house to see how badly I was wounded. I thought that perhaps God had busted my lip! He had disciplined me for my critical speech. Then while looking in the mirror, I began to laugh—not just a little giggle, but a loud, joyful shout of thanks that God loved enough to discipline my bitter tongue. Some say this was just a coincidence. I don't think so!

God disciplines those whom He loves, so we can rejoice when He shows His great love for us. We should expect and welcome His correction even in our thoughtless speech, so we can be "perfect." Has God lovingly disciplined you? Rejoice!

Dear Father and Lord of all, we want to be perfect, like You in every way. One area in which we need improvement is our speech. We confess our weakness and welcome Your discipline as we strive to "keep our whole body in check." In the name of Jesus, we pray. Amen.

Fresh Water Spring

Can both fresh water and salt water flow from the same spring? (James 3:11, *New International Version*).

Scripture: **James 3:7-12**
Song: **"Make Me a Channel of Blessing"**

A paradox is defined as something that is self-contradictory, which seems to violate its own nature or to be opposite of what is expected. James says the tongue is that way. Sometimes it offers positive, encouraging, supporting, godly speech, while at other times it tears down, is bitter and negative. It is a paradox.

We know that the water in a natural spring, whether the water is sweet or brackish, will always be the same. It will not be sweet today and brackish tomorrow. Down the road from our house is a pipe sticking out of the side of the hill. Water flows constantly from this pipe. Day and night people bring bottles to take home the sweet, pure water. They know the water will always taste good. Legend has it that this water even has healing properties.

Some people are like this beautiful spring of fresh water. They are delightful to be around because they are consistently positive, affirmative, and encouraging. Their words are pleasant and satisfying. We can all be a source of healing when we use our tongues to bless and not curse. Let's be a spring of fresh water for God today.

Dear heavenly Father, *thank You for showing us how to be consistent in all of our ways. Please help us to bless, rather than curse one another. In Christ's name we pray. Amen.*

Trash Passers?

Peacemakers who sow in peace raise a harvest of righteousness (James 3:18, *New International Version*).

Scripture: **James 3:13-18**
Song: "Take My Life and Let It Be"

Without being disrespectful to the Scriptures, someone recently paraphrased a part of the Lord's Prayer: "and forgive us our trash-passes as we forgive those who pass trash against us." This play on words reflects pretty well the teaching of our Lord. When a believer is maligned, divine wisdom, wisdom that comes down from Heaven, insists that we be pure and not ambitious, envious, bitter or disorderly.

It is popular today to say we should be pro-active and not re-active. We are responsible for our actions and attitudes that we choose how we will respond. That is what James teaches in this passage. Verses in the Old Testament dealing with this subject indicate there are two paths and that all people must choose which path to walk the path of wisdom or the path of foolishness. We reach crossroads nearly every moment in which we choose how we will respond. Either we "pass trash" or we sow peace.

The harvest of righteousness comes from measured, merciful words of wisdom.

Dear Father, please help us to choose our path carefully. We want to sow in peace in order to raise a harvest of righteousness. Fill us with Your wisdom, mercy. In the name of Christ, we pray. Amen.

Praise Him!

Praise our God, O peoples, let the sound of his praise be heard (Psalm 66:8, *New International Version*).

Scripture: **Psalm 66:8-15**
Song: **"O for a Thousand Tongues to Sing"**

We praise what we love and appreciate. Parents praise children; children may praise parents, siblings, and friends. A musician may praise the music of Beethoven; an art enthusiast may praise the work of Monet; a lover of nature may praise the beauty of the Alps or the grandeur of the Grand Canyon. Praise is a natural human expression.

In his *Reflections on the Psalms*, C. S. Lewis maintains that the worthier the object, the greater the delight in praising; in Heaven angels and men will be perpetually engaged in praising God. True, without doubt. But the appropriate response of men and women on earth, in this life, is to continually praise God.

Praise is expressed not only in words and songs and acclamations; it is expressed through deeds, offerings, and the fulfilling of vows. "I will come to your temple with burnt offerings and fulfill my vows to you" (v.13).

We offer to You, O God, a sacrifice of praise. We are not worthy of Your love and mercy, but we want to join every creature in praising Your holy name. In Jesus' name, we pray. Amen.

September 22-28. **Ron Henderson** retired after 40 years of teaching English at the college level. He and his wife, Gerri, have two children and ten grandchildren.

God Hears a Sincere Prayer

If I had cherished sin in my heart, the Lord would not have listened (Psalm 66:18, *New International Version*).

Scripture: **Psalm 66:16-20**
Song: **"Something for Thee"**

There are some prayers that God does not hear. Jesus teaches in Matthew 6:5 that "When you pray, do not be like the hypocrites, for they love to pray standing in the synagogues and on the street corners to be seen by men." When their prayers are finished, the hypocrites have their reward. Bystanders have heard and may be impressed, but God has not heard and is not impressed. In Luke 18, Jesus tells the parable of a Pharisee and a tax collector that went up to the temple to pray. Characteristically, the Pharisee prayed about himself: "God, I thank You that I am not like other men–robbers, evildoers, adulterers—or even like this tax collector" (verse 11). By contrast, the tax collector wouldn't even look up to Heaven. He beat his breast and said, "God, have mercy on me, a sinner" (verse 13). The tax collector went home justified before God; the Pharisee did not.

It's obviously possible to impress men with long, loud, razzle-dazzle public prayers. But God will not hear such prayers. He hears and answers the prayers of a sincere and humble heart.

We thank You, God, that You hear our prayers. We can affirm with the hymn writer: "nothing in our hands we bring; simply to the cross we cling." In Jesus' holy name, we pray. Amen.

The Deceitfulness of Riches

But the worries of this life, the deceitfulness of wealth and the desires for other things come in and choke the word, making it unfruitful (Mark 4:19, *New International Version*).

Scripture: **James 5:1-6**
Song: **"Be Thou My Vision"**

Back in the mid-70's, a certain major league baseball player signed a five-year contract for two million dollars. One of his responses to the contract was "Now I can have anything I want." When Michael Jordan was playing basketball not many years ago, he was earning about three hundred thousand dollars per game, which means that he would have earned about two million dollars in two weeks. Bill Gates is light years beyond Jordan financially. I suppose Jordan and Gates have about everything they want, materially.

It's worth noting, perhaps, that there is nothing inherently evil about a ten-dollar bill. The problem is human greed. It is very difficult in our materialistic culture not to desire riches and to put trust in them. Some people desire the things that money can buy. And millions of people want to get rich quick. They buy lottery tickets for the miniscule chance of winning.

Today's Scripture text presents a scathing rebuke, even condemnation, of the wealthy who have trusted in riches.

We praise You, dear God, because You have given us material blessings. As we count our many blessings, give us clear vision of the spiritual blessings You give. In Jesus' name, we pray. Amen.

Clothe Yourselves in Humility

All of you, clothe yourselves with humility toward one another (1 Peter 5:5, *New International Version*).

Scripture: **1 Peter 5:1-6**
Song: **"O Master, Let Me Walk With Thee"**

Some people give attention to their wardrobes. They are concerned about what they wear. Do you feel that you must have several suits, ties, or shoes? Are you one of those ladies who have 40 pairs of shoes that are color-coordinated with 40 purses? Well, there are times and places for appropriate, attractive clothes. Peter, of course, is speaking metaphorically, and in this sense there are other kinds of clothing that the Christian needs to be concerned about.

It is possible, for example, to clothe oneself with pride or arrogance; with selfishness or a judgmental spirit; with worry, impatience, or despair. There are some clothes, however, that the child of God should wear. Job says: "I put on righteousness as my clothing" (29:14); Paul urges the Colossians to "clothe yourselves with compassion" (3:12); and he admonishes the Romans to "clothe yourselves with the Lord Jesus Christ" (13:14). Peter urges his readers to "clothes yourselves with humility." Is humility one of the garments that we wear daily?

Heavenly Father, we give You praise because You are clothed in splendor and majesty. Help us to remember that through baptism we clothed ourselves with Christ. Help us to clothe ourselves with compassion and humility. In His holy name, we pray. Amen.

Grace for the Humble

God opposes the proud but gives grace to the humble (James 4:6, *New International Version*).

Scripture: **James 4:1-6**
Song: **"There's A Wideness in God's Mercy"**

What does it mean to be humble? To be characterized by humility? There are some things it does not mean. Emily Dickinson played with the idea in one of her poems: I'm nobody! Who are you? / Are you-Nobody-too? Dickinson was being ironic. Some people put on a show of humility; some may simply be demonstrating a warped self-image. C. S. Lewis suggests in *The Screwtape Letters* that humility means self-forgetfulness rather than a low opinion of one's talents and character.

In a biblical sense of the word, being "humble" means having a proper sense of one's place or station in life. The person who has genuine humility knows how to submit how to serve how to put others ahead of self. Paul writes to the Romans, "Everyone must submit himself to the governing authorities" (13:1). To the Ephesians, Paul writes, "Submit to one another out of reverence for Christ" (5:21). To the Galatians: "serve one another in love" (5:13). In James, we read, "Submit yourselves, then, to God" (4:7). Behaviors and attitudes like these prompt God to give grace to the humble.

We come before You, Father, recognizing You as Lord and offering ourselves in service to You. Help us by Your grace to continually submit our wills to Yours. Through Christ we pray. Amen.

The Reward for Humility

Humble yourselves before the Lord, and he will lift you up (James 4: 10, *New International Version*).

Scripture: **James 4:7-12**
Song: **"Revive Us Again"**

Have you had the experience of being in a checkout line in a grocery store where several people are in front of and behind you? Suddenly, a new lane opens. The normal outcome is that the last person in your line becomes the first customer in the newly opened lane. "The last shall be first." If most people are like me, they think, "That's not fair." Well, grocery lines are not exactly what Jesus was talking about, but He just might have made a parable out of this experience if such lines had been a part of life in first century Galilee.

It is comforting to know that being first in the eyes of men is not the final word; and Jesus was often at pains to drive this point home. In His conclusion to the parable of the workers in the vineyard, Jesus says, "So the last will be first and the first will be last" (Matthew 20:16).

Jesus set the example. Having taken on "the very nature of a servant. ... God exalted him to the highest place and gave him the name that is above every name" (Philippians 2:7, 9). The promise of Scripture is that if we humble ourselves before the Lord, He will exalt us.

Heavenly Father, we praise Your name and we give ourselves in service to You. Give us the spirit of service exemplified in the life of our Lord Jesus. Help us to persevere. Through Christ we pray. Amen.

God Is in Control

I desire to do your will, O my God; your law is within my heart (Psalm 40:8, *New International Version*).

Scripture: **James 4:13-17**
Song: **"Take My Life and Let It Be"**

A well-known athlete of a few decades ago liked to announce to the world: "I am the greatest!" He was a little ahead of his time. Today there are all kinds of athletes and entertainers, as well as a multitude of public and private persons, who are happy to make similar claims. Such behavior is a degenerate form of a trait of the America character once described as "rugged individualism." You've heard claims such as: "He's a self-made man," or, "He pulled himself up by his own boot straps." Some people like to think that they can make it on their own.

There's nothing wrong with individual effort, of course. But boastful trust in self is misguided. James reminds us that we are not in charge of tomorrow. It is surely common sense to make plans, to anticipate, to chart a course for our lives, and to work toward goals. With James, we should always say, "If it is the Lord's will, we will live and do this or that" (4:15). Let's recognize that God is ultimately in control.

Help us, dear Lord, to be rid of every form of boasting and arrogance. Help us to recognize that we are totally dependent on You for our daily bread and for every other good gift we enjoy. Through Christ, our Savior, we pray. Amen.

God's Treasured Possession

For you are a people holy to the LORD **your God. The L**ORD **your God has chosen you out of all the peoples on the face of the earth to be his people, his treasured possession** (Deuteronomy 7:6, *New International Version*).

Scripture: **Deuteronomy 7:6-11**
Song: **"The Church's One Foundation"**

It is said that dated coins began in Lydia in what is now Turkey during the reign of King Gyges (c. 685-652BC). Coins have been found in Iran and China from the middle of the 700's BC. Some coins used in Nepal in the 18th century AD were so small that 14,000 of them weighed one ounce. Those would surely have been easier to carry than one of the Swedish copper coins of the 17th century AD that weighed 43 and one-half pounds.

I have collected several jars of foreign coins. Mostly, they are the coins left over when I've left one country for another. I wonder if I have a rare, valuable coin.

God chose the Israelites as His treasured possession. Peter used similar imagery when he spoke of Christians (see 1 Peter 2:9). If God treasures His people, should we not appreciate our worth and treasure one another?

Dear Father, when the people of Israel encamped at Mount Sinai, You said that if they obeyed You they would be a treasured possession out of all the nations. Help us to realize that You have chosen us also for obedience and blessing. In the name of Jesus, we pray. Amen.

September 29, 30. **Ward Patterson** is a Christian educator and author of numerous books and articles. He lives in Cincinnati, Ohio.

Ambitious for Holiness

Speak to the entire assembly of Israel and say to them: "Be holy because I, the LORD your God, am holy" (Leviticus 19:2, *New International Version*).

Scripture: **Leviticus 19:1-5**
Song: **"Take Time to Be Holy"**

Agnus Benigus Sanrey was a 17th century French theologian who wrote a huge and ponderous volume with the sole purpose of establishing the correct pronunciation for one word, *Paracletus*, translated "Comforter" in the New Testament. The history of mankind has its share of inconsequential endeavors. We humans often give great effort to things of little eternal value.

What is the major ambition that controls us? Is it a desire to be considered wise or loving or successful or significant? Some people are ambitious for power, others for wealth, and still others for fame. Others are ambitious to serve, to relieve suffering, or to impart love.

The Bible declares that one of our greatest ambitions should be to replicate in our lives the holiness of God. Phillips translates Hebrews 12:14 "Let it be your ambition to live at peace with all men and to achieve holiness 'without which no man shall see the Lord.'"

Holy God, help us to set our hearts on living holy lives. Help us to be pure in our thoughts, motives, and ambitions. Let our actions show that we know You. In Christ's holy name, we pray. Amen.

My Prayer Notes

Devotions™

Hear my prayer,
O LORD, give
ear to my
supplications: in
thy faithfulness
answer me

(Psalm 143:1).

October

*Photo by Julie Riley is of Cheryl Frey.
associate editor in Standard
Publishing's adult curriculum
department.*

Refined by Fire

These have come so that your faith—-of greater worth than gold, which perishes even though refined by fire—may be proved genuine and may result in praise, glory and honor when Jesus Christ is revealed (1 Peter 1:7, *New International Version*).

Scripture: **1 Peter 1: 1-7**
Song: **"Guide Me, O Thou Great Jehovah"**

Often we are quick to label people. The apostle Peter is often labeled as impetuous. It is true that during Jesus' ministry, Peter spoke when he might have been better served to keep silent. Yet, Peter was a natural leader, a man of passion, and a man of great possibilities.

It was Peter who was chosen by God to preach the gospel on the day of Pentecost and to take the gospel to the Gentiles at the home of Cornelius.

The writings of Peter reveal him in his maturity, as he counsels and encourages the church.

The Emperor, Nero, blamed the Christians for the burning of Rome, and persecution spread. Peter writes to give Christians hope and encouragement.

Have you ever wondered why we suffer? While Peter does not attempt to answer this question, he does point to the fact that faith, like gold, is refined by fire.

Dear Father, *the sufferings that come our way bewilder us, but we are certain of Your loving concern. In Christ's name, we pray. Amen.*

October 1-5. **Ward Patterson** is a Christian educator and author of numerous books and articles. He lives in Cincinnati, Ohio.

Seeing the Invisible

Though you have not seen him, you love him; and even though you do not see him now, you believe in him and are filled with an inexpressible and glorious joy (1 Peter 1:8, *New International Version*).

Scripture: **1 Peter 1:8-12**
Song: **"Heavenly Sunlight"**

Have you ever wondered how Jesus expressed joy? Did His eyes sparkle? Did He break out in song? In Luke 10:21 we are told that Jesus was "full of joy through the Holy Spirit" when He heard the report of the seventy-two followers He had sent out to surrounding villages. While Luke goes on to tell us what Jesus said to them, he does not tell us what joy looked like in the face of Jesus.

I like to be around joyful people. Joy can be contagious. It lifts our spirits and restores our sense of well being.

The joy, love, and faith of the persecuted Christians to whom he wrote impressed Peter. Though they had never seen Jesus in person, yet they had committed to Him.

The writer to the Hebrews described faith as being "certain of what we do not see" (Hebrews 11:1).

The Christians of the first century faced life and death with a certain trust in Jesus whom they had seen only through eyes of faith. Let's be as faithful as they.

Dear Lord, help us to live our faith with full realization that there is more to life than the things which we can see and handle. We thank You for the example of Christians throughout history who have been faithful in good times and in bad. In Jesus' name, we pray. Amen.

Strangers in the World

Therefore, prepare your minds for action; be self-controlled; set your hope fully on the grace to be given you when Jesus Christ is revealed (1 Peter 1:13, *New International Version*).

Scripture: **1 Peter 1:13-21**
Song: "My Soul, Be on Thy Guard"

Do you ever feel out of step with the culture that surrounds you? If so, you may relate well to the Christians to whom Peter wrote in the first century. Nero led an intense persecution of the Christians that took the lives of many faithful people.

Peter addressed the Christians as "strangers in the world" (1 Peter 1:1) and "aliens and strangers in the world" (1 Peter 2:11), and urged them to live their lives "as strangers here in reverent fear" (I Peter 1: 17).

I know what it is like to be a stranger. I motorcycled from southern India to Europe over a period of seven years. I did not know the local languages and customs. I was ignorant of the food. I was often reduced to being like a child, dependent on others and uncertain of what was going on around me. It is not always fun to be a stranger and foreigner. Yet, that is the position Christians find themselves in as we live here on earth.

Peter urged Christians to be alert and ready for action, to be self-controlled, and to set their hope on Jesus.

O Father, draw us near when we feel alone. Protect our minds from evil. Bring our desires into conformity with Your will. You are our guide. Help us to be like You. In Jesus' name, we pray. Amen.

Love Portrayed

Now that you have purified yourselves by obeying the truth so that you have sincere love for your brothers, love one another deeply, from the heart (1 Peter 1:22, *New International Version*).

Scripture: **1 Peter 1:22–2:3**
Song: **"It's Just Like His Great Love"**

Donald Grey Barnhouse once said, "Love is the key. Joy is love singing. Peace is love resting. Long-suffering is love enduring. Kindness is love's touch. Goodness is love's character. Faithfulness is love's habit. Gentleness is love's self-forgetfulness. Self-control is love holding the reins." We might add that forgiveness is love forgetting. Mercy is love showing kindness. Hospitality is love providing. Fellowship is love interacting.

Suppose you were a sculptor who was commissioned to create a statue expressing the idea of love. What would you carve? A mother and father with a child? Someone helping an elderly person to walk? Someone giving food to a starving person? A bride and groom at the altar? A woman sewing a dress for her daughter? A father throwing a ball to his son? A parent kissing his or her child goodnight? A child running into the arms of a parent? Just how would you portray love?

Opportunities to portray love will come to us today. Let's keep our eyes and heart open for them.

Loving Father, *we thank You for Your enduring and living Word. Help us to show love to others. In the name of Jesus, we pray. Amen.*

Chosen to Declare Praise

But you are a chosen people, a royal priesthood, a holy nation, a people belonging to God, that you may declare the praises of him who called you out of darkness into his wonderful light (1 Peter 2:9, *New International Version*).

Scripture: **1 Peter 2:4-10**
Song: **"We Gather Together"**

When I was in grade school we began many games at recess by choosing sides. I never wanted to be a chooser, for that role would require me to express preferences among my friends. I did, however, want to be chosen very early in the process. I dreaded the possibility that I would be passed over again and again until one of the choosers ended things by saying something like, "You can have Patterson."

Choosing sides could be either very affirming or very cruel. It was certainly an effective way to find out where one stood in the pecking order of popularity.

Peter reminded the Christians that they were a chosen people. They were God's special people, holy, and set apart to Him. He chose them to declare His praises and called them out of darkness into His wonderful light.

How do you think these truths would be a comfort to Christians during a time of persecution? How do you think they can be an encouragement to us?

Dear God, You have given us value and called us to lives of holiness. You have extended Your mercy to us and given us light for our path. Thank You, gracious Father. In the name of Christ, we pray. Amen

My Little Sunshine

Never be lacking in zeal, but keep your spiritual fervor, serving the Lord (Romans 12:11, *New International Version*).

Scripture: **Romans 12:9-18**
Song: **"Give of Your Best to the Master"**

While growing up, my family was blessed by the presence of many missionaries. One such man was Brother Gerald Murphy from Kingston, Jamaica. He would say to me as I followed him around the house, "You're my little sunshine."

Brother Murphy stayed in our home during Vacation Bible School at the church. He had the gift that today's passage shares: the gift of meeting people at their need.

Brother Murphy comforted me when I fell off my brother's bike and got hurt. I can still remember those acts. He knew how to show love in word and deed.

Brother Murphy had a zeal for service. He was a true servant that reached out to young and old alike, planting lasting seeds. I am thankful that my life was changed because of him. I hope others see that kind of zeal in me.

Precious Father, may I spread sunshine in the lives of those around me today by meeting them at their need. May my zeal not be lacking. Thank You, God, for being my source of joy and strength. You alone can help me take my eyes off of myself and onto the needs of those around me. In the name of Jesus, my Savior, I pray. Amen.

October 6-12. **Kristy Steppe** and her husband, Jeff, live in Williamsport, Pennsylvania. She serves in the women's ministry in her church, teaches first grade, and travels to speak and sing at various churches.

Passing the Right Test

Examine yourselves to see whether you are in the faith; test yourselves. Do you not realize that Christ Jesus is in you— unless, of course, you fail the test? (2 Corinthians 13:5, *New International Version*).

Scripture: **1 Peter 2:11-17**
Song: **"Is Thy Heart Right With God?"**

In my sophomore year of high school, I was in Mrs. Smith's etymology class. Unfortunately, the difficult tests she had a reputation for giving over the years had a wide circulation around the school. I was not aware of that fact until one particular day.

A girl in my class, who was an office volunteer, made copies of our upcoming test—with the answers. Mrs. Smith stepped out of the room, and copies of the test began to be distributed. I kept my head down as a test was placed under my nose. I looked up into that girl's eyes and shook my head, as I said, "No." All eyes focused on me. Then I was in the "hot seat."

At that moment, I became an alien to my classmates. I did the opposite of my peers. I got a C on the etymology test. But that was not the test that really mattered.

Let us make sure we are examining ourselves to be ready for THE test—God's FINAL.

God, You are the only source of truth. May we weigh every action against Your Word and Your character. Thank You for the spiritual tests that make us stronger. Help us to abide in Jesus Christ our Savior, who alone is our answer. In His holy name, we pray. Amen.

Good Fruit, Bad Fruit

But the fruit of the Spirit is love, joy, peace, patience, kindness, goodness, faithfulness, gentleness and self-control. Against such things there is no law (Galatians 5:22, *New International Version*).

Scripture: 1 Peter 3:8-12
Song: "Higher Ground"

My dad loves to tell the story of my siblings' trip to the orchard when they were little. My parents purchased some apples and put them in the back of the car. On the trip home, my dad caught Tana and Harold taking a bite from each apple and throwing them out the window.

When I think about that story, I know that "throwing away the fruit" could teach a useful lesson.

I am prone to nibble on rotten fruit. Maybe that fruit is a negative comment that was made about me. I dwell on it until a nasty retort or look can be given in return. God tells us to not repay evil with evil. If someone gives you rotten fruit, give it a toss—and not in their direction.

Let's take a daily trip to God's orchard, His Word, to pick a bushel of the Spirit's fruits. We know the ones: love, joy, peace, patience, kindness, goodness, faithfulness, gentleness, and self-control.

Precious Lord, thank You for being the vine. May we bear much fruit for You and Your kingdom. Help us to endure the times of pruning, even those times when we are at another person's mercy. Help us to be gracious people who only bear sweet fruit, never rotten. In Jesus' holy name, we pray. Amen.

The Rainbow Connection

For Christ died for sins once for all, the righteous for the unrighteous, to bring you to God (1 Peter 3:18, *New International Version*).

Scripture: **1 Peter 3:13-22**
Song: **"He Took My Sins Away"**

My neighbor, Dee was a very fascinating person. She raised wolves as a hobby. She also collected Indian relics. It was fun to talk with her about an interest in something about which most people knew little.

One day, while visiting Dee at her home, it began to storm. After the rain, a beautiful rainbow appeared. I recognized it for what it was—God's promise to us, and I made a comment to that effect. Dee did not understand. She wasn't a believer and didn't know the promise of the rainbow.

Dee began to question me not only about the rainbow but also about its Maker. I was thrilled. God provided the rainbow and allowed me to help make the connection for my neighbor. The covenant God who keeps His promise with the rainbow is the same God who made a wonderful covenant with us by the way of His son, Jesus. This covenant isn't remembered by a rainbow in the sky but by a cross on a hill.

Thank You God, for all Your wonderful, majestic ways. We praise You for Your beauty and Your creativity. We thank You for Your love that loved enough to die. Thank You for keeping Your every promise. We love You Lord. In the name of Jesus, our Savior, we pray. Amen.

Checking the Mail

Let us fix our eyes on Jesus, the author and perfecter of our faith, who for the joy set before him endured the cross, scorning its shame, and sat down at the right hand of the throne of God (Hebrews 12:2, *New International Version*).

Scripture: **1 Peter 4:1-6**
Song: **"Draw Me Nearer"**

One summer many years ago, I lived to receive letters. My fiancé and I were apart for seventy-nine days, and letters were our source of communication.

I have often thought it would be nice of God to send us personal letters. One of the letters might go something like this:

Dear *(insert your name)*,

Greetings from Heaven! I am writing to let you know what you'll be doing over the next twenty years and the many things that will happen to you and your family.

Love,

God

He doesn't send personal letters to tell us every detail of our future, but the Word is our love letter from God. It lets us know that life is about having the right attitude, a likemindedness of Christ. Let us be encouraged that we have a Savior who has identified Himself with our earthly struggles, yet remained in His Father's will.

Gracious heavenly Father, help us to stay away from the things of this world that desire to choke out the Word planted in us. In Jesus' holy name, we pray. Amen.

Silence Is a Language Too

If anyone speaks, he should do it as one speaking the very words of God (1 Peter 4:11a, *New International Version*).

Scripture: 1 Peter 4:7-11
Song: "Jesus Is All the World to Me"

Most of us have experienced loss or pain. When we experience a hurt, we need time to heal. Some things are helpful in our grieving process while others are not. Remember the story of Job? When his friends first arrived, they were silent because they saw how great his grief was. Excellent idea. They should have stayed quiet.

A few years ago, my husband and I suffered the loss of an adoption. It was heartbreaking. Several people said things that hurt us even more. I understand that was not their intent but that's what happened. Not one person only cried with us. Not one person only hugged us without using words. When we love others deeply, we hurt with them. We share their tears. This is God's language: the language of love.

Why are we tempted to talk so much and quote Scriptures to hurting individuals? As the old saying goes, "Silence is golden." Sometimes it is a golden friend who remains silent when we are suffering.

Father, our Abba, we need Your help. We desire to love others and speak Your language of love. Lord, when we are tempted to give pat answers and use idle talk, help us to keep silent. Show others Your love through us. Thank You for Your wonderful love that lifts us out of the slimy pit. In the name of Jesus, we pray. Amen.

Be Prepared

Therefore put on the full armor of God, so that when the day of evil comes, you may be able to stand your ground, and after you have done everything, to stand (Ephesians 6:13, *New International Version*).

Scripture: **1 Peter 5:7-14**
Song: **"Standing on the Promises"**

Do you remember the hairdo called the beehive? Women had their hair wrapped and spun into a high tower. My mom and grandma often spent their entire Saturday morning getting their hair done.

By getting their hair done on Saturday they were always ready for church on Sunday. With all the hair spray that was used to keep the beehive in place, come wind or rain, that hair was not going to move.

Just as a beehive hairdo can stand up to almost any weather condition because of its preparedness, likewise an armor-fitted Christian is prepared for Satan's attacks. In the writings in Ephesians, we are given a list of how to prepare ourselves for spiritual battle because the enemy is seeking whom he may devour.

If we are not prepared and alert, how will we stand? We won't. We want to be left standing. Stand firm in His promises. Every promise is true!

Father in Heaven, You are truth. We long to worship You in Spirit and in truth. Guide our steps every minute lest we fall into temptation. Thank You for caring about every detail of our lives and bearing our burdens. In Jesus' holy name, we pray. Amen.

Like a Tree Planted by the Water

Blessed is the man who trusts in the LORD, whose confidence is in him. He will be like a tree planted by the water that sends out its roots by the stream (Jeremiah 17:7, 8, *New International Version*).

Scripture: **Jeremiah 17:5-10**
Song: **"Trust and Obey"**

Once while traveling in Israel on the main route from Jerusalem to Jericho, we turned off onto the old Roman Road, a narrow, twisting two-lane highway. It took us through the arid, parched Judean hills. We stopped at a spot where a huge deep and narrow ravine amazed the tourists. The guide said the stream at the bottom was the Brook Cherith where the prophet Elijah hid from Jezebel and was fed by the ravens (1 Kings 17:1-5).

Across the ravine was a narrow strip of bright green foliage. A spring at the top of the ravine looked dramatic between the luxuriant growth and the parched hillsides. The trees and shrubs had their roots in the cascading water from the spring, while little or no plant growth appeared in the surrounding area.

When we have the roots of our lives in the Word of the Lord and when we trust Him, our lives are verdant and green, even if the world around us is dry.

Dear Father*, feed us with the Water of Life that our days may bear fruit for Jesus. In His holy name, we pray. Amen.*

October 13-19. **J. David and June Lang** have been directors of Christian Seniors Fellowship since 1987.

Green Trees

The righteous will flourish like a palm tree: he shall grow like a cedar of Lebanon (Psalm 92:12).

Scripture: **Psalm 92:5-15**
Song: **"Help Somebody Today"**

I frequently address gatherings of senior adults. Some are ready to retire; others have retired and are bored with inactivity. Still others have traded retirement from a life-long profession into a busy job volunteering or functioning full- or part-time in another occupation.

The 92nd Psalm is one of my favorite Scriptures to encourage older saints to continue in productive work for the Lord. We are living longer, healthier, and in some cases wealthier. Many have passed the "three-score years and ten," continuing to advance in wisdom, knowledge, and even intelligence.

Let's accept the promise of this psalm to continue bearing fruit. We can do volunteer work, short-term missions, and ministries in the church and community.

One couple we know scheduled three or four trips a year to various mission stations. A few years after they began volunteering, we saw them at a missionary convention and could not believe how much younger and healthier they appeared. If you don't want to get old, then serve the Lord and stay fresh and green.

O loving Lord, make our lives a living, loving, productive tool in Your Kingdom. We want to serve You today. In Jesus' holy name, we pray. Amen.

A Faithful Life

I pray that out of his glorious riches he may strengthen you with power through his Spirit in your inner being, so that Christ may dwell in your hearts through faith (Ephesians 3:16, 17a, *New International Version*).

Scripture: **Ephesians 3:14-21**
Song: **"Faith of Our Fathers"**

James Orval Stevison was led to Christ early in his life. He and his wife, Ethel, built their married life around Christ and the church. Orval, as he was called, was active in local, state, and national Christian Endeavor. Later he became an elder in the church and for years taught a men's Bible class. Ethel directed and taught in the children's department of the church.

Two children were born to the Stevisons, one of whom is an elder; the other is my wife. Her faithfulness is a tribute to godly parents. Now our children and grandchildren continue the way of the parents and grandparents. They all have found a way to serve the Lord. We praise God for the faithfulness of this young couple who built their lives around Christ.

All this love and service rises to the glory of Christ. His love abounds everywhere and rises in glory through the faithful lives of His saints. It continues to the third and fourth generations.

Loving Father and Lord of all, *thank You for godly parents and their faithfulness through the years that is passed on from generation to generation. In the name of Jesus, our Savior, we pray. Amen.*

Walk in the Spirit

The Spirit himself testifies with our spirit that we are God's children (Romans 8:16, *New International Version*).

Scripture: **Romans 8:9-17**
Song: **"Spirit of God, Descend Upon My Heart"**

How can we tell if we're walking in the Spirit of the Lord? Each of us is one person made up of both spirit and physical flesh. When we accept Christ and desire to obey His Word, we receive the gift of the Holy Spirit. Our spirit is joined with the Holy Spirit, who enters our life to help us to overcome sinful desires. Satan may tempt us to cheat on exams or taxes, and even do evil things. But God speaks to our spirit and counters that temptation. The Spirit is our shield and our protector. The choice is still ours, but evil is overcome by good. We don't have to give in to the devil.

Walking in the Spirit means making godly choices. Righteousness and truth speak to us through the Word, but motivation begins with the Spirit. It is one thing to know to do right; it is another to choose the right. By the Spirit's help we can resist evil and do good.

Dear heavenly Father and Lord of all, we know that we often make the wrong choices. Please help us to choose the right and act in a godly manner. Help us to learn to listen to the Spirit so that as we live our daily lives, those around us will see and witness the love of Christ in us. May our lives be a witness to the world of You, O God. In the name of Jesus Christ, our Savior and Lord, we pray. Amen.

Check-up Time

But grow in the grace and knowledge of our Lord and Savior Jesus Christ (2 Peter 3:18a, *New International Version*).

*Scripture: **2 Peter 1:1-7***
*Song: **"Higher Ground"***

As our children were growing up, we periodically would have a height and weight check. Each child in turn would stand against the chart we had posted on the wall to see how much taller he or she had become. Then we would enter the name of that child at the level he/she had achieved. Each child would stretch to reach as high as possible, and it was not unusual to see one sneak heels onto the baseboard molding to seem taller. The bathroom scales were approached with the same optimism. They celebrated each pound gained with delight. (Now they want to go the other way!)

How do we measure our spiritual gifts? Perhaps we should mount a growth chart near our mirrors and do a regular check-up to see if we are gaining. We can ask: Is my faith growing? Have I made any progress with the patience list? Am I gaining in self-control? How have I demonstrated brotherly kindness? Regular self-examination can help us keep our eyes on the goal of growing into productive fruit-bearers.

***Dear heavenly Father**, how easily we forget our good intentions! Thank You for Your patience with us when we falter. Help us to be good fruit bearers. Help us to let the world see You through us. In the name of Jesus, the Savior of the world, we pray. Amen.*

Follow Through

He has showed you, O man, what is good. And what does the Lord require of you? To act justly and to love mercy and to walk humbly with your God (Micah 6:8, *Now International Version*).

Scripture: **2 Peter 1:8-15**
Song: **"True-Hearted, Whole-Hearted"**

Preschool Brian was in trouble. His mother said, "Brian, how many times have I told you not to do that?" He innocently replied, "But you didn't tell me this time."

The Apostle Paul was concerned that the Christians would not remember the truths of the gospel that he had taught them and might fall away. Like the prophet, Micah, who in our verse for today told the people, "this is what the Lord requires," Paul had just listed specific fruit that Christians should bear. He also knew that memories need constant jogging, and he worried about what would happen to them when he wasn't around.

I am thankful for Bible school teachers and youth leaders who taught me to memorize Scriptures. Knowing the Word and practicing the Word, however, are two different things. Often when I read the Scriptures or hear a challenging sermon on a particular subject, I vow to do better in the future. Alas, I don't always follow through.

The formula is simple: meditate on God's Word, inventory your progress, and practice, practice, practice.

Heavenly Father, *help us to overcome a lazy, rebellious spirit and act responsibly to do what is right. In Jesus' name, we pray. Amen.*

Obey the True Scripture

Above all, you must understand that no prophecy of Scripture came about by the prophet's own interpretation. For prophecy never had its origin in the will of man, but men spoke from God as they were carried along by the Holy Spirit (2 Peter 1:20, 21, *New International Version*).

Scripture: **2 Peter 1:16-21**
Song: **"Standing on the Promises"**

It is said that there was a man who had a hobby of writing prose that sounded like verses from the Bible. He also had a print shop and actually made lead plates and printed his "scripture" into a book. An unscrupulous man saw value in those plates, stole them, and later caused them to appear with a declaration that he had found "new scripture" that had been deposited on earth by angels. He subsequently founded a new religion based on those so-called "divine revelations" which has since attracted thousands of followers.

Peter is clear that no divine Scripture came from a prophet's own interpretation, and no prophecy came from human sources. All true Scripture came from men who were moved and inspired (God-breathed) by the Holy Spirit. How tragic it would be if everyone, or even key leaders, produced their own scripture!

Father in Heaven, *may the Word of God speak to us clearly and surely and may we ever be aware of false scriptures and false doctrines produced by men. Help us to always look to Your Word for the truth. In the name of Jesus Christ, our Savior, we pray. Amen.*

Heading Straight for Home

Forgetting what is behind and straining toward what is ahead, I press on toward the goal to win the prize for which God has called me heavenward in Christ Jesus (Philippians 3:13, 14, *New International Version*).

Scripture: **Hebrews 10:19-25**
Song: **"The Way of the Cross Leads Home"**

In the years when my children were growing up, our family lived in Rochester, New York. But since my parents and other family members lived in Springfield, Ohio, we made many trips back and forth between the two places. Each time we set out, all of us were eager to get to "Grandpa and Grandma's house."

As we traveled, there were attractions that might have tempted us to go in another direction–a fireworks factory for my son, a petting zoo for my daughter, or a closer look at Lake Erie for my husband and me. But our stops were few in number. Our hope of getting to Springfield kept us on the most direct path to our destination.

When our eyes are set on a goal, we do not allow ourselves to be sidetracked. This is also true spiritually as we fix our sight on reaching our eternal destination.

Heavenly Father, *help us to set our hearts on things above so that we won't swerve off the path that leads to You. In Jesus' name. Amen.*

October 20-26. **Cheryl Frey** is a Chistian writer living in Cincinnati, Ohio.

Rich or Wise?

I pray also that the eyes of your heart may be enlightened in order that you may know . . . the riches of his glorious inheritance in the saints (Ephesians 1:18, *New International Version*).

Scripture: **1 Corinthians 1:4-9**
Song: **"Great Is the Lord"**

Would you rather be wealthy or wise? There are indications that most people choose wealth. Characters in movies are more apt to say, "Show me the money" than "Teach me the truth." Most of the people watching "Who Wants to Be a Millionaire?" are saying, "I do!"

Would it surprise you to know that in God's kingdom we can be both rich and wise? The riches God provides won't necessarily show up in our bank accounts. But because of God's grace we "have been enriched in every way" (1 Corinthians 1:5, *New International Version*).

What riches are these? One is knowing what to say and when to say it (v. 5). Many rich people would give a lot of money for such ability. We also have the promise that we will "not lack any spiritual gift" (v. 7) in order to do the work God has given us. Best of all, we will be "blameless" (v. 8) on the day we stand before Christ's judgment throne.

We are rich indeed!

Loving Father, open our eyes to see all the riches that are ours in Christ Jesus. In His holy name, we pray. Amen.

God Says "Yes!"

And this is what he promised us—even eternal life (1 John 2:25, New International Version).

Scripture: 2 Corinthians 1:18-22
Song: "To God Be the Glory"

When our children are small, it seems like we spend a lot of time saying "no" to them. "No, no! Don't touch that—it's hot." "No, you can't have your dessert until you finish your supper." "You want to bring that creepy, crawly thing in here? No way!"

As we read the Ten Commandments, we see that nine of them contain some form of "Thou shalt not." Jesus tells us in the Sermon on the Mount not to pray like the hypocrites, not to store up treasures on earth, and not to worry. We continually struggle against sinful desires. The Scriptures tell us, "No, no. Don't do it!"

But just as we enjoy those times when we can say "yes" to our children, God delights in the many ways He can say, "Yes," to us through His Son Jesus Christ. "Yes, I will forgive your sins and cleanse you by the blood of the Lamb." "Yes, I will call you my child because you believe in His name." "You want to live forever in the presence of the Lord? Yes, you will."

In Jesus Christ, all God's promises are "Yes."

Dear Lord and Father of all, when we think of all the promises You have given and fulfilled through Your Son Jesus, our hearts overflow with love and gratitude. Thank You for saying "Yes" to us. In Jesus' holy name, we come before You. Amen.

Our Timeless Bible

Heaven and earth shall pass away, but my words shall not pass away (Matthew 24:35).

Scripture: **Isaiah 55:8-12**
Song: **"Thy Word Is a Lamp"**

One way that man tries to diminish the power of God's Word is to declare the Bible irrelevant to the present age. The Bible stories are dismissed as myths and legends written long ago for another time and people. Atheists have mocked the "outmoded rules" known as the Ten Commandments by saying, "I bet nobody even pays much attention to 'em, because they are too old."

But God's Word still has great power to work in people's lives today. The lost sinner who has read a verse of Scripture and had it pierce him like a sword knows that God's Word has power to convict and lead to repentance. The grieving widow who recites the 23rd psalm to herself before falling to sleep each night knows the comfort and peace it brings. The prisoners of war who reviewed all the Scripture they knew to hold on to their sanity would attest to the power of the Bible to give meaning to life even in the worst of circumstances.

God has given us His Word to convict us, to comfort us, and to conform us to the image of His Son.

Almighty God, give us the desire to daily read Your Word and take it into our hearts. Then it can work in us powerfully as it changes us and transforms us. Through Jesus, who is the Word, we pray. Amen.

Reserved for Fire

In just a very little while, "He who is coming will come and will not delay" (Hebrews 10:37, *New International Version*).

Scripture: **2 Peter 3:1-7**
Song: **"Beyond the Sunset"**

Although there are those who see signs of the "last days" everywhere they look, most of us see life going on as it always has. We get caught up in the sameness of our daily routine, and we expect life always to go on as it is now. We might agree with the scoffers of Peter's day: "Everything goes on as it has since the beginning of creation" (2 Peter 3:4, *New International Version*).

But we should not forget that as God destroyed the world by water, He has promised to destroy it by fire. That promise should help us put life in perspective.

The story is told about a pastor who was able to buy a brand new car. He was so thrilled with it that he was out polishing it every night. He discovered a scratch that someone had put down the side of it. As he was fussing in the driveway, his teenage son came out and saw what had happened. Putting his hand on his dad's shoulder he said, "Dad, it's OK. Someday it's all gonna burn."

Let's hold lightly to possessions and keep hope alive in our hearts as we await the fulfillment of God's promise.

Father and Creator of all, Your Word is true and Your promises are sure. Help us to stay faithful to You as we look forward to the time when all will be fulfilled. In the name of Jesus, we pray. Amen.

A Father's Promise

Then shall they see the Son of man coming in a cloud with power and great glory (Luke 21:27).

Scripture: **2 Peter 3:8-13**
Song: **"One Day"**

When I was six and my brother was four, we heard about a wonderful place out in California called Disneyland. Although it was far away from our home in Ohio, we asked our dad if he would take us there. He thought about if for a minute and said, "Yes. Someday I will take you to Disneyland."

Each year as summer rolled around we would mention Disneyland, and Dad would say, "Someday." But as the years went by, the hope of Disneyland became a fading memory. My brother and I stopped talking about it.

Then the summer I turned 14, Dad announced that we were going on a one-month camping trip out West. Included among all the other sights we would see would be a two-day trip to Disneyland. Dad kept his promise.

While a father's promise sometimes looks uncertain, our heavenly Father's promise is sure. In His Word He has promised that Jesus will come again. He will keep His promise.

Heavenly Father, what a comfort it is to know that we can have absolute confidence that You will keep every promise You made to us in Your Word. Let the certainty of the Lord's Second Coming cause us to live purposefully each day. In Jesus' holy name, we pray Amen.

God's Patience with Sinners

The Lord . . . is patient with you, not wanting anyone to perish, but everyone to come to repentance (2 Peter 3:9, *New International Version*).

Scripture: **2 Peter 3:14-18**
Song: **"Amazing Grace"**

One of the most amazing stories from the Old Testament that illustrates the patience of God is the account of the life of Manasseh, king of Judah. During most of the fifty-five years that he reigned, Manasseh was guilty of the most disgusting and despicable of sins. Not only did he engage in idol worship, sorcery and witchcraft, but he also brought these evil practices into God's own temple. The Scriptures sum up his life by saying, "He did much evil in the eyes of the Lord" (2 Chronicles 33:6, *New International Version*).

Because of Manasseh's sin, God allowed him to be carried into captivity. Manasseh repented of his evil acts and called out to the Lord for forgiveness. With almost unbelievable mercy God forgave him and even restored him to his throne in Judah.

Let us remember God's patience with sinners, even one as bad as Manasseh. God never gives up on any sinner. Often the sinner totally gives up on God.

Holy God, we praise You for Your heart of love. Give us perseverance as we pray for the lost. Enable us to be patient and merciful toward them until they come to salvation through Your Son Jesus. In His holy name, we pray. Amen.

Smell Good

Walk in love, as Christ also hath loved us and hath given himself for us, an offering and a sacrifice to God for a sweetsmelling savor (Ephesians 5:2).

Scripture: **Ephesisans 5:1-10**
Song: **"We Bring the Sacrifice of Praise"**

Smells fix themselves in the memory. Yeast-raised rolls in the oven generate an unforgettable aroma. Someone's gracious hand is ready to "make an offering" to a loved one, family or friend.

Righteousness has the aromatic beauty of life and joy. James was a beautiful perfume to the Father, "a sweetsmelling aroma" of a sacrifice of love. God smells the delightful aromas of His children's offerings. The fruit of the Spirit offered fully ripe and lovely pleases the heavenly Father.

A life of love, "as Christ also has loved us," makes a "sacrifice to God" that He lovingly accepts. Love smells good. Let us send a fragrance of loveliness heavenward.

God, we want Your nose to be filled with the sweet smell of our fruit of the Spirit offered to You. Help us to be a "sweet-smelling aroma" like Your Son. In the name of the One who gave the gift of love to all mankind, we pray. Amen.

October 28-31. **Ron Davis** is a editor, educator, and writer who, lives in in Cincinnati, Ohio with his wife, Ruth. they have two daughters and two grandchildren.

Joiners and Joy

Join with us in the fellowship that we have with the Father and with his Son Jesus Christ. . . . that our joy may be complete (1 John 1:3, 4, *Today's English Version*).

Scripture: **1 John 1:1-5**
Song: **"Blessed Be the Tie That Binds"**

God created people with a driving social need. God wanted fellowship with His created beings. He wanted Adam and his kin to have the same intimate blessings that He, the Father, had with the Son and Spirit. Both Israel in the Old Testament and the church in the New are God's gracious provision for mutually encouraging fellowship. When He is fully permitted into the mix, the fellowship expands exponentially. Deep joy results from deep fellowship.

Many clubs offer a substitute fellowship. But apart from the third element of fellowship, the upward fellowship with God, fellowship will fade to mutual misery. Every person needs relationship with God; that one-to-One union brings joy. Every person needs relationship with other people. But when other people also have relationships with God, joy is complete.

God of divine fellowship of Father, Son, and Spirit, may we join in the joy of fellowship with You. Help us to show the joy of life. In the name of Your son, Jesus, we pray. Amen.

Black Forest Nightmares

Yea, though I walk through the valley of the shadow of death, I will fear no evil: for thou art with me; thy rod and thy staff they comfort me (Psalm 23:4).

Scripture: **1 John 1:6-10**
Song: **"Stepping in the Light"**

Bad things happen when one goes walking in the dark. At home, in the middle of the night, toe gnomes have their hammers and bricks ready. Outdoors, a friendly walk in the woods after sunset becomes a sprain-and-strain obstacle course.

No one chooses to walk a dark path in the physical realm. Lanterns, torches, flashlights, glow sticks—any source of light is welcome.

In the spiritual realm, many choose to walk a dark path. Unlit by the Light, the path may as well be traversed with the eyes closed and covered with a black mask. Disaster looms. Sooner or later, there is a headlong fall. The Black Forest of sin, where the shadow of death lurks and swallows, should terrify the bravest heart.

Why would anyone choose to walk life's path without light? There is not even a shadow when one is walking in the Light and toward the Light. Let us walk in the Light!

Father of Light, *thank You for Your Son who is the Light of the world. Give us the wisdom to love light. Give us the wisdom to walk in it. In Jesus' holy name, we pray. Amen.*

Giant Sandals

Jesus of Nazareth . . . went about doing good (Acts 10: 38).

Scripture: **1 John 2:1-6**
Song: **"O for a Closer Walk With God"**

Children often walk like one of their parents. Shoulders are held in a mirrored way. Hands are swung or rested in a characteristic pose. Some amble. Some meander. Some stride. Some shuffle. Some trudge. Some tiptoe. To see the child is to see the parent.

John declares the same truth and goal for the Father's spiritual children: "Walk as Christ walked." It is not a matter of posture but a matter of style, lifestyle.

The question becomes, "What does one notice as he walks? What does one stop to do?" To walk as Christ walked is to see people with needs. To walk as Christ walked is to stop with a kind word and a deed of grace. To walk as Christ walked is to stand straight in righteousness. To walk as Christ walked takes one into confrontation with sin and sinners.

To walk with Christ takes one into the very presence of God. That was His direction. That was His destination. Walk with Christ. There is no better walk. There is no better destination.

We walk into Your presence, O God, because we come in the footprints of Your Son. Give us grace to walk as He walked, in loving service, full of good deeds. In His holy name, we pray. Amen.

Nothing New

"This is My commandment, that you love one another as I have loved you" (John 15:12, *New King James Version*).

Scripture: **1 John 2:7-11**
Song: **"Love Divine, All Loves Excelling"**

Today we want "new and improved." John, the apostle, though, has nothing new, no new command.

Jesus made it clear when He was asked about the greater commandments—love God and love one another (see Matthew 22:35-40). If one loves God, he will do what is right. If he loves a person, he will do what is right toward that person. That is the essence of love.

John, possibly sixty years after he first heard Jesus state the truth, has nothing to add. From the hostile occasion of Matthew 22 to the loving occasion of 1 John 2, love works best. What problem—universal, political, congregational, and personal—cannot be resolved if each one loves the other? Racism disappears. Injustice withers away. Economic inequity fades. Family wrangling dissolves into the dust of the floor, as parents do what is loving toward their children and children respond in loving submission and obedience.

Faith is critical. Hope keeps life meaningful. Love is greatest. Love one another and fulfill the law of Christ.

God who loves, we have opened and rejoiced in the gift of Your Son. Let us demonstrate that same love toward one another. For the glory and honor of our Lord in whose name we pray. Amen.

Devotions

All thy works shall praise thee, O Lord; and thy saints shall bless thee

(Psalm 145:10).

November

Photo by Chuck Perry is of a farm in Indiana.

Easy to Love

Do not love the world or anything in the world. If anyone loves the world, the love of the Father is not in him (1 John 2:15, *New International Version*).

Scripture: **1 John 2:12-17**
Song: **"Who Is on the Lord's Side?"**

The world is easy to love. It wraps tantalizing gifts and writes everyone's names on the tags. Satan manages a complimentary toy store: free gifts for all! He wants desperately for all to love him. He wants every person to be unbound by the stifling restraints of self-control.

God owns and operates a free tool shop: complementary gifts to every worker. He wants all to obey Him. Satisfying gifts for everyone. He wants all people to be bound by their love for Him.

Why is it easy for the Christian to love the world? In John's words, we have known Him, and we have overcome the wicked one. There should be absolutely no appeal remaining in the tawdry toys on the wicked one's shelves. Whether children or fathers, young or old in the faith, we know better. "For all that is in the world . . . is not of the Father, but is of the world. And the world passeth away" (1 John 2:16, 17).

Father, whom we have known in Christ Jesus, give us eyes that focus on the glories of Heaven. Help us grow in self-control and obedience. In the Suffering Servant's name we pray. Amen.

November 1, 2. **Ron Davis**, is a Christian writer who lives in Cincinnati, Ohio.

Anchored

And now, little children, abide in Him, that, when He shall appear, we may have confidence, and not be ashamed before him at his coming (1 John 2:28).

Scripture: **1 John 2:26–3:3**
Song: **"The Solid Rock"**

Technological change accelerates. "Pop" music is just that, as evanescent as soap bubbles. Dot.coms last little longer than the echo of their hype.

Abiding, resting, and staying—all are difficult in the world. Keeping the same job, living at the same address, maintaining a marriage and family, deepening a spiritual relationship—all are contrary to the emotionally restless milieu of modern life.

The Spirit says: abide. Stay when the world says, "Come!" Rest, when the culture says, "Look busy!" Abide, when the society says, "Doubt and waver!"

If truth were relative, if maturity were undesirable, if depth were foolish, then abiding is nonsensical. Any stability, steadfastness, or absolute anchor is suspect.

But nothing makes more sense than abiding in Christ. He is the same yesterday, today, and forever. If one is going to take a stand, what better place than the Rock?

Rock of Ages, we have put our feet on You and Your promises. Give us daily grace to abide in Christ Your Son. We await His appearing. Even so, come, Lord Jesus, in whose name we pray. Amen.

The Power of Love

[Love] always protects, always trusts, always hopes, always perseveres (1 Corinthians 13:7, *New International Version*).

Scripture: **1 Corinthians 13:1-7**
Song: **"O Love, That Wilt Not Let Me Go"**

Other than the apostles themselves, Augustine (354-430 AD) is considered the greatest theologian in the history of the church. The early life of Augustine did not suggest he would be a spiritual leader. His mother, Monica, was a Christian. Augustine grew up with no interest in what he considered the superstitious follies of his mother.

From his North African home he went to Carthage for a university education and took a mistress, by whom he had one son. When he took a teaching job in Milan, Monica followed him there, constantly praying for his conversion. She often invited him to attend church with her, but he normally refused. Then one day he heard the great preacher Ambrose. His conversion soon followed, and his intellect went on to dominate Christian theology.

Monica prayed, hoped, believed and endured. Because of her steadfast love for her son, he ultimately came to share her faith. Her influence on him is a sparkling example of the power of love.

***Dear Father**, help us to pursue those things in life that will credit positively toward the purposes of Your kingdom. Guide us to bring honor to Your son, in whose name we pray. Amen.*

November 3-9. **Dr. James North** is a professor at the Cininnnati Bible Seminary. He and his wife live in Cincinnati, Ohio.

Love Is for a Lifetime

Love never fails (1 Corinthians 13:8a, *New International Version*).

Scripture: **1 Corinthians 13:8-13**
Song: **"Oh, How I Love Jesus"**

True love never diminishes. It just keeps on going and going. Some time ago I knew an elderly man who demonstrated this in the care of his wife. I had seen pictures of them as a much younger couple, and the wife was quite attractive. But when I knew them, her face no longer had the fresh bloom of youth. Her hands had what one commercial refers to as "those horrid age spots." In addition, she was going through the stages of a progressively debilitating disease. It reached the point where she was unable to take care of herself, even the most basic of her functions.

But the man's love for his wife never flagged. He took care of her every need. She became the center of his existence. He gave up most of his free time to be with her, even when it was questionable that she even knew he was there. Yet he never complained, and he never even questioned his priorities. He loved her! Of course he would spend as much time as possible with her—until time finally took her away. Love is like that; it endures to the end.

Thank You, heavenly Father, for Your love that will surround us for a lifetime. We know we can never be completely worthy of Your love, but help us to be eternally consistent and faithful in our service to You. In Jesus' holy name, we pray. Amen.

November 5

Self-Sacrifice

We ought to lay down our lives for the brethren (1 John 3:16b).

Scripture: **1 John 3:11-17**
Song: **"Blest Be the Tie That Binds"**

The American Civil War was a period of unparalleled tragedy and loss in our history. Yet it also contained vignettes of incredible heroism and devotion. Richard Kirkland was a private in the Second Regiment of South Carolina Volunteer Infantry. At the Battle of Fredericksburg he was in the front lines behind a stone wall when the Union troops charged up the hill toward the entrenched Confederates. Thousands were killed in the assault, and more were wounded, many falling within hearing distance from the Confederate lines.

Some hours later Kirkland could no longer take their pleas for water and succor. He gathered up numerous canteens from his fellow Confederates, filled them with water, and jumped over the wall. Exposing himself to the Union fire he began to give sips of water to wounded and dying men. The Union troops saw what he was doing and held their fire. For an hour and a half no shots were fired as Kirkland aided the wounded. His actions at Fredericksburg demonstrated the compassion of a man who was willing to lay down his life for friend and foe.

Dear Father, we acknowledge that Jesus gave His life for us. Help us to live in such a way that we can demonstrate our willingness to sacrifice personal wants and instead serve the needs of others. We ask this in the name of Jesus. Amen.

Love Is an Active Verb

Let us not love with words or tongue, but with actions and in truth (1 John 3:18, *New International Version*).

Scripture: **1 John 3:18-24**
Song: **"Make Me a Blessing"**

My wife's birthday is next week. After more than forty years of wedded bliss, I have learned something about love. It doesn't do a whole lot of good if all I do is say "Honey, I love you," and then spend each evening watching television or reading a book while she washes the dishes, works around the house, or does various other things. If I spend no time with her, do not become involved in her daily activities, do not communicate with her, then my words of love fall rather flat.

Words of love require some action to reinforce them. God's message of love to us was underscored by the actions of Jesus going to the cross. Our words of compassion to a neighbor are weak unless they are supported by appropriate actions. Even though my wife has everything, she will be hurt if I do not provide some kind of birthday present on the appropriate day. It need not be much, but it must be something. Words require action.

Dear Father in Heaven, thank You that Your love for us was graphically demonstrated in action, not just in comfortable words. Guide us today that we may put our words into action and thus demonstrate our love for others. Give us the grace to rise above our selfishness. In Jesus' name, we pray. Amen.

The Gift of Love

Every good and perfect gift is from above, coming down from the Father of the heavenly lights (James 1:17, *New International Version*).

Scripture: 1 John 4:1-7
Song: "Love Divine, All Loves Excelling"

How many good gifts do you enjoy in life? A "gift" is anything that you have that you did not earn. Many enjoy the gift of health. Those who don't have it know how precious is this gift. Some have the gift of numerous friends. Others have the gift of beauty. They didn't earn it; it's merely the result of genetic chemistry. Some have the gift of musical talent. Although they may work hard to develop it, they still started out with a gift which some of their atonal friends would envy.

Love is also a gift. When someone loves us, it is rarely because we deserve it. A spouse—in spite of the dirty socks, the snores and our often petty behavior—loves us. Mothers love their children. Friends love each other in spite of their well-known faults. The epistle of James tells us (1:17) that every good and perfect gift comes from the Father. God loves us. That's a gift. We didn't deserve that one either. This is a gift that we can multiply by giving it to others as well.

Heavenly Father, *You have showered us with so many good and perfect gifts. Help us to be truly grateful for these, and be willing to share with others the resources You have given to us. In Jesus' name, we pray. Amen.*

Defining God

God is love (1 John 4:8b).

Scripture: **1 John 4:8-12**
Song: "Jesus Loves Me"

Some few years ago there was a fad to complete the following sentence: "Happiness is..." The options suggested were often creative and stimulated warm feelings. "Happiness is a warm puppy." "Happiness is taking a walk holding the hand of a loved one." "Happiness is sleeping in on Saturday morning." "Happiness is scoring a hole-in-one." "Happiness is a Minnesotan lounging on a Hawaiian beach in January."

How would you complete the sentence, "God is..." Children learn the prayer "God is great, God is good." We can be more creative than that. Abraham could say, "God is my provider." Martin Luther sang, "God is my fortress." We sing, "God is a shelter in a time of storm."

The Apostle John put it in even more basic terms. "God is love." God is our sustainer, our nourisher, our guide, our friend, and our Savior. Of all the things that God is in the lives of those who believe on Him, none compares to the simple but comprehensive statement that God is love. When we say, "God is love," we have said it all.

Dear Father, thank You for Your love which defines our very relationship. Thank You for defining love in such a way and showing us that this is a wonderful gift of Your all-encompassing love. May we also define ourselves by the way we extend Your love to others. In the name of Jesus, we pray. Amen.

Trading Gifts

We love because he first loved us (1 John 4:19, *New International Version*).

Scripture: **1 John 4:13-21**
Song: **"My Jesus, I Love Thee"**

At this time of the year, some people are already working their way through their Christmas gift-buying lists. And that list often reflects the giving pattern established in recent years. It is necessary to give Aunt Harriet a nice gift because she gave us a really great gift last year. We take Cousin Joe off the list because he hasn't given us a gift for some years.

But what would it be like to give a nice gift to the family outcast? What if we give a nice gift to Crazy Harry every year, and he doesn't even send a "Thank You" note? We normally don't operate like that. We give to those who give back to us. But imagine what would happen if Crazy Harry finally came into his right senses and realized the gifts he has received over the years. He would be overwhelmed and want to give back.

We are Crazy Harry. For years we took for granted all the gifts that God gave us. When we finally realize the source of all this plenty, we are impelled to want to return the affection. We love, because He first loved us.

Dear Father, thank You for the gift of Your Son, Jesus, and the gift of eternal life. May we never take it for granted. Lead us in such ways that we may also share this gift and thus deepen the relationships within Your family. In the name of Jesus, we pray. Amen.

A Faithful Walk of Faith

By faith we understand that the worlds were framed by the word of God, so that things which are seen were not made of things which do appear (Hebrews 11:3).

Scripture: **2 Corinthians 5:4-9**
Song: **"My Faith Looks Up to Thee"**

My mom would never have described herself as a naturalist or an environmentalist. Still, she had a familiarity with the world around her. She got me up in the middle of the night to watch the Northern Lights. She taught me to ponder the flight of the wild geese, marvel at an owl and her owlets lined up on the high-tension lines in the alley. We watched the ants' struggle and talked of what ants teach us.

"We can't see God," she said. "But God is! I know it! Just look at what He has made!"

I know Him too, Mom. From you, the testimony of His world around me, and from the pages of His Word.

Today I want to say, "Happy Birthday, Mom." But I can't. She has ended her walk of faith. Every day I try to give her a present she would relish—an appreciation of God's world and the faithfulness of my own walk of faith. "Happy Birthday, Mom!"

Our Father, thank You for the gift of life, so that I may enjoy all things and still know the longing to be clothed with immortality. In Jesus' name, I pray. Amen.

November 10-16. **Sandra Ziegler** is a Christian writer, living in Cincinnati, Ohio.

Following Directions

For God so loved the world that he gave his one and only Son, that whoever believes in him shall not perish but have eternal life (John 3:16, *New International Version*).

Scripture: **John 3:11-21**
Song: **"It's Just Like His Great Love"**

Sometimes I see in Scripture the human side of Jesus almost as clearly as I usually see the divine. I can almost feel what Jesus was feeling when he said to Nicodemus, "I have spoken to you of earthly things and you do not believe; how then will you believe if I speak of heavenly things?" (John 3:12, *New International Version*). I've been in about that same place myself!

More than once "Read-the-Directions" me has locked horns with "I'll-Figure-It-Out" volunteers who had their own ways to do things.

The difference between Jesus' approach and mine is that I usually react. I toss down the directions and stomp off in a huff! Jesus, on the other hand, went on patiently, just as He had intended to do, to tell what He knew, and what a message it was!

I'm glad Jesus didn't stomp off, but stayed to tell us what He knew!

Our Father, thank You for Jesus, the Son of Man, who was lifted to death on the cross so that He could be lifted to life everlasting, not just for me, but for everyone who believes in Him. With a grateful heart, in His name we pray. Amen.

Hope Through a Child's Eyes

Since we have been justified through faith, we have peace with God through our Lord Jesus Christ, through whom we have gained access by faith into this grace in which we now stand (Romans 5:1,2, *New International Version*).

Scripture: Romans 5:1-5
Song: "Take the Name of Jesus With You"

Emily was only five. She was dressed in her Sunday best. She quietly sat down in the first row in front of the casket on one of the chairs placed there by the mortuary for her uncle's funeral. Quietly, she sat looking at the casket. Seeing her there alone, her grandmother slipped over and sat down beside her. "Hi, Honey."

"That's not really Uncle Neil, Grandma," said Emily with all the confidence of a child's simple faith. "He's really in Heaven. That's where you go when you die."

"Yes," agreed her grandmother. "I know."

In a few simple moments and a few simple words, Emily and her grandmother gave voice to and claimed for themselves that hope which all Christians share and Scripture promises will never disappoint—the peace and assurance God made possible through His Son and available to all whose hope is in Jesus.

Our Father, most of the time we take the peace and joy that are Your gifts to us for granted. But in those moments when we come face to face with death, we remember and we are grateful for Your unspeakable gift of hope. In the name of Him who loved us so much He died for us. Amen.

I Have Called You Friends

I have called you friends, for everything that I learned from my Father I have made known to you.... This is my command: Love each other (John 15:15,17 *New International Version*).

Scripture: **Romans 5:6-11**
Song: **"What a Friend We Have In Jesus"**

My doorbell rang. I slipped on my scuffs and a robe and grabbed some tissues for my nose. "Gladys," I said with surprise as I opened the door. "What are you doing here? You know I am sick."

"May I come in?" she asked. "I stewed up a chicken and made you some homemade chicken vegetable soup. If you're hungry, I'll heat some of it for you now!"

Wow! Homemade chicken soup. Just what the doctor ordered. How pampered can you be? But then, that's not the only time Gladys was there when I needed her. She's my friend. Friends do things to help each other. That's why a friend is a wonderful thing to have!

The apostle Paul knew something about friends too. That's why he could write to the Romans in chapter five to tell them, "We are happy in God through our Lord. Through Him we are now God's friends again."

Heavenly Father, *this is Your friend. I just knocked to say "hello," and to let You know that I care about this relationship that we share together. No one can have a friend without willingly investing of one's self in the friendship. Thank You for calling me friend. In Jesus' name, I pray. Amen.*

Doing the Unexpected

Who is he that overcometh the world, but he that believeth that Jesus is the Son of God? (1 John 5:5).

Scripture: **1 John 5:1-5**
Song: **"Faith Is the Victory!"**

In the aftermath of the World Trade Center on September 11, 2001, I was reading today's Scripture.

I found myself pondering what would be the result if we did the unexpected and showered our enemies with humanitarian aid, turning the other cheek. After all, the one who wins against the world is the person who believes that Jesus is the Son of God. And whoever loves the Father loves His children and shows it by keeping God's commands.

It's not always easy for me to love all the Father's children. I'm always trying my best to pick and choose. Especially when I feel one of them is my enemy I really balk at the idea of loving. Isn't it interesting that by believing in Jesus and loving God enough to live by what He commands, I can learn to love his children?

A couple of weeks after the attack of September 11, I read that the U.S. had resumed humanitarian aid to Afghanistan. I liked that!

O Father, I'd like to get over being such a slow learner that I can never remember to turn the other cheek. Not that I want to be tormented by Your other children to learn it, but I do want to grow more loving day by day. In Jesus' holy name I pray. Amen.

November 15

Tell Me the Truth

While he was still speaking, a bright cloud enveloped them, and a voice from the cloud said, "This is my Son, whom I love; with him I am well pleased. Listen to him!" (Matthew 17:5 *New International Version*).

Scripture: **1 John 5:6-12**
Song: **"Tell Me the Story of Jesus"**

I was hiding in the closet when Mom found me. "Come out of there," she said. "And tell me the truth. Does you are hiding in the closet have anything to do with a police car next door?" She knew that Robert was prone to trouble, and I was often in it with him.

I took one look at her and knew I had better tell the whole story, and it had better be true. I told her about going for a walk with Robert and about him throwing a brick at the neighbor girl.

Whether you're in a pickle or not, telling the truth is always the right policy. But I learned that day that I didn't want there to be a next time. You should choose your friends carefully because you can get into trouble fast when you don't.

God gave us a great truth that helps us stay out of trouble and make the right friends. He said, "This is my Son. I love him. He pleases me. Listen to Him!"

Heavenly Father, *help me to listen to Your Son so carefully that I will never have trouble seeing the truth through His eyes. In His holy name, I pray. Amen.*

You've Got Mail!

I write these things to you who believe in the name of the Son of God so that you may know that you have eternal life (1 John 5:13, *New International Version*).

Scripture: **1 John 5:13-21**
Song: **"Love Divine, All Loves Excelling"**

Except for a barrage of junk mail and bills, my mailbox is mostly empty these days. It didn't used to be so. Once I could almost always find a letter from family or a friend. I could read the letter and keep it or toss it. I relished my mail. But times have changed. You'd think I would mind, but I don't. I have another mailbox now.

My new mailbox is seldom empty. Oh, it gathers its fair share of junk too. But it also fills up with short, caring notes from my family and friends. Some I hear from regularly, but others pop into my digital mailbox and fill me with surprise and delight. Sometimes I hear from someone I haven't heard from in years.

I don't get long letters, but I get more, and the news is up to the minute. With a click of my mouse and my favorite words, "You've got mail," I know I'm in touch.

Whether it's a digital letter at my new address or a letter called First John, I read it with interest and pleasure for the assurance it gives me that I am loved beyond measure and never forgotten.

My Father, thank You for the assurances of love that I receive not only from Your Word but also from Your people who grace my life. In the name of Jesus we pray. Amen.

November 17

For Better or for Worse

Let us rejoice and be glad and give him glory! For the wedding of the Lamb has come, and his bride has made herself ready (Revelation 19:7, *New International Version*).

Scripture: **Philippians 3:10-15**
Song: **"Anywhere With Jesus"**

On my wedding day, I thought I loved my wife. Everyone thinks that on his wedding day, but no one really knows what love is there until it's tested. It's an incredible thing when you think about it, to stand at the altar and link your fate to another person, for better or for worse, without a clue about the challenges you will face. But for people in love, it's enough simply to know, "wherever you are, that's where I want to be."

In today's passage, Paul expresses the desire to be with Jesus "for better or worse." When you love someone, you want to share with that person and to know about his or her life. Paul wants to have a complete experience of Jesus Christ, including both the joys and rewards as well as the sufferings and hardships. Because his ultimate desire is to be with Christ forever, he's willing to follow Christ today, even if the path is one of hardship.

Husband of my soul, I declare my love for You and thank You for allowing me to be part of Your holy bride, the church. May my heart remain unswervingly loyal to You as the trials and joys of life test my love for You. Amen.

November 17-23. **Andrew Wood** is a teacher at the Cincinnati Bible College in Cincinnati, Ohio. He and his wife, Laura, are parents to daughter, Hannah Elise.

Some Assembly Required

Join with others in following my example, brothers, and take note of those who live according to the pattern we gave you (Philippians 3:17, *New International Version*).

Scripture: **Philippians 3:16-21**
Song: **"More About Jesus"**

I've learned an important rule-of-thumb about buying unassembled furniture. I first learned this as a college student when I bought a computer desk. Of course there are directions. They lost me on page one by insisting that I start with the little printer stand. As if a handyman like me would need to practice on something SMALL!

I jumped ahead to the desk and started putting pieces together. I soon discovered that the screws were unlike any I had seen before—none of my screwdrivers would work on the funny little hexagonal hole in the top of each screw. Finally, in frustration I got out my hammer and turned those funny little screws into funny little nails.

Paul urges us in today's Scripture to "follow the directions" by emulating him and other godly people. We can try to come up with our own way to do things, but we, and God, will like the results better if we just follow the directions!

Lord Jesus, may I be attentive today to the instructions You have given me in Your Word. May I be diligent to obey You in all things, knowing that Your commands are not burdensome, but are meant for my ultimate joy and fulfillment, in this life and in eternity. Thank You, Lord. Amen.

My "Brown Thumb"

So then, just as you received Christ Jesus as Lord, continue to live in him, rooted and built up in him, strengthened in the faith as you were taught, and overflowing with thankfulness (Colossians 2:6, 7, *New International Version*).

Scripture: **John 15:1-7**
Song: **"All Creatures of Our God and King"**

I'm not good with plants. They often die on my watch. When I was nine, my aunt gave me my first plant. I put it in the trunk of the car on our five-hour drive home... in December.

Usually a Schefflera plant is hard to kill. Just dump some water on it and soon a rainforest growing will be from a 10-inch pot. So imagine my shock recently when our new Schefflera started to die. Changing the watering schedule, fertilizer and light didn't help. Finally, I pulled it up from the roots only to discover that the stalks had no roots. They were just cuttings crudely jammed into the soil. Without their connection to the mother plant, these cuttings didn't have much of a chance—at least not at my house.

The world can be an inhospitable environment, but if we keep our connection to the true Vine, we can flourish wherever God plants us.

Creator of Heaven and Earth, I praise You for the intricate design of nature, with each part working together according to Your plan. Help me to remain connected with Your Son. Give me energy and wisdom to follow Him. In His name, I pray. Amen.

Truth or Dare

Speaking the truth in love, we will in all things grow up into him who is the Head, that is, Christ (Ephesians 4:15, *New International Version*).

Scripture: 2 John 1-6
Song: "I Would Be True"

In the classic slumber party game "truth or dare," teenage girls present one another with a choice between telling the truth about some secret or performing an outrageous act. It's a game designed by its very nature to produce giggles, red faces ... and friendship.

In today's text, John challenges us not to choose between "truth or dare," but to choose "truth and a dare." The word "truth" occurs five times in the first four verses. He wants to impress the importance of remaining true to God. He goes on to follow this challenge with a dare: dare to live a life of love.

The apostle hasn't made it easy for us. If I take a stand for the truth, won't I offend some people?

Funny...that's the same dilemma God faces when we sin. He hates sin and must take a stand against it, yet He loves us and doesn't want to lose a relationship with us. He solved that dilemma by sacrificing what was dearest to Him, all because of His unstoppable love for us.

God of truth, give me opportunities this day to speak words of grace and truth and to communicate love through my words and actions. May I learn to keep these priorities in balance in my life, following the example of Jesus my Lord, in whose name I pray. Amen.

Walking the Snake Path

Then we will no longer be infants, tossed back and forth by the waves, and blown here and there by every wind of teaching and by the cunning and craftiness of men in their deceitful scheming (Ephesians 4:14, *New International Version*).

Scripture: **2 John 7-12**
Song: **"Blessed Assurance"**

One of our family's traditions when we visited my Granny's house was to take a walk in the afternoon to the pond. It wasn't much of a pond—just a shallow pool big enough to attract bullfrogs and mosquitoes.

Once on our walk, my five-year old cousin impatiently ran ahead, hoping to be the first to spot a frog. As the rest of the family followed, Granny suddenly froze and pointed up ahead. There, almost invisible in the leaves, was an enormous copperhead—a deadly and aggressive snake. My cousin hadn't even noticed it, and fortunately, it had chosen to ignore her as she stepped over it.

In our spiritual lives, the time of greatest danger is when we feel we know just what Jesus wants and so we run ahead to pursue it. But if we keep in step with Him, He will navigate us through the dangerous paths.

It's a dangerous path we trace through this world. I'm glad we have Jesus to lead us through it.

My Savior, thank You for Your care and guidance. Point out to me areas of danger and falsehood so that I may avoid them and draw closer to You. May I delight in following You and always be attentive to the direction You are leading. Thank You, Lord. Amen.

Be Faithful to the Truth

I have no greater joy than to hear that my children are walking in the truth (3 John 4, *New International Version*).

Scripture: 3 John 1-8
Song: "Faith of Our Fathers"

"You're having a girl." The technician operating the ultrasound machine said it so matter-of-factly, as if commenting on the weather. But in that instant, my heart did a flip-flop, and my mind began to race ahead with dreams for my daughter's future.

What kinds of dreams do we have for our children? Most parents hope their children will grow up to "make something of themselves," but how do we measure success?

John writes, "I have no greater joy than to hear that my children are walking in the truth." John's spiritual children did not have to reach the top of the corporate ladder to impress him. They could be unemployed, but his joy would still be complete in the knowledge that they were faithful to the Lord. Oh that I might be that kind of father! May I be proud of my daughter for her faithfulness and devotion to the Lord. Let me say, "She really let God make something of her."

Father, thank You for giving us different priorities than the hectic world around us. May our daily lives and our words encourage others to focus on spiritual matters and not to expend all their energy and attention on temporary, fading things. Thank You for being that kind of Father to us. In the name of Jesus, we pray. Amen.

Clash of the Titans

But many who are first will be last, and many who are last will be first (Matthew 19:30, *New International Version*).

Scripture: **3 John 9-15**
Song: **"A Shelter in the Time of Storm"**

Watching a clash of titans may be entertaining on the big screen, but it's no fun in real life, especially when it happens in the church. Today's text gives us a glimpse at just such a situation in one of the early churches. On the one hand we have Diotrephes who "loves to be first" and creates havoc as he uses his church position for selfish ends. Demetrius, on the other hand, is "well spoken of by everyone," a man of integrity and respect whose godly reputation precedes him.

What can we do when titans clash? John advises, "do not imitate what is evil but what is good." Sometimes the best we can do is just stay out of the way, but at those times we are not to be inactive in our faith. We continue seeking out godly examples and follow them in doing well. Fortunately, we can know that just as civilization survived the dinosaurs, the church will ultimately outlive earthly conflicts.

Protector of my life, *thank You for sheltering us in times of conflict we have witnessed and experienced. May we be imitators of godly examples such as Demetrius, and may we be that kind of example to others by living a life of integrity and peace. In the name of the Prince of Peace, we pray. Amen.*

True Safety

In that day shall this song be sung in the land of Judah; We have a strong city; salvation will God appoint for walls and bulwarks (Isaiah 26:1).

Scripture: **Isaiah 26:1-6**
Song: **"A Mighty Fortress Is Our God"**

Many years ago, people began to build walls around their towns and cities, making them less vulnerable and easier to defend. Walls would slow down an attacking force, and give defenders a superior place from which to fight back. This advancement helped the progress of civilization, for the citizens who were so protected were able to concentrate more of their efforts on learning, agriculture, and trade. They were surer that the next day would not bring sudden destruction.

The promises God makes to us are our defenses and our protection. If we accept Jesus as His Son and the Lord of our lives, we will live with God forever. We do not need to live in fear of what the future may bring, for the One who created all has given us assurance of our eternal salvation. We are free to live righteous, happy lives and to use the gifts that God has given us, knowing that our souls are safe, forever shielded by God's mighty power.

Dear God, *keep us ever close to You, and help us show others the refuge we have found in You. In the name of Jesus, our Savior and Lord, we pray. Amen.*

November 24-30. **T.A.Bell** is a Christian businessman living in Cincinnati, Ohio with his wife, Kelli, and their four children.

Real Contentment

Lord, thou wilt ordain peace for us: for thou also hast wrought all our works in us (Isaiah 26:12).

Scripture: **Isaiah 26:7-13**
Song: **"Blessed Assurance"**

These days most of us are blessed with goods, riches, entertainment, and opportunities in life that were unimaginable years ago. The average person in much of the western world today owns many appliances that make much of the drudgery of life easy. We can read about, view images of, and travel to any part of the globe that we are interested in. There is a whole spectrum of activities with which we can occupy ourselves.

Yet all these worldly riches and pursuits do not give us true contentment or inner peace. God created the world for us to live in, but it is not an end unto itself. God alone provides meaning to why we are alive and purpose for our existence. We are created not randomly, but in His image, and are not robots preprogrammed to obey, but unique individuals endowed with free will, so that when we choose to follow Him, we add glory to His creation, and will live with Him forever.

Today, may we perform good deeds and charitable acts for others, and live in such a way that the world will find the true and living God who gives life meaning.

O Heavenly Father, how magnificent You are to have given us the gift of life. Help us to remember in our daily lives what our purpose on earth really is, and that You are our peace and strength. Amen.

Fear Not

He shall not be afraid of evil tidings: his heart is fixed, trusting in the Lord (Psalm 112:7).

Scripture: **Psalm 112:1-8**
Song: **"Hiding in Thee"**

After the fall of the Soviet Union and the rapid prosecution of the Gulf War, there seemed to be a lull in news of major conflict. Maybe times had finally changed, and oppression, cruelty, and hatred were at last seen as the counterproductive, dead-end policies they are. Many were shocked to find that there are still deep hatreds and avowed enemies that see America as the ultimate evil nation. There are now many reports of troubling events within and beyond our borders, and a renewed understanding that people exist who seek to do us harm.

It is natural to feel concern, even anxiety when hearing and viewing news of destruction, war, and death. Yet we are consoled by the Scriptures and by prayer. God knows we are weak, but He wants us to be free from fear. Our hope for the future is not based on promises of man, but on the everlasting Word of our Creator, who has fulfilled each and every promise throughout history, and who guarantees eternal salvation to all who accept redemption through His Son Jesus Christ.

Dear Almighty Father, guard us and keep us from harm, and assure us that we are safe in Your care. Show us how to be strong in small challenges and large, and hear us as we call on You. Amen.

Listen Carefully

He that hath an ear, let him hear what the Spirit saith unto the churches (Revelation 3: 13).

Scripture: **Revelation 3:7-13**
Song: **"Teach Me Thy Will, O Lord"**

One Saturday I called to my children, who were playing upstairs, "When you clean your rooms we'll go for ice cream!" The next thing I knew the three pre-teens were charging downstairs yelling, "We're going for ice cream! Hooray!" After a moment they saw I hadn't moved, and they looked at me quizzically. I reminded them, "What I said was, 'When you clean your rooms we'll go for ice cream.'" Some minor grumbling accompanied their ascent back upstairs, but half an hour (and clean rooms) later we were in the car and headed for the ice cream parlor.

My children sometimes practice "selective hearing." They discern the words "ice cream" and miss "clean your rooms." We sometimes do this too. It is easy to read an uplifting psalm and to neglect an epistle that tells us to obey God's teachings. We are blessed when we remember to review the teachings and admonitions God gave to the early church. It is also our guidepost for today.

Heavenly Father, *help us to put our earthly ways aside and listen to You. We know that following You is not always the easiest path, but it is the one true road that does not vary. Let Your constancy bring us peace in a changing world. In Christ's name, we pray. Amen.*

Don't Flag

And let us not be weary in well doing: for in due season we shall reap, if we faint not (Galatians 6:9).

Scripture: **Galatians 6:1-10**
Song: **"Bringing In The Sheaves"**

Any exertion, by definition, is not easy. When we exercise, we breathe heavily, perspire and get physically tired. When we work at a job, we might not perspire, but we definitely get physically and mentally tired. Why undergo the struggle? There are rewards, of course. After exercising, our bodies feel better; after working, we are paid for our efforts. These are obviously worthwhile activities we can do that benefit ourselves. Sometimes the benefits of helping others can be less obvious.

Jesus tells us that we are to help those who will not repay us and to love those who do not love us. These things are not easy to do. The exertion is great, and the returns are not immediately apparent. Even so, we are to overcome our fatigue and keep putting others' needs ahead of our own. If we do, we will earn rewards in Heaven that far exceeds anything attainable on Earth. There can be no greater satisfaction than that which comes from helping even one other soul to find God's salvation.

O Lord, keep us ever mindful in our daily lives that we should work for You. Show us how to love others and to repay evil intentions with good deeds. Give us the stamina to do Your will. Amen.

Try Harder

Beloved, when I gave all diligence to write unto you of the common salvation, it was needful for me to write unto you, and exhort you that ye should earnestly contend for the faith which was once delivered unto the saints (Jude 3).

Scripture: **Jude 1-13**
Song: **"Faith of Our Fathers"**

We all need encouragement to do our best. How much better do we perform when someone urges us to try harder? Parents who are positively involved with their children's activities inspire them to achieve academic and other successes. Sports teams often have a squad of cheerleaders to provide support to the players on the field striving for victory. Business managers, teachers, and medical personnel are much more successful when they encourage those for whom they are responsible. Some people even hire a personal trainer to achieve fitness goals that would be difficult to attain alone.

God knows we all have spiritual goals to achieve, and that we are in need of His assistance. He has given us His Son to redeem us, the Holy Spirit to inspire us, and His Word to instruct and to guide us. Even so, we have to do our part. We are to strive for the deep faith of the saints, and if we do we will find ourselves prepared to withstand all the challenges we experience in life. Let us face life today knowing that God will provide.

Heavenly Father, *help us stand firm in Your love. Give us strength to trust in Your guidance and to hold fast to Your promises. Amen.*

Grow Tall

Keep yourselves in the love of God, looking for the mercy of our Lord Jesus Christ unto eternal life (Jude 21).

Scripture: **Jude 16-25**
Song: **"Lead Kindly Light"**

Outside an office complex where I was working years ago, I saw landscapers planting young trees and flowers. Two of these trees were nearby my window. Through the seasons, I watched both trees take root and grow. One tree had an advantageous position—it received better waterings and more maintenance, but mainly it received more sunshine. Three years went by, and eventually I changed jobs. When I left, the two trees were distinctly different. The tree in the shade looked almost unchanged from the day it was planted, but the other tree was much taller, thicker, and leafier.

We are living beings as are the trees, and God's love is our sunshine. When we don't live with God as our inspiration, we remain small and stunted. But when we live in the light of His love, we prosper and flourish. This is a direct promise from God. We need to grow our faith so we can use our gifts and talents to work for God's purpose. Doing so gives our life on Earth meaning and prepares us to live with God in Heaven forever.

Dear Lord, *teach us to walk always in Your light. Help us to grow our faith and be useful to You. Show us ways to serve Your will. In Jesus' holy name, we pray. Amen.*

My Prayer Notes

_____

_____

_____

_____

_____

_____

_____

_____

_____

_____

_____

_____

_____

_____

_____

_____

_____

_____

_____

_____

Devotions

Jesus came that
we might all
have peace.

December

*Photo by Chuck Perry was taken
of a first snowfall.*

December 1

Do You See Who I See?

You, dear children, are from God and have overcome them, because the one who is in you is greater than the one who is in the world (1 John 4:4, *New International Version*).

Scripture: **1 Samuel 1:1–11**
Song: **"I Know Whom I Have Believed"**

Hannah's life certainly wasn't all that she could have hoped for it to be. She did have a husband who loved her, but her husband had another wife who did everything she could to make Hannah's life miserable. On top of that, Hannah wasn't able to have children, and she wanted children desperately. And her husband wasn't exactly sympathetic because he couldn't see why he wasn't all that Hannah could possibly want.

In our time, Hannah would be considered a candidate for intensive counseling. Hers was certainly a dysfunctional situation. But Hannah knew that the answer to her problem was not in human wisdom. She saw God as the only One who could solve her problem.

All of us face times of discouragement. The way we handle those times will say a great deal to those around us. Do we focus on the problems, on human solutions, or on God? Where we look will determine what we see.

Dear God*, often we get caught up in our lives and in our own power to control those lives. Help us to turn everything over to You, knowing that You can handle it. In Christ's name, we pray. Amen.*

December 1-7. **Paul Friskney**, his wife, Ann, and their children, Hannah and Ben, live in Cincinnati, Ohio, where he teaches at Cincinnati Bible College.

Prayer for Peace

Eli answered, "Go in peace, and may the God of Israel grant you what you have asked of him" (1 Samuel 1:17, *New International Version*).

Scripture: **1 Samuel 1:12-20**
Song: **"God Will Take Care of You"**

God has given our family several opportunities to work in Kosova. It has been very rewarding, but it has its challenges. For example, communication is very limited. One time, we needed to talk with a Czech organization working in the same area. We had a small window of time, and the people we needed were continually on the move, so we didn't know where to find them.

We knew that we needed to turn the whole thing over to God. We prayed, and right away we felt the peace of knowing that He would handle it. And He did. The next day, we returned home after a trip to the city and found the leaders of the Czech organization having just finished changing a flat tire right in front of the house.

What a tremendous answer to prayer! But even more significantly, God gave us His peace first. In the same way, Hannah was able to return home in peace even before God gave her a child. Can we receive His peace before we receive His answer?

Dear Father, patience isn't always easy for us as humans. Please help us to wait in peace for You to meet our needs according to Your plan. Help us to rely completely on You in everything. Then help us to have open eyes to see You at work. In the name of Jesus, we pray. Amen.

If You Have Received, Give!

Each man should give what he has decided in his heart to give, not reluctantly or under compulsion, for God loves a cheerful giver (2 Corinthians 9:7, *New International Version*).

Scripture: **1 Samuel 1:21-28**
Song: **"Give of Your Best to the Master"**

We all think about giving during the Christmas season. We think about what we will give and what we will receive. Sometimes, we get caught up in trying to buy everything that is needed to make the holidays perfect. But on those occasional days when we're able to keep the right perspective, we think about the greatest Gift that we have received: the Child whose birth we celebrate.

Hannah also received the gift of a child. She had prayed for him, and when God answered her prayer, she was overjoyed. To show her thankfulness for that great gift, she carefully prepared her son for a life committed to God. She knew that with the gift came a tremendous responsibility to use that gift for God.

Hannah's gift pales in comparison to what we have been given in Christ. He provides the perfect example for life, and through His death and resurrection He offers us forgiveness and eternal life. What will you give back to show your gratitude for what you have been given?

Dear Father, the gift of Jesus is a greater one than we could ever have imagined that You would give to us. Help us to be so thankful for that gift that it will be evidenced in how we live our lives and in how we give. In the name of Jesus, our Lord and Savior, we pray. Amen.

Lives of Praise

There is no one holy like the Lord; there is no one besides you; there is no Rock like our God (1 Samuel 2:2, *New International Version*).

Scripture: **1 Samuel 2:1-5**
Song: **"Praise Ye the Father"**

Nothing touches my emotions like a story of someone who praises God in spite of negative circumstances. For example, Paul and Silas in the book of Acts singing in prison, or Corrie ten Boom and her sister Betsie praising God in a concentration camp. The sense of complete commitment that such stories convey is overwhelming.

Bringing Samuel to the Tabernacle does not seem like such a negative situation until we consider how Hannah might have viewed it. She could have thought about the fact that she was giving away what might be the only child she would ever have. She could have thought about the torment she was likely to receive from her husband's other wife. But she didn't. She focused on who God is and how He could use Samuel in His service.

No matter the circumstances of our lives, positive or negative, they can bring praise when we focus on God and how those circumstances can be used for His glory. Knowing that He is in control brings praise in our hearts.

Dear God, help us to praise You always in all circumstances. The fact that You are worthy of praise never changes, so help our praise never to stop. May we see the wonderful aspects of Your nature that lead us to praise You. In the name of Christ, our Savior, we pray. Amen.

I'll Take Care of It

Are not two sparrows sold for a penny? Yet not one of them will fall to the ground apart from the will of your Father (Matthew 10:29, *New International Version*).

Scripture: **1 Samuel 2:6-10**
Song: **"His Eye Is on the Sparrow"**

What's your favorite Christmas movie? One of mine is *It's a Wonderful Life*. This story of self-sacrifice and loyalty stirs and comforts at the same time. But another Christmas film by the same director, *Meet John Doe*, has a message that I like even better. It takes a similar story of an average man fighting against the rich and powerful, then climaxes in a Christmas Eve scene focused not on the joy of friendship but on the fact that we don't have to rescue mankind because Jesus already did.

In her joy, Hannah recognized that God not only provided for her but also controls the whole world. He cares for the poor, the lonely, and the lost more than we ever could. Does that mean that we aren't responsible to help those in need? Of course not. God has called us to fulfill His vision for what should take place in this world. But the future of the world doesn't depend on any human, and we don't deserve the credit for any good that does take place. God is still in control.

Dear Father, sometimes we think of ourselves as more important than we are. Please help us remember that You always have been and always will be in charge of all life. Help us to look to You for solutions for the problems around us. In the name of Christ, we pray. Amen.

More Than I Could Imagine

For the Mighty One has done great things for me—holy is his name (Luke 1:49, *New International Version*).

Scripture: **Luke 1:46-50**
Song: **"It Came Upon a Midnight Clear"**

I love being a father. As I grew up, I differed from many boys in that being a father was one of the main things I looked forward to in adulthood. Yet even after all those years of looking forward to the prospect, I found that I hadn't come close to imagining all of the joys and challenges that would be involved in that role.

One of the most beautiful Christmas songs of the last several years, *"Mary, Did You Know?"* by Mark Lowry and Buddy Greene, considers what Mary thought of as she looked forward to the life of her Son, Jesus. While she almost certainly didn't understand everything that was ahead, she did realize that God had chosen her for a very special task.

Many times we want to know more about the past, present, and future before we praise God. If this must happen, we'll never get around to praising Him. Instead, we need to praise Him now, anticipating all that He will do in and through us. What can you imagine happening? He can easily surpass that. Have you praised Him today?

Dear God, *You see everything more clearly than we can that there's really no comparison. May we learn to trust You completely even before we know any of the details and praise You for who You are, not waiting to see what You do. In the name of Christ, we pray. Amen.*

December 7

A Conquered World

The LORD reigns, let the earth be glad; let the distant shores rejoice (Psalm 97:1, *New International Version*).

Scripture: **Luke 1:51-55**
Song: **"Crown Him With Many Crowns"**

We're told that when Alexander the Great reached his goal of world conquest, he sat down and wept because there were no more worlds to conquer. Similar things happened to other world conquerors. Whether they reached their goals or not, they eventually ran their course and faded away. But we serve a God who surpasses all earthly leaders. In fact, as Mary recognizes in her song of praise, He takes power away and gives it as He chooses. All rulers have to answer to Him for the way that they use their positions of leadership.

On the other hand, God provides care and strength for those who are left powerless by the world's system. He fills "the hungry with good things" (Luke 1:53) and has made His people "more than conquerors" (Romans 8:37). He has a purpose for our lives that can be fulfilled when we turn our lives over to Him completely. Do you know His purpose for your life? What choices are you making right now that will help you fulfill that purpose?

Dear Father, what a relief to know that You stand above all powers! We live triumphantly because we are on Your side. Help us to share that message with others so that they might become "more than conquerors" as well. In the name of Jesus, we pray. Amen.

Get Ready! Be Prepared!

John replied in the words of Isaiah the prophet, "I am the voice of one calling in the desert, 'Make straight the way for the Lord'" (John 1:23, *New International Version*).

Scripture: **Isaiah 40:3-11**
Song: **"Give of Your Best to the Master"**

The world was clamoring for hope. The times were troublesome. There was political and social unrest everywhere and fear mingled with anger. "What we need is a Savior!" the Israelites cried disparagingly.

"Take comfort," Isaiah encouraged them. "Your Savior is coming. Misery will be turned to joy. The sovereign and holy Lord is coming!"

The troublesome times continued to the days of Roman rule, and again the Israelites murmured. "Where is the Savior Isaiah had so boldly proclaimed was coming?" Many tried to take matters into their own hands. Others wallowed in despair. Then in the midst of all this chaos arose an unlikely figure preaching a new-yet-old message. "Get ready! Your Messiah is coming!"

The Messiah came. He saved. He left a promise.

Today, times are troubling. People are crying out.

The message is still the same. "Get ready! Be prepared! The Savior is coming again."

Dear Father, *we look forward to Your return. May our anticipation be shown by our actions. We pray in the name of Jesus. Amen.*

December 8-14. **Pam Coffey** is a minister's wife and mother. She and her husband, Mark, have twin sons.

December 9

Be Faithful

Be faithful, even to the point of death, and I will give you the crown of life (Revelation 2:10b, *New International Version*).

Scripture: **Luke 1:5-11**
Song: **"O Thou in Whose Presence"**

Talk about a shock of a lifetime! Zechariah knew that such things happened. He had studied Scriptures and had read about God's miraculous works in the past; but can you imagine how he must have felt? He and his wife had remained pious and had done things "God's way" all their lives. Yet there were no children. He could probably hear the whispers as he walked back and forth to his duty, but what were he and Elizabeth to do? He would do the only thing he knew to do. Remain faithful.

Then an angel appeared and, even though we know the rest of the story, Zechariah didn't. What if that angel never appeared? What if a son had never been born to them? What if their lives continued just as before—never changing—always longing. What do you think Zechariah and Elizabeth would have done?

Would they have given up at some point, crying out, "It's worthless! Everything I have been or have done is all a waste!" Would they have rejected God?

Obviously God knew their hearts and He blessed them for their faithfulness.

Heavenly Father, sometimes we question our success and even Your love for us. Please forgive us. We ask that You help us remain faithful to the end. In the name of Jesus, our Savior, we pray. Amen.

Point to the Promise

And he will go on before the Lord, in the spirit and power of Elijah, to turn the hearts of the fathers to their children and the disobedient to the wisdom of the righteous—to make ready a people prepared for the Lord (Luke 1:17, *New International Version*).

Scripture: **Luke 1:12-17**
Song: **"Lead On, O King Eternal"**

Prayers had been heard and a promise of a child was given. As some may say, it was "worth the wait."

This was no ordinary child. His job description was overwhelming and his parents had an awesome responsibility in raising him.

How do you raise a child who is to be the forerunner of the Messiah? What principles in evangelism do you teach him? What strategies on dealing with guilt and repentance do you chart out before him? How do you teach him to dress for success? What do you tell him about the dangers of conflict, and being "close minded"?

God surely guided John's parents as they loved him and taught him. Through the power of the Holy Spirit in the life of John, the world was introduced to Jesus. Zechariah and Elizabeth's "promise fulfilled" pointed to God's promise fulfilled in His very own Son.

We may not be like John, but that job is ours also.

Heavenly Father, *we know that we need to point the world to Jesus, but sometimes we fall short. Teach us and guide us as Your own children. We submit to You. In the name of Jesus, we pray. Amen.*

In His Time

"For my thoughts are not your thoughts, neither are your ways my ways," declares the Lord (Isaiah 55:8, *New International Version*).

Scripture: **Luke 1:18-25**
Song: **"Never Alone!"**

"A son? We will give birth to a son? Impossible! Now, if you had told us this twenty years earlier, I wouldn't have too much trouble picturing this, but now?"

Okay, Zechariah really didn't say this in these exact words, but the thought came out. At this point in his life, the easier task would seem to be to just remain faithful than to deal with a fulfilled long-awaited dream.

We are limited by time. God isn't. Though God created time and uses it to perform His works, He can also step right over that tightly wound boundary that keeps us trapped, and can set our heads spinning.

Zechariah felt that trap of time and gave in to doubt. But doubt was transformed back to trust and God performed His mighty work in Elizabeth.

Is time trapping us? Let's trust in the God who transcends all time and all human finiteness. We can say, "I don't understand, Lord, but I trust in You." Then we can rejoice, as trust becomes full bloom in victory.

We are so human, God, and are filled with limitations. We thank You for creating us—even in our humanity—but we ask for Your help to reach beyond ourselves to understand You more and trust You more. May Your will be done in us through Jesus, we pray. Amen.

God Is Gracious

"Do not be afraid Zechariah; your prayer has been heard. Your wife Elizabeth will bear you a son, and you are to give him the name John" (Luke 1:13, *New International Version*).

Scripture: **Luke 1:57-66**
Song: **"Wonderful Grace of Jesus"**

John—God is gracious. We had a son named John—Jonathon, exactly. Jonathon was physically impaired and lived only 23 days. Those days he was alive were not only painful, they were rich. God had visited us and given us a gift in the form of a son. Though we did not understand the working of God's plan, we knew His was perfect, and—if even for a little while—our lives would be blessed by his presence. That's why we still hold on to the name plaque we set above his little hospital bed—"Jonathon—Gracious gift of God."

Zechariah and Elizabeth must have marveled as they held their own little John—gracious gift of God. What a joy he was! How he had blessed their lives already! And to think that he would herald the Savior of all mankind!

John lived out his ministry before he died. Our Jonathon lived out his little ministry before he died. One prepared the hearts of the people for the Messiah. The other prepared the hearts of his parents for a deeper relationship with that same Messiah.

Almighty God, *we rejoice and thank You for Jesus Christ. Please help us to be used as a gracious gift of Yours for Your glory, we pray in the name of Jesus, our Savior. Amen.*

One Name

And this is His command: to believe in the name of His Son, Jesus Christ, and to love another as He commanded us (1 John 3:23, *New International Version*).

Scripture: **Luke 1:67-75**
Song: **"Glory to His Name"**

Zechariah knew. The curtain had been raised and he—through the Holy Spirit—saw the big picture. Even though he was delighted in the birth of his son, his song of praise was not just for himself, but for the salvation of his people. Ancient promises were being revealed before his very eyes.

It all pointed to Jesus—Immanuel—God with us—the Holy One of Israel.

Jesus is the focal point of all history. Acts 4:12 says, "Salvation is found in no one else, for there is no other name under heaven given to men by which we must be saved." And John 1:12 tells us, "Yet to all who received Him, to those who believed in his name, he gave the right to become children of God" (*New International Version*). It is Jesus who will enable us to serve without fear in holiness and righteousness.

Jesus is the way to forgiveness and the hope of eternal life. He is our Savior. That was Zechariah's message. That was John's message. It is our message, too.

Lord Jesus, *You are the Holy One of Israel. You are the only way to eternal life. You are the Lion of Judah and the sacrificial Lamb. May we proclaim Your name to the world. Amen.*

Prepare Your World

How beautiful on the mountains are the feet of those who bring good news, who proclaim peace, who bring good tidings, who proclaim salvation, who say to Zion, "Your God reigns!" (Isaiah 52:7, *New International Version*).

Scripture: Luke 1:76-80
Song: "Send the Light"

John did what he was called to do. He prepared the way for the Lord. Was he voted the most eloquent speaker and the best-dressed man in all of Judea? Hardly! Was he considered as "The most likely to succeed" by religious leaders? Not in a stone's throw!

Was he truthful? Yes. Was he humble? Yes. Was he effective? Without a doubt. Was he human? Of course. Yet he remains a hero and his message rings loudly, "Repent! Prepare the way for the Lord!"

Are we following his example? Is his message ringing out from our lives? Will some reject and make fun of this message? Absolutely. Will others listen and allow God to prepare the way in their hearts? Yes! Even if only one turned to the Lord, it would be worth it—for the Redeemer is coming back and some day He will say, "Well done, good and faithful servant. Enter in."

Go; prepare your world for the Messiah.

Dear Father, we await the return of Jesus. In fact, we can hardly wait! Please give us courage and strength as we boldly proclaim Your name with passion and joy and love! We pray this prayer in the name of the Savior of the world, Jesus Christ. Amen.

The Power of Belief

Do not let your heart be troubled. Trust in God, trust also in me (John 14:1, *New International Version*).

Scripture: **John 14:1-5**
Song: **"Trust and Obey"**

In the disciples' darkest hour, Jesus said that their faith would give them comfort. But what is the object of their faith? First Jesus said, "You believe in God." The fact is most people in the world believe in a Supreme Being. It helps us navigate life, believing there is one who rules, who is stronger, kinder, and more holy than we are.

Jesus goes further. He says, "Believe also in me." Jesus is telling them that it is appropriate to couple faith in God with faith in His son. Here is where God becomes specific. He is not just a vague concept. The Scripture teaches that Jesus is the divine cloaked in flesh.

Jesus goes on to tell the disciples that they have a future in eternity. Jesus prepares the way. Jesus comes again to receive us. Jesus will fellowship with us. So there in a nutshell are the three beliefs that sustain in any crisis. Don't be afraid. You have a father, a friend, and a future.

Dear Lord, help me to see that faith in the future brings power to the present. I serve You here, knowing that if life assaults me with its worst, the best is yet to come in Heaven. I pray this in the name of Jesus, who has gone ahead to make a place for me. Amen.

December 15-21. **J. Michael Shannon** teaches at Cincinnati Bible College. He and his wife and children live in Cincinnati, Ohio.

How to Know God

Philip said, "Lord, show us the Father and that will be enough for us" (John 14:8, *New International Version*).

Scripture: **John 14:6-10**
Song: **"The Church's One Foundation"**

It is the desperate dream of humanity to know God. Philip said what must be one of the great understatements of all time, that it would be enough. Jesus' answer is startling in its claim. Jesus says, "Anyone who has seen me has seen the Father." If God really wanted to help us know Him, what better way to reach us could there be than to come to us in the flesh?

A man had been estranged from his childhood friend for many years. He decided to make his peace. He saw the old friend's name in a phone book. He went to the address and knocked on the door. A young man answered and the man asked for his friend. The young man said, "I am his son, and I'm sorry to tell you that he passed away about a year ago." The man broke into tears and started to leave, when he had a flash of insight and turned back. "Wait a minute," said the old man, "let me look at you for a spell. I want to see if I can see some of your father in you." So with Jesus, we can look at Him and see the Father.

Father, I believe in You, but confess sometimes I long to see You face-to-face. The saints of old were filled with fear at that thought. I fear too, but long for You nonetheless. Thank You for the gift of Your son, who helps me to see You clearly. And it is in His name I pray. Amen.

Getting to Know God

I tell you the truth, anyone who has faith in me will do what I have been doing. He will do even greater things than these, because I am going to the Father (John 14:12, *New International Version*).

Scripture: **John 14:11-15**
Song: **"Take My Life and Let It Be"**

Our verse for today contains an extraordinary promise. It is so extraordinary that we really don't believe it. After all, Jesus healed the sick, calmed a storm, and raised the dead and thousands of other things we would not presume to do. Our problem is that we focus only on the miracles.

The greatest thing Jesus did was provide salvation. The promise that we will do greater things is based on Jesus returning to the Father. He wants us to know that as He works in us and through us, we will be a part of these greater things. Jesus went to the cross and rose again, and we can proclaim His salvation to a lost world. Jesus enabled the disciples to travel farther than He traveled. He enabled them to speak to more people than He spoke to while here on earth.

The work is all about Him and is done under His authority and with the blessing of His Holy Spirit.

Father, I submit myself to let Him work through me. It humbles me to know that He entrusts great work to His followers. We depend upon Your Spirit and we give all the glory to You and Your son, in whose name we pray. Amen.

Someone to Stand Beside You

I will ask the Father, and he will give you another Counselor to be with you forever (John 14:16, *New International Version*).

Scripture: **John 14:16-20**
Song: **"Thou Didst Leave Thy Throne"**

The disciples of Jesus had to face His absence. Jesus, cognizant of their concern, promised that the Father would send another counselor. Notice he said "another." Jesus had been their counselor, but another would be coming. The other counselor was the Holy Spirit. He is the Comforter we have today.

The word *comforter* also means that He will stand beside us and is there to share our tears. Now we can see how both the word *comforter* and *counselor* fit very well with the Holy Spirit.

When we don't know what to do, God's Spirit is within us to help us develop wisdom. When we are happy, God's Spirit is within us to enhance the celebration. When we are deeply saddened, the Spirit is within us to give a sense of comfort and courage. Jesus was there to stand beside the disciples in their need. In Jesus' absence the Holy Spirit provides help to all who follow Him. With all we have to face in this life, isn't it nice to know that we have someone to stand beside us?

I thank You, Father that You have not left us orphaned. No matter how lonely we may feel, the fact is that Your Spirit is ever with us. As the old song says, "Blessed quietness, holy quietness, what assurance in my soul." In the name of Jesus, we pray. Amen.

December 19

Moving in

Therefore the Lord himself will give you a sign: The virgin will be with child and will give birth to a son, and will call him Immanuel (Isaiah 7:14, *New International Version*).

Scripture: **Isaiah 7:10-17**
Song: **"The First Noel"**

Dr. John Rosen was a psychiatrist with a very non-traditional technique in therapy. He had remarkable success with catatonic patients. Many of his patients would simply lie in bed in a fetal position. Rosen put a cot on the ward and moved in with the patients. He would see them every day. Sometimes, when he stopped by a patient's bed, he would take off his coat and tie and crawl in beside them. He would put his arms around them and embrace them. Often he said not a word. A number of patients responded and returned his love.

When we say that Jesus is called Immanuel, we are saying that Jesus is "God with us." What does that mean? In Christ, God moved into our ward. In Christ, He shared our sick room. In Christ, He reached out to people who weren't reaching out to Him.

Jesus is "God with me." He is there. That is what Christmas is all about.

Father, we are grateful that even though in many ways we have said, "Leave us alone!" You would not. You came to us because we were in desperate need. A need so desperate we didn't even know what the problem was. Thank You for the abiding presence of Your Son, in whose name, we pray. Amen.

Why No Room?

And she gave birth to her firstborn, a son. She wrapped him in cloths and placed him in a manger, because there was no room for them in the inn (Luke 2:7, *New International Version*).

Scripture: **Luke 2:1-7**
Song: **"Nothing Between"**

It is a simple detail that had no spiritual significance, yet preachers and poets have found that the phrase, "no room" resonates in our time. In His own time, the religious leaders had no room for Him. His hometown had no room for Him. The temple had no room for Him. Even the world had no room for Him. That's why they placed Him on a cross.

What about today? Is there room for Him in our public life, our homes, and our personal lives?

Christ wants to come into our hearts and be a part of our lives. As the song says, "Where meek souls will receive him still, the dear Christ enters in." Even the smallest heart can be expanded when Christ is invited in. Even the most crowded heart can be put in order, if Christ is allowed to do His work. When we hear His knock may we say, "Come in, Lord, there is always room for You." Let us celebrate this season of Christmas by allowing Him to enter into our hearts today.

O Lord, may what we have read find lodging in our hearts so that it might find expression in our lives. As we make room for Your Word and insights into Your Word, we make room for You and Your son, in whose name we pray. Amen.

Don't Forget Joseph

When Joseph woke up, he did what the angel of the Lord had commanded him and took Mary home as his wife (Matthew 1:24, *New International Version*).

Scripture: **Matthew 1:18-25**
Song: **"Silent Night"**

If you did a word association with the birth of Jesus, you might come up with scores of names and terms before you would come up with the name Joseph. We rightly honor Mary. God chose her. But God also chose Joseph. Since Jesus' birth was miraculous, *Joseph* was not genetically related to Jesus, but he was his father in every other way. We know Joseph had qualities that would make him an ideal father for the Son of God. When Mary was pregnant and Joseph didn't understand, he had a mind to put her away privately. He knew his legal rights, but he was filled with compassion and refused to humiliate Mary. When the angel told him to take Mary as his wife anyway, Joseph trusted and obeyed. He was a man of faith and a man of submission to God. During this season we will think much of Mary. She will be mentioned in song, Let's also remember Joseph. But most of all, we want to remember it is Jesus' birthday.

Dear Father, as we strive to live our lives for You, may we display the commitment of Joseph—a commitment that is mixed with compassion, a commitment that is sustained by trust. In the name of Jesus who once held Joseph's hand, we pray. Amen.

Predictions

And righteousness shall be the girdle of his loins, and faith-fulness the girdle of his reins (Isaiah 11:5).

Scripture: **Isaiah 11:1-5**
Song: **"If Jesus Had Not Come"**

Another year is drawing to a close. As it does we not only remember all that has happened but also we look forward to what the New Year will bring. Newspaper columnists of all varieties begin to make their predictions—who will be in the sports playoffs, which political leaders will be in power, whose marriages will last, which songs or movies will win awards. Of course while various people may agree on a few things there are many conflicting opinions as to what the future really holds.

When God tells us what the future will bring, there are no variations. In this passage of Isaiah he tells of the coming of God's Son. What a glorious event for people to await—the arrival of God's Son and the truth and righteousness He will bring to earth and to each human heart. What a deep abiding love is offered to us by our God, who is always faithful, always just, and whose righteousness endures forever.

O Father God, keep us ever mindful of Your will. Thank You for giving us the greatest gift of all, Your Son, Jesus. Help us to follow Him now and in the New Year. In His holy name, we pray. Amen.

December 22-28. **K. D. Bell** is a wife, mother, writer and artist living in Cincinnati, Ohio. She and her husband, Todd, have four children.

The Son of God

And there came a voice out of the cloud, saying, This is my beloved Son: hear him (Luke 9:35).

Scripture: **Luke 9:28-36**
Song: **"Crown Him with Many Crowns"**

When I was younger I was so proud to be my father's daughter that I couldn't imagine ever taking the last name of my husband. My father was a tall gregarious minister who shared his faith and lived his life with such drama and gusto that I never wanted to leave his shadow. I was once asked to come up with some small flaw, in order for his friends to tease him—and I couldn't. I wanted everyone to know that I was his child.

How magnificent to know that Jesus is the Son of God. How incredible He must have felt to hear His Father's voice from Heaven claiming Him as His own chosen son. What a great gift has been given us that we, through the blood of Jesus, are claimed by God to be His children. What an honor is ours to be the sons and daughters of the Creator of the universe. How proud we should be to proclaim to the world the love of our Father and the salvation He has given to us.

Heavenly Father, *how proud we are to be Your children! Thank You for this great gift You have given each of us through Jesus. Let us always share with others our joy in the Lord. In the name of the Father, Son, and Holy Spirit, we pray. Amen.*

A Promise Fulfilled

Behold my servant, whom I have chosen; my beloved, in whom my soul is well pleased (Matthew 12:18a).

Scripture: **Matthew 12:15-21**
Song: **"Joy to the World!"**

Are you ready for Christmas? Is the tree decorated, the lights twinkling in the dark? Are the presents wrapped and ready to be placed under the tree? Have you mailed out your cards and wished all and sundry the joy of the season? More importantly have you found the time to pause and reflect on the true spirit of Christmas?

God prepared the greatest gift of all in His Son Jesus. For centuries He readied His people, teaching them the signs that would show all of us, then and now, that this truly is His Son, God dwelling among us, living a life to show us how to live, dying for us to take away our sins so that we might stand blameless before our Creator, resurrected so that we might live eternally. God, through the Scriptures, told us Christ was coming. He showed the many ways Scripture was fulfilled by the life of Christ. God became flesh and dwelt among us, teaching us of His grace and His love and His peace. What a deep joy is ours! Hallelujah!

Dear heavenly Father, thank You for sending us Your precious Son to live among men and to show us how to be good stewards of the most precious gift of life. Help us to share the joy we have through You. In the most holy name of Jesus, we pray. Amen.

Born Again

And lo a voice from heaven, saying, This is my beloved Son, in whom I am well pleased (Matthew3:17).

Scripture: **Matthew 3:13-17**
Song: **"There's a New Song in My Heart"**

I was eight years old when I made my way down the church aisle singing that great old hymn *"Just as I Am."* My father, who was the minister, was waiting for me with open arms and a smile full of love and pride. The event was particularly special for me because my earthly father was expressing the same emotions that my heavenly Father was. Knowing that I was accepting the son of God as my personal Savior filled me with true joy. I remember coming up out of the water and feeling like a new creature. I felt God's love and forgiveness and something had definitely changed inside of me that day when I accepted Jesus into my heart.

When God saw His Son, Jesus Christ, fulfilling "all righteousness," He let the world know just how proud He was of His Son. The Spirit of God descended like a dove, and a voice was heard from Heaven saying, "This is my beloved Son, in whom I am well pleased."

Heavenly Father, on this one of the most special days of the year when we pause and remember the baby You sent to the world to become our Savior, we give praise, honor, and glory to You. Thank You for the spiritual new birth You offer to the entire world through Your Son, Jesus. In His holy name, we pray. Amen.

Just Like My Father

For the Father loveth the Son, and showeth him all things that himself doeth (John 5:20a).

Scripture: **John 5:19-24**
Song: **"O To Be Like Thee!"**

Everyday I watch my toddler as she struggles down the road to independence. It isn't always easy to know how to behave, particularly when your closest sibling is eight years older than you are. Most of all she looks to me as her role model. She loves it when she realizes we are both wearing hats or we're both sitting together reading books or we both ate the carrots on our plate first. "Look at me I'm just like Mommy" she sings out as she clops around the house in my old shoes. Children are such a joy and a responsibility as we, and others, see us reflected through them.

Jesus reflected the perfection of God the Father. Together along with the Holy Spirit they show us the way we should try to be. May we strive everyday to become more like our heavenly Father. When we put on His righteousness, we begin to live the lives He wants us to live. It is when we follow His example of love that the world can better understand the heavenly Father.

Dearest heavenly Father, *let us everyday awake and sing out "Today I will be just like You!" Teach us Your ways. Show us Your truths. Let the world see You in us today. In Your Son's holy name, we pray. Amen.*

Growing With God's Favor

And the child grew, and waxed strong in spirit, filled with wisdom; and the grace of God was upon him (Luke 2:40).

Scripture: **Luke 2:40-44**
Song: **"O, for a Faith That Will Not Shrink"**

"Good, better, best never let it rest 'til your good is your better and your better is your best" is a quote my husband often recites to our children to encourage them to always try harder and to spur them into applying themselves in everything they do. We want them to live up to the potential God has instilled in each of them. How proud we are when we see our children doing their best. How happy they are to know that they have given their best effort.

God gave each of us unique gifts and talents. We are His children and He wants us to always do our best in all that we do. When we use the gifts He has given and seek to be filled with His Spirit, we show others that special piece of God that is a part of us when we do His will. May God find us living the lives He wants for us. May we daily strive to live by His holy standards.

Heavenly Father, create in each of us a heart ready to do our best so that others might see You living in us. Help us to always put You first. Help us to never turn our backs on the gifts You have instilled in us. May we always find favor in Your eyes. In Jesus' name, we pray. Amen.

Right Where You Belong

How is it that ye sought me? wist ye not that I must be about my Father's business? (Luke 2:49).

Scripture: **Luke 2:45-52**
Song: **"All People That on Earth Do Dwell"**

Have you ever felt so comfortable in a situation that at that moment and that place you know you truly belong there? Maybe it was a family gathering and the love and fellowship was so complete you knew that if even one member of the family hadn't been present the moment would have been lessened. Maybe it was a moment at work where you knew your talents and expertise had been utilized in such a way that you knew no one else could have finished the task with such success. Maybe it was the time a perfect stranger began to share the grief of losing a loved one, and you were there to offer compassion and release.

We may not always know how God will use us or where He wants us to be. We may not always realize how the gifts God has given us bring comfort and joy to others. But God puts us where we belong. He puts us where He wants us to be. All we need to do is open our hearts to His will and let Him lead us.

Dear Father God, *place us where You want us to be. Teach us to be free in sharing Your love with others. Help us to use the talents and gifts You have given us so that others may know You better. May we always be where we truly belong. In Jesus' name, we pray. Amen.*

December 29

Liberation Day

For to me, to live is Christ and to die is gain (Philippians 1:21, *New International Version*).

Scripture: **Romans 8:18-23**
Song: **"My Faith Looks Up to Thee"**

The ironclad vessel Monitor was sunk in the Atlantic Ocean off the North Carolina coast on December 31, 1862. Recently, its engine was recovered and moved to the Mariner's Museum in Newport News, Virginia. It was placed in a special solution to slow the deterioration of time and to prepare it for a lengthy restoration process.

Our human vessels are no different than the Monitor. Disease and old age rob us of strength and former glory.

The apostle Paul says this painful process is like childbirth. It is all a part of the transition we are making to our eternal home in Heaven.

Physical illness is not the only source of pain and suffering. The secret to contentment can be found in Paul's practice of comparing the present with the future. Temporary trials mean nothing when we compare them to the glory of eternal life.

Cheer up! Freedom is not far away. On liberation day God will give you a new body.

Dear Father, *sometimes the aches test my patience and attitude. Help me to keep my eyes focused on Heaven. Make me a blessing. Amen.*

December 29-31. **Larry Ray Jones** is Senior Minister of a church in Newport News, Virginia. He and his wife, Jane, have two children, Nathan and Laura.

What Is God Doing?

You intended to harm me, but God intended it for good to accomplish what is now being done, the saving of many lives (Genesis 50:20, *New International Version*).

Scripture: **Romans 8:24-28**
Song: **"Under His Wings"**

The story of Joseph teaches us to wait on God. Joseph's jealous brothers sold him into slavery. They returned to their father and spun a fantastic lie to explain his disappearance. Years later, a famine struck the land, and Joseph's brothers went to Egypt to buy grain. God had a surprise waiting for them. Joseph had not only survived, but was second in command to Pharaoh as the manager of Egypt's food supply.

God never promises a quick end to circumstances that test our faith and patience. What He does promise is good results. Sometimes these results might also take us through the frightening valley of personal reflection as God changes us from the inside out. He often does this to prepare us for greater service.

What good thing is God doing in your life right now? Maybe the answer to this question is clear. Chances are, though, it is still a mystery. In time, you will understand His plan and you will be thankful you continued to love the Lord and trust Him with your future.

Dear Father, we trust You and know You will give the spiritual strength needed. Give us the grace to cope with circumstances we can not change. In the name of Jesus, our Savior, we pray. Amen.

You Can Depend on God

The Lord is my rock, my fortress and my deliverer; my God is my rock, in whom I take refuge. He is my shield and the horn of my salvation, my stronghold (Psalm 18:2, *New International Version*).

Scripture: **Romans 8:29-33**
Song: **"A Mighty Fortress Is Our God"**

Kirk Puterbaugh boarded a plane leaving Atlanta, Georgia soon after the World Trade Center attack on September 2001. As he sat with a handful of passengers awaiting take-off, a large college student appeared in the doorway. Following him was an entire football team on their way to a football game in Hampton Roads, Virginia. Mr. Puterbaugh felt overwhelmed, by the immense size and build of the players. But something was about to happen that impressed him even more. As the plane engines accelerated a voice in the back of the plane shouted, "heads." On that command every player bowed his head and the team prayed the Lord's Prayer.

God justified us by paying our debt through the blood of His Son on Calvary. If God has expressed His love for us in Jesus, surely He will be faithful until the last day when we are raised to eternal glory.

God, who is able to protect us, has called us. "If God is for us, who can be against us?"

Dear God, we know we should not fear, but we lose confidence. Give us the spiritual grit to remain faithful in situations as You remind us of the victory we have in You. In Jesus' name, we pray. Amen.